A SMILE ON
THE
FACE OF GOD

To Maureen

God bless

By the same author:

BROKEN WINDOWS, BROKEN LIVES

A SMILE ON THE FACE OF GOD

Adrian Plass

HODDER AND STOUGHTON
LONDON SYDNEY AUCKLAND

Where it seemed appropriate to do so, I have changed the name of
various people and localities.

Quotations of Bible passages have been taken from the
Authorised Version and the Revised Standard Version of the
Bible; quotations from Anglican services are generally from the
Book of Common Prayer.

Copyright © 1990 Adrian Plass

First published in Great Britain 1990.
This edition 1991.

The right of Adrian Plass to be identified as the Author of
the Work has been asserted by him in accordance with the
Copyright, Designs and Patents Act 1988.

10 9 8

British Library Cataloguing in Publication Data
Plass, Adrian
A smile on the face of God.
I. Title
248.4092

ISBN 0 340 51387 X

Printed and bound in Great Britain

Hodder and Stoughton Ltd
A Division of Hodder Headline PLC
338 Euston Road
London NW1 3BH

This book is dedicated to
Margaret Ilott and Bridget Plass,
who work so hard
to make stories possible for others

Contents

Preface

Nearly five years ago, before I ever wrote anything, I phoned a man who had been in the book business for years and asked him how to be a successful writer. He said that above everything else, I would need a 'Great Subject'. As far as biography is concerned, I suppose he was implying that fame or public significance are the ideal qualifications for the central character in such a book.

Philip Ilott is not a famous person. Hardly anyone has heard of him. A lot of people have asked me why I wanted to write about such an obscure character, and why I should expect anybody else to want to read about him. A clue to the answer lies in this book's title. More than anyone else I have ever met, I see in Philip a living expression of the compassionate smile with which God regards his suffering children. From the first day that I encountered this unusual Anglo-Catholic priest, I was intrigued about his background and development. Had he always shone and sparkled as he now did? If not, how had it happened? What had made him special?

Long before we first talked about a book, I had wanted to write about Philip's life. When one day he told me that he had refused a publisher's request to write an autobiography because of ill-health, I tentatively suggested that I might do it for him. His enthusiastic response was the first step towards the completion of this book.

Philip has travelled a very difficult road, and some stages of his journey do not show him in a particularly good light. He and I believe that this is important. There are enough shiny, seamless testimonies about, without adding another one to the list. This is a story about the way in which a man and his ministry can be divinely nurtured, side by side, like parallel straight lines that are ordained to meet miraculously one day. I hope it will show how mistaken we are to assume that God will only use us when we have achieved some minimum level of virtue. I hope that it will also show how irrelevant denominational differences are when the Holy Spirit is lovingly, powerfully working through people like Philip.

Since *A Smile on the Face of God* appeared in its first edition I have received many positive and encouraging letters from readers. One or two people, however, have expressed concern and puzzlement about Philip's recollections of various phases of his life.

'It wasn't quite like that,' they say.

Confusingly, such statements have often been paralleled by comments from people who say, 'it was *exactly* like that,' referring to precisely the same period, or set of incidents. I suspect that any attempt to describe something as complex as the life of another human being is bound to be fraught with that kind of problem, but in this case there are other factors.

First, the book is a history of Philip's perceptions of his own life, not the kind of hologrammatic picture of reality that is produced by combining several independent views of the same event or events. Thus, folk who knew Philip Ilott at a certain time in his life may remember him as being cheerful and contented, whereas, inwardly, he was suffering agonies of inadequacy and unhappiness. It is through Philip's eyes that we view these experiences.

Secondly, emotional and physical disability has dogged Philip throughout his life. Some of the significant happenings of the past are visible only through the mist of pain or depression that accompanied them. Again, we look with Philip at the shape of his own past as he sees and recognises it.

For every mote of unintentional inaccuracy that might be detected in Philip's account, there is a beam of honest intent that cannot but illuminate.

Philip is a very special person. I am pleased and honoured to be able to share him with you.

1

War Damage – A Child Abused (1936–1945)

Little Philip Ilott hated Adolf Hitler. Not because of any differences in political ideology; not even because the mad dictator threatened to occupy and enslave a large proportion of the free Western world. Nothing so trivial motivated the intense anger that the six year old boy felt towards the leader of Nazi Germany. Philip hated Hitler because he stopped daddy from being at home all the time. Daddy was away being a soldier in the war. But Philip really needed him now, because strange and terrible things were happening. They happened at night in the dark, and they frightened him.

Only two things made them stop. One was Adolf Hitler's aeroplanes coming over to bomb Newcastle. When that happened a siren sounded and everyone had to hurry down into the air-raid shelters and spend the night there. Philip wasn't afraid of bombs. He would rather be blown up than have to spend the night in his own house – much rather. Sometimes, as the daylight began to fade, he would sit perfectly still in his perfect bedroom, and ask God to make Mister Hitler send the bombers to attack Newcastle. He didn't even mind if a bomb fell on his house while he was in it. That would be the end of everything, and a good job too!

The other thing that made the frightening nights stop was daddy coming home. It was so exciting when daddy came home! He got such a funny, unusual warm feeling in his tummy when he saw 'I love you – I'm so glad to see you' coming out of daddy's eyes. It didn't last long, because the rows came next, and daddy wasn't allowed to be with him properly once the rows had started. He was only allowed to smile at him and ask if he was alright. But those coming-home times were wonderful, especially the bit when daddy hugged him tight and said, 'Hello, Chick!' That was daddy's special name for him. Nobody else called him Chick – nobody. But the best thing about daddy coming back, the thing that took away the worrying all through the day, and the miserable fear in the night, was that as long as daddy was home on leave Philip slept in his own bed in his own bedroom – and not with mammy . . .

He just hadn't been able to understand it. At first, when daddy went away to be in the war, he was glad that mammy wanted him to come and sleep in her big bed, on the side where daddy usually lay. He was glad because he thought it might mean that mammy loved him after all.

He did try to make mammy love him, he really did. He walked very carefully round the house, making sure he didn't break any of the precious things, and he did his best to keep as clean and smart as she was. Mammy was a *very* smart lady with shiny hair who wore dead foxes and shoes with big long heels. She smoked posh cigarettes in a long thin black tube, and her nails were bright shiny red, as though she'd dipped the tips of her fingers in a pool of blood.

He knew how important it was to mammy that things *looked* right, and he always tried to help, but it was so easy to get it wrong and make her shout at him, or say things that made him feel silly and small, or shut him in his room or in the cupboard under the stairs with the light off until he'd learned his lesson. That was the worst thing; standing like a statue in the blackness – with his eyes stretched open wide, trying to see things – too frightened to move in case he knocked something over and made her angry again when she came back. He hated that.

Sometimes he thought that a long time ago he must have done something so bad, so horribly wrong to his mammy, that she was punishing him for ever by not letting him be important; by only letting him be in the way, or a nuisance. He wondered what it could have been. Perhaps it was what he'd said in the pram that day. He always went white inside when he thought back to that awful day – the very first thing he remembered in the whole of his life.

He was a very little boy, sitting in his pram in the sunshine outside the house. A lady came walking along the pavement. He watched her as she came closer and closer. She had a long hooked nose and a pointed chin, like in the pictures of witches he'd seen in books. He didn't like her. When she got to his house, she stopped and came up close to the pram. She said, 'Hello, darling, you're a lovely little baby, aren't you?'

Philip wanted to make her go away, so he said the first words that jumped into his mouth: 'Bugger off!'

The witch's face went cold and hard. She knocked on the door of the house, and mammy came out. Mammy said sorry and did a little not-real laugh when the witch told her what had happened. Afterwards, indoors, mammy had been very angry, but he couldn't seem to remember what she said. He wondered where he'd heard the bad words. He was only ever with mammy.

Being rude to the witch might have been the horribly wrong thing that mammy would never forgive him for, but he didn't think so really.

There was something else, something that happened even before that. He could never remember just what it was, but sometimes, when he looked into a mirror to make sure he was alright for mammy, he would touch a funny little dent in his cheek with the tip of his finger, and then it would ever so nearly come back into his mind, but not quite.

Perhaps it was something to do with that. Perhaps . . . Perhaps not.

There was something even deeper and farther back, something he couldn't see with his eyes or his mind or his memory. In the nights after the really bad days, lying awake in the dark, he could feel it – a deeper darkness inside him, full of a lost, hopeless sobbing that would never come to the top and never be properly cheered up. Something to do with belonging – or rather, not belonging – something right back at the beginning . . .

Sleeping next to mammy, it seemed as if everything was going to be alright after all. Maybe this was where being happy started. Mammy would start to notice him and do things with him. It would be like it was supposed to be with a mummy and her little boy. But after a while the things that happened – the things that mammy did – seemed wrong and frightening. They made the lines on his forehead go tight and worried when he thought about them. He didn't want to be mammy's teddy bear. Why did there have to be a night-time at the end of every single day? Why couldn't the war end and daddy come home for ever?

Later, when he started going to school, and mammy got a job that she went to every day, there was a new thing to get used to. It was the shed.

Mammy's house was easily the most important thing in the world. She cleaned it and dusted it and arranged things in it so that it was just the way she wanted it. Sometimes she pushed an ornament along the mantelpiece for a tiny, tiny, tiny distance with the tip of one of her red nails, until it was in exactly the right place.

It didn't seem to make her very happy having everything so clean and tidy, but if something was moved or dirtied it was worse than anything that Mister Hitler could do. She often told Philip how difficult and annoying it was to have a little boy who insisted on creasing chairs by sitting in them, or touching walls or table-tops or door handles with fingers that might not be as clean as they could possibly be. Sometimes he thought she would really like to stand him in the middle of the living-room carpet at the beginning of the day and leave him there until bedtime, when she had a use for him.

Now that she was going to work, mammy told Philip, she couldn't possibly let him come back into the house after school. He would have to go into the garden shed and wait there until she came home in the evening. That way there was no danger of the house being hurt or messed up while she was away.

He was to let himself into the shed with a key that she'd give him, sit at a little desk in the middle of the floor, and make himself some bread and jam with the things she'd leave out ready for him. And when daddy came back for his next holiday from the war, Philip wasn't to tell him about going to the shed every day; and he wasn't to tell him what happened with mammy and him at night; and he wasn't to tell him how mammy locked the front-room door all the time so that Philip couldn't practise on the white piano with his fingers that might not be quite clean; and he wasn't to tell him how his toys – especially the fort and the puppet theatre made specially for him by daddy – were all packed away as soon as daddy went back to the war; and he certainly wasn't to tell him how sad and lonely he felt, because that would use up some of daddy's kindness, and all of daddy's kindness belonged to mammy and nobody else.

At first the shed was a bad place. It was winter, and therefore quite dark when Philip came home from school. After he had unlocked the shed door, he would move fearfully into the darkness and feel around with his foot for the desk. Then he would run his hand along the flat piece on top, searching for the box of matches that was always there. It was a huge relief when he touched it and picked it up and listened to the matches rattling inside as he gave it a shake. Then there would be a blinding little explosion as he rasped a match head along the rough yellow strip on the side of the box, and a little spluttering sound as he held the flame against the wick of his stub of candle in a brass holder. He would shake the match out and place it carefully in the base of the candle-holder.

It was now time to do the bread and jam. The cutting and spreading and eating had to be done very carefully.

Sitting in the little pool of light thrown by his candle, munching slowly and watching the shadows leap and dance on the shed walls, Philip knew that mammy would check for crumbs later. (The inside of the shed was almost as squeakily clean as the inside of the house.) When he had wiped his mouth carefully, while leaning over his plate, he would stand up, take the candle-holder in his hand, and check every inch of floor under and around the desk to make sure that mammy would have no cause for complaint.

Last of all, he would sit back in his chair, with Sebby in his arms, and wait for mammy to come home. Sebby was a Panda who loved him and never said anything. His name was short for Sebastian. Philip had once read a story about a horse called Sebastian and had liked the name.

It wasn't until Philip had been going to the shed for quite a long time that he realised he was beginning to feel angry as well as sad. The feeling started very small, like a tickle in the throat before you get a cough, then it grew and grew until it had to come out somehow.

He was angry with daddy because he never stood up to mammy when she had tempers. Last time daddy was home, he had come into Philip's bedroom when he thought Philip was asleep and had knelt down by the bed and cried and cried as if he was a little baby. Why did he do that? Why couldn't he be strong and in charge, like daddies were supposed to be?

He was angry with himself, too, because *he* couldn't stand up to mammy either. He went all weak and wobbly whenever he tried to say or do or be what he wanted in front of her. She was strong and huge inside, like a giant. He was small and silly and didn't really count.

Most of all he was angry with mammy – so, so angry with mammy for not loving him, for not noticing how he tried, for making him only what she wanted, for not letting daddy love him properly, for making him go all tight inside whenever he thought of the nights when she used him like a dolly, without feeling anything . . .

He decided to sack her.

Sometimes, on a Saturday evening, he and mammy would sit down to listen to *Saturday Night Theatre* on the wireless. Philip didn't always understand what it was about, but that wasn't important. It was one of the only times when it felt as if he and mammy were really doing something together, even if they didn't actually talk. One of the plays had been about somebody losing his job; he told another person that he had been 'sacked' by his frightening boss.

Philip became the frightening boss of his shed. Each evening, after the bread and jam had been eaten, and the floor checked for crumbs, he would sit very straight in his chair behind the desk and would interview mammy. Mammy would come crawling through the door all white and shaky and kneel in front of the desk, begging to be allowed to stay.

'No!' shouted the frightening boss. 'You're sacked! I'm sacking you for being bad! D'you understand? You're sacked! Sacked! Sacked! Get out!'

The feeling of sacking mammy was wonderful. It came right from deep down in his stomach and shot out of his mouth like those pictures of oil spurting out of the ground. He loved to watch mammy staggering out into the darkness beyond the shed door, bent and unhappy because of things that *he* had said to her. Sometimes she would stop at the door, turn around, and ask him if he would be in bed with her that night, doing the things that worried him.

'Not tonight, mammy – not tonight! Get out! Out!'

Mammy wasn't the only one to get the sack. School-teachers tiptoed timidly into the shed, and were quickly sent out into the big wide world with no job and a look of surprise on their faces because they hadn't realised that little Philip Ilott, who sat so pale and still at his school desk, was one of the most important and powerful people in the whole of Newcastle. He really showed them!

Daddy too. Daddy got sacked sometimes, but it was more difficult with daddy because mammy was always sacking him anyway. Daddy was the one who should have been doing the sacking, then Philip wouldn't have to do it. Oh, daddy . . .

Now that Philip was taking charge of the inside of his shed, he thought it would be nice to have some friends to talk to as well as all the people who had to be sacked every day. There was Sebby of course. He had to be smuggled in most days because mammy thought he should really stay in the room where Philip slept. He didn't like to call it his bedroom. It wasn't his, and it wasn't a bedroom. It was one of mammy's perfect places where he was allowed to sleep when daddy was home. Sebby was the only thing in the room that was specially his. He liked to have Sebby in the shed with him, but there was someone else now; someone who you couldn't see, but who was just as real as Sebby; someone who he'd learned about from granny.

Granny.

Granny was mammy's mummy, and Philip loved her with every bit of himself because she was all the things that mammy had never been. She was someone to share secrets with and cuddle up to whenever he was allowed to visit her in the flat where she lived with grandad, who was very deaf and needed to be shouted at. It was the best thing in the world to nestle up to granny's soft comfortable body, to lay his face against the red, black and white check dress that she often wore, and to ask yet again (although he always remembered really) what her dancing lady brooch was made of. He just liked the words.

'Ivory and marble, my little bairn,' she would answer softly. 'Ivory and marble.'

He was allowed to see granny once each week, usually on Saturday afternoons. But first he had to do mammy's shopping. Mammy didn't want to go into the shops, because she might meet common people from the council estate near where they lived. So Philip would set off every Saturday morning, holding the shopping bag that was almost as big as he was and saying over and over again, quietly to himself, 'Six-four-five, six-four-five . . .' That was their special cheque number at the Co-op, so you had to know it if you were going to buy things.

Sometimes mammy would tell him to go into particular shops and ask for things that were under the counter because of the war; things like eggs and tomatoes. Philip didn't much like doing that, but you never argued with mammy.

Then, in the afternoon, the world started to shine like a diamond as he climbed on to the bus and set off across the city to the place where granny lived.

Granny's front door was at the top of two very high steps, and it had a long black curly iron knocker that he could just reach if he held on to the door handle with one hand and stretched up with the other.

Soon he would be sitting on his granny's lap, listening to the kettle singing happily on the hob, and telling granny all the things that had been happening inside him since they last met. It was so safe and happy there, sitting in the gaslight, staring into the flames of the fire that always burned beneath the long stone mantelpiece that was covered with a strip of green material with tassels on the ends.

On either side of the fire were the big old ovens that weren't used for cooking any more. Philip knew that granny used one of them to warm up her nightclothes before going to bed. He liked to think about that – granny cooking her nightdress.

He always stayed to tea on Saturdays. There would be home-made bread that had a golden smell, and cake, and sweets, and a lovely feeling of being at home which he never felt in mammy's house.

After tea he might play bagatelle on the beautiful board that grandad had made. Grandad had also made the nails that the balls bounced off, because he used to work in a place called an iron foundry where you could do that sort of thing.

Philip even enjoyed going to the lavatory at granny's. You went through the scullery, where the washing was done in a great big copper, and out into the yard where the toilet was in a little shed.

At granny's you didn't have to stay still in one place all the time. You could get up and move around and sit down again, and say things, and not be careful all the time. It was all wonderful, but the best thing was the stories.

Granny was very good at stories. All sorts of stories. The best ones came from the Bible. Philip's favourite was the story of David and Goliath.

Snuggled up to granny, smelling her fresh, clean granny smell, and trying to see pictures in the flaming coals, he never tired of hearing how the young David, unprotected by armour or a shield or a spear or a sword, set out to challenge the huge Philistine champion, armed only with a sling. He especially liked the bit when Goliath laughed at the brave young shepherd boy, casting scorn on the Israelites for sending such a puny challenger out to the field of battle.

Goliath was mammy, and David was Philip. Philip saw it all in the fire.

There was mammy standing on one side of the valley, huge and strong, sure she could never be beaten. Then, catching sight of Philip on the opposite side, mammy, and the whole of the Philistine army watching from the top of the hill behind her, would laugh and laugh at his silly girlish loincloth thing, and the pathetic little sling dangling from his hand. They would still be laughing as he trotted down the hill to choose a flat white stone from the bed of the stream that ran through the valley; and they would laugh even more as he whirled the sling round and round his head, faster and faster until it was time to let the stone fly, like a tiny white arrow, straight towards mammy's head.

How quickly the laughing stopped as the missile found its mark, and mammy started to topple slowly down towards him with a surprised expression on her face. She was so high that when she landed her head was right next to Philip, and suddenly he was taller than her. The next bit was good, too – when all the Israelites crowded round, clapping him on the back and saying, 'Well done, Philip! You're a hero, and no mistake . . .'

When Philip asked granny how she knew these exciting Bible stories, she said it was because she was a Christian, and Christians liked to read the Bible because it taught them about God and his Son Jesus, and about some of the people who believed in Jesus and talked about him after he'd been killed by the Roman soldiers for saying he was the king.

Philip decided that if granny was a Christian, he liked Christians. He asked her if there were any stories about people who believed in Jesus that had happened after the Bible was finished. It was then that Philip heard, for the first time, about the person who was to be his favourite friend in the silent half-darkness of the shed. His name was Saint Alban.

Alban was an officer in the Roman army at a time when the Romans were still in charge of Britain. He lived in one of the main cities, a place called Verulamium. Philip couldn't say that word very well, but he enjoyed rolling the sounds round his mouth, trying to get it right. Granny said that people weren't quite sure exactly when

Alban was alive, but it was probably about two hundred years after Jesus died.

One day Alban had a visitor, someone he'd never met before. His name was Amphibalus, and he was looking for somewhere to hide because he was being chased by a soldier who wanted to arrest him. Alban found the man interesting, so instead of taking him prisoner he asked what crime he had committed.

'I am a Christian priest,' said Amphibalus, 'and, as you probably know, a message has come from the great emperor Diocletian in Rome, to say that it is against the law to follow Jesus now. When I am caught I shall be condemned to death and beheaded unless I stop being a Christian, and that I will never do.'

There was something about Amphibalus that made him different from anyone else Alban had met. There was a strength and a gentleness and a sureness that he would have liked to have had himself. All that evening Alban asked his guest questions about this Jesus Christ that he followed, and, by bedtime, he was himself almost ready to believe.

That night, as he lay awake in the dark, God spoke to Alban, telling him that Jesus had died for him as well, so that his sins could be forgiven and his life changed. By the time morning came, Alban believed for himself that Jesus had come alive again after being crucified and put in a tomb. He had become a Christian.

After being baptised, he asked Amphibalus to leave his cloak behind, and he sent the Christian priest away to a safe hiding place. Later that morning, when the soldier who was searching for Amphibalus tracked him to Alban's house, there was only Alban there, wearing the cloak left by the priest.

'The man you are looking for has gone,' said Alban, and he drew the cloak more tightly around him. 'I too have become a Christian, so you may arrest me in his place.'

Nothing that anyone said would make him change his

mind. His fellow Romans did their best to persuade and threaten him into giving up his new faith and making sacrifices to the Roman gods, but Alban refused to do either. He was condemned to death, led to the top of a hill where, granny said, a tower now stood in the town of St Albans, and beheaded by the Roman executioner. Alban was a martyr. He had died for what he believed in.

The story of Alban was even better than the one about David and Goliath. Curled up like a baby on granny's lap in the warm kitchen, Philip was almost sure that he could have done just what Alban did. He too could be brave and strong, giving away his life for someone who needed help as much as Amphibalus had done. Out in the cold, or back in mammy's house, he wasn't quite so sure. It was hard to be brave when you didn't feel loved.

The best thing about knowing Alban's story was that it gave him a new friend in the shed. Alban had died knowing that he would come alive again and be with Jesus, so he wasn't really dead at all, even though you couldn't see him. Talking to Alban became the most important part of being in the shed after school. It wasn't like talking to Sebby, who you knew was really only a toy made of cloth, and stuff inside, with glass beads for eyes. It was a secret friendship with a real person who was more like an elder brother than anything else; a brother who cared and was with you when things made you sad, and shared in your happiness if something good happened. Alban, brave and true, was someone to come home to. He wasn't a game. He was really there. Philip knew that he would always be there.

Granny knew other things besides stories. She knew about things that had happened to Philip when he was very, very little. She might even know what the very bad thing he'd done to mammy was. One day, sitting on her lap as usual, he asked her a question: 'How did I get this little dent in my cheek, granny?'

Granny didn't answer for a long time, then she said,

'I'll tell you one day, Philip. You don't need to know that just now, my bairn.'

He asked her again on another day, and again and again, but she always said the same sort of thing: 'One day . . . No need to know now . . . Some things better left . . .'

'I want to know *now*, granny,' he said at last. 'Tell me now!'

She still hadn't wanted to tell him, but he made her. Granny tried to make it sound like a sort of accident, but he knew by the way she talked what had really happened. It was mammy who had hurt his face by touching it with a red-hot poker because he wouldn't do what he was told.

He must have been very, very little at the time though. He didn't remember anything about it. Nothing. He wondered what it was that he hadn't done when he was told, but granny didn't know.

He felt more angry than he had ever felt. The next time he was in the shed he sacked mammy as soon as she came through the door. But it wasn't enough, so he went out into the garden and bashed down lots of mammy's plants with a long whippy cane. The next day, when mammy found the broken plants, he said he thought there must have been a storm in the night, or while she was at work. He could see that mammy was puzzled. She thought she knew that little 'couldn't-hurt-a-flea' Philip would never dare do such a thing.

'Maybe there *was* some kind of freak storm,' she said, more to herself than to him.

Philip smiled inside. He had won for once.

But mammy won most of the time, and the war seemed to be going on for years and years and years. Granny and Alban were still his only real friends. Now, daddy was hardly allowed to play with him or do things with him at all when he was home from the war.

Philip often told Alban how much he wished he could discover that he was adopted – that it had all been a big mistake. Mammy, who took no notice of him, and wished he wasn't there, was not really his mother: *that* was the reason it had all gone wrong.

Once, when daddy was on leave, and he and mammy had gone out for the morning, Philip did something very dangerous. He looked through the bureau where mammy and daddy kept their most private papers, longing to find something that would say he was adopted. Hardly daring to breathe, he rooted through piles of letters and bills and other printed things he didn't understand, putting each one back exactly where it had been, his hair almost standing on end with the fear of mammy coming back to find him committing such a terrible crime. There was nothing at all, no trace of the letter he had hopefully imagined so many times –

Dear Mrs Ilott,
    Thank you very much for saying you will adopt Philip. His real mother will miss him very much . . .

Perhaps the war would go on for ever. Perhaps nothing would ever change very much. Perhaps he would have to set fire to his shed before anyone really took any notice of him. He never knew what embarrassing thing mammy would make him do next. Standing by the carefully tidied and closed bureau, he felt his cheeks redden as he remembered the other day when mammy had made him go out with a bucket and spade to pick up piles of manure after a horse had gone past. He had felt so silly scraping away in the middle of the street just because mammy didn't want any of the neighbours to see *her* doing it. Probably the neighbours were all watching from behind their curtains, laughing at him and secretly wishing that they could come out and pick up some of the nasty stuff to put on *their* gardens. Why had mammy made him do that when usually she wouldn't even let him play in the street because it was common?

Nowadays, although he only just realised it, he quite liked to go into his shed at the end of the day. Apart from granny's flat, it was the only place where he could be in charge for a little while. There was Sebby, and the people to be sacked, and thoughts about granny; and best of all there was Alban – the brother he had always wanted so much – never pushing him away, always keen to listen.

The shed was a place where Philip Ilott could be a star, instead of the meanest, most anonymous bit-player in the crowd; it was a very small world, but for a long time it was all he had.

2

Worship, Woolworth's and 'Nellie from the Tenements' (1945–1954)

The war ended, and things changed a lot. Most of the changes were good; some were very good.

First, daddy was home for ever from the army. That meant the end of being in the shed after school, and, best of all, it meant no more nights with mammy in the big double bed.

The rows between mammy and daddy didn't change. They were just as bad or worse than they'd ever been, now that Philip was older and daddy didn't have to go away any more.

Daddy worked in a solicitor's office in the city every day, but that still left the evenings and weekends for fights and arguments. Sometimes Philip thought mammy and daddy might kill each other when the fighting got really bad. At other times he thought they might kill him, but only if he got in the way when they were going at each other. The rest of the time he wasn't noticed much.

He knew that daddy would have liked to do more with him, perhaps even be quite loving, but mammy was too greedy and too clever. He was beginning to see it now. Daddy had to pay for any peace he got by giving mammy the most and the best of everything. There wasn't much left for Philip.

One *very* good change was connected with the cathedral choir.

Philip had started going to Sunday school when he was quite little. He was sent every Sunday afternoon. Mammy never came with him or went to church herself. It always felt as if she had just found a way of getting rid of him for a while each Sunday. But he quite enjoyed it, especially when it led to him becoming a member of the church choir. Singing was something he did well, and you could feel things when you sang out loudly with the others. But the really exciting thing, the thing that happened when Philip was nine and the war had just ended, was passing an audition to sing in the cathedral choir.

It all started with an advert in the local paper, inviting people who were interested to come along to the cathedral to see if they were good enough to sing in the choir. Philip went, not very hopeful, and sang as well as he could. He could hardly believe it when he heard that he had passed his audition and would be able to sing regularly in the cathedral.

It was one of the very few times in his life so far when mammy had been pleased with something he'd done. She said she was 'thrilled' at the news, and proud of him for succeeding with something so important. Her praise trickled into a tiny corner of the bottomless pit that had been empty in him for so long, and triggered a succession of fantasies in which mammy sat enraptured in the great cool cathedral, ecstatically enjoying the sound of her son's voice as it fluted through the solemn vastness of the beautiful building.

Actually joining the choir was pure joy. It was like walking straight into a new family, full of boys of his own age and a bit older; boys who chattered and scuffled and behaved normally. It took his breath away to think that he could be part of what seemed to him such a richly happy band of folk. He didn't even mind the unofficial initiation ceremonies too much, although it was all rather strange. First he was debagged. That was what they called taking your trousers off by force. Then they put his head in the lavatory and pulled the chain, and, last of all, he was thrown into a prickly holly bush.

Philip would have cheerfully gone through a lot worse if it meant earning the friendship of his initiators. All his life he had longed to have a brother. Alban was the first, and now there were all these new friends. Secretly he thought of them as being real brothers, part of him, just as he was part of their lives, and he loved them in a way which would certainly have surprised them if they'd known.

Life changed beyond recognition because of the choir. Every day after school Philip would hurry straight down to the cathedral for tea in the Chapter House with the other boys, then it would be time for choir practice, and finally the office of Evensong would be sung on every day of the week except Saturday. In addition, of course, there were all the Sunday services at the weekend, and, a little later, the beginning of regular confirmation classes during the week. Daddy took him to those. Mammy never did, but Philip had a private burning hope that when the time came for him to be confirmed, she would be in the cathedral to see the bishop lay hands on him.

Services on the Sunday were full of excitement and mystery. It was what they called an Anglo-Catholic cathedral, which meant there was a lot more to look at than there had been in the church where Philip used to go to Sunday school. There were wonderful processions, full of colour and sound; there were priests dressed in richly embroidered robes; there were candles burning and bells ringing; and the sweet smell of incense filled the interior of the building until it seemed that the air itself was decorated with that pungent scent. The whole place was alive with a God-receiving bustle, and Philip, chosen to be a part of it, began to feel more at home among this solemn but dazzling ritual than he had ever felt before.

He loved wearing his own choir outfit – the normal black and white for ordinary occasions, but red and sometimes even purple for the more special services. It gave him immense pleasure. There was something about putting on a uniform that pleased him deep down inside. It meant that people could see what he was just by looking at him. They could tell he belonged somewhere; a place where people would say things like 'Oh, good, Philip's here', or 'Philip's here – now we can start . . .' He felt more real with his uniform on, and much more confident.

Sometimes, during the cathedral services, he would gaze at the shining blue, red and gold vestments worn by the priests and wonder how it must feel to dress up in that kind of splendid uniform and give Jesus to the people in a tiny wafer of bread and a sip of holy wine. That must be so strange and wonderful. It was almost impossible to imagine being that important – having that much power. He tried to picture himself doing it. It was not easy.

Another thing he loved was going on the cathedral choir camps. It was the very first time he had stayed away from home. All the boys slept in a big bell-shaped tent, watched over by the choirmaster, Mr Malcolmson, to make sure they didn't come to any harm or get up to any tricks. Philip liked the cooking best. It was done over a real fire, and all the vegetables had to be washed and prepared by the choristers. That was his favourite job of all, especially as he might be able to eat a whole Oxo cube if one happened to be left lying around. Philip absolutely *adored* Oxo cubes.

Choir camp was a lot easier and far more enjoyable than school, but there was still that haunting dread of dirt, outside or inside. You couldn't help a bit of dirt when you were camping, but Philip found it very difficult to be dirty. Even when he thought for a moment that he didn't mind some mud on his knees or a grubby face, it was too easy to imagine mammy appearing from

among the trees and looking at him as if he was something disgusting.

That was one of the things that made school a not very
happy place. Take cross-country for instance. Philip was
a very useful cross-country runner, and he liked racing
along, beating weather and people and ground conditions, for the same reason that he enjoyed singing. It
was shouting with your legs and your lungs. It felt good.
But you got dirty. It was the same with rugger. You got
dirty. That meant two worrying things.

First, you had to take your running things or your
rugby shorts and top home to mammy. She always
looked at them and you as if you were something the
dog had done, then she got angry and shouted at you
for making work.

The second worrying thing was having to shower with
the other boys after a games afternoon. Philip hated the
other boys seeing him with no clothes on, and he was
embarrassed about seeing them. Despite what had happened while daddy was away at the war, mammy always
talked about bodies and private parts as if she'd just put
her hand into something smelly and nasty. Philip was
amazed at how easily the other boys stripped off and
abandoned themselves to the pleasure of a hot shower.
For him it was a weekly nightmare. He was deeply
ashamed of his maleness.

When he was eleven, Philip was confirmed at a service
in the cathedral, together with a number of other boys
of similar age. Now that the choir and the cathedral were
the most important things in his life, it seemed very right
and natural to go through this special form of being
taken properly into the family of the church, and it
was the beginning for Philip of feeling a new sort of
understanding about God.

God, as such, had not played a great part in his life
up to now. Mammy never went to church or talked
about that sort of thing, and daddy was too busy working
out how to stop mammy from shouting at him to be very

bothered about who made the world and kept it spinning round.

Philip had never sacked God in the shed. He wouldn't have dared. Apart from occasionally asking him to make Mister Hitler bomb Newcastle, he'd hardly ever spoken to him. On the other hand, granny was someone who loved God and read about him in the Bible. He'd often thought that the 'loveness' surrounding granny was probably something to do with God. Then there was Alban, who had gone to his death like a brave lamb, just because being loyal to God's Son was more important to him than being alive. Granny and Alban were pretty good adverts for God, Philip reckoned, but he had never felt that God was there like a person right next to him.

His two years in the cathedral had changed that a little. Surrounded by his chorister brothers, immersed in the richness and mystery of the services, he had begun to sense an impossibly vast presence moving around and through the people and the music and the prayers. Sometimes it even moved through him. It was powerful and strong, not like his own father, and it was peaceful as well. That wasn't like his own father either.

Now, at his confirmation, something new happened. In some extraordinary way he felt that God was making him one of his children – that it was now alright to call God Father. He didn't really understand what was happening, but he knew that the most important part of him had taken a step forward. Bit by bit he was building a new family to take the place of the one that had disappointed him so much. Alban and the choristers were his brothers, God was his Father, and the cathedral was his home. He wondered how much bigger the family might get. Surely you couldn't have a new mother?

Alas for Philip's fantasies of mammy witnessing the important moments of his life at the cathedral. Granny and grandad and daddy were there to see him confirmed, but mammy never came to hear him sing, or see the bishop lay hands on him, or anything . . .

Daddy gave Philip a key to the front door of the house when he was twelve. It was partly because daddy thought Philip ought to have a key, and partly because he needed one to get into the house after school, but also so that, at holiday times, he could make the fire and get the tea ready and put two pairs of slippers by the fire for when mammy and daddy came home from work.

Philip quite liked being in the house at holiday time when mammy and daddy were at work. There was a delicious feeling about safe aloneness.

Once, greatly daring, he invited a school friend over to the house while his parents were out, and suggested they should get the stepladder upstairs in order to explore the loft. Philip knew nothing about lofts. He had never been in a loft. With his first step he put his foot through the floor of the loft. The hole in the loft floor also turned out to be a hole in the bathroom ceiling near where the toilet cistern was. He was absolutely terrified. What on earth would mammy say? Once again, though, his reputation for mild compliance saved the day. To his amazement, and showing no signs of suspicion, mammy swallowed his feeble tale about the noise of the flush bringing the ceiling down. Philip didn't feel any guilt. Winning was too rare for that – too satisfying.

It was the same with mammy's black satin bag, the very elegant one that she wore only when she wanted to look extra smart. One day in late summer, when Philip was thirteen, mammy had said or done something to bring all the sleeping anger in him raging to the surface again. It was like choking on feelings – you had to do something to get the breath going again. When everyone was out, he slipped upstairs, found mammy's satin bag, tucked it out of sight under his jumper, then ran quickly out of the house and into a nearby field where blackberries grew.

Making his way along the brambly hedge in the warm, early September sunshine, he picked all the biggest, ripest, juiciest berries he could find, until the black bag was crammed full with fruit. Then, sitting on the grass by the bushes, he ate every single blackberry until the bag was empty again. Then he looked at the inside of the little cloth container. It was covered with juice and bits of blackberry. Smeared and dirtied and ruined. Not clean and smart and useful any more. He had done it, and she would never know. He threw the bag away and went home full of peace and blackberries. Mammy never connected the loss of her bag with Philip, but it must have puzzled her.

Philip was beginning to learn another way to get anger and tension out of himself, besides cross-country running and singing in the choir and visiting granny's and doing things behind mammy's back and talking to Alban. It was something that happened during the services at the cathedral, during what he was beginning to call 'worship'. Since his confirmation he had begun to know that someone outside himself was listening, not only to the sounds he made in song or prayer, but to the much deeper and more resonant sound of the real needs and feelings inside him. Sometimes, during a service, especially perhaps in the course of certain psalms which quite blatantly and grittily echoed the hurts in his heart, it was as though the harshness and tension were lifted out of him, just as the psalmist almost invariably made his way upwards through darkness and out into the light of praise.

* * *

Philip's academic career was not a distinguished one. Frequent nagging reminders that his place in the Dame Allen school cost a lot of money each term didn't help very much. Nor did the constant conflict at home.

Apart from his success in cross-country races, there were few rewards for Philip in the arena of school. Painting, drawing and music were talents that were beginning to emerge, but it was difficult to see how a future career could be based on these skills, especially as National Service was the inevitable destiny of every young man when he reached the age of eighteen. For a while he nursed a secret and quite passionate desire to become an actor or entertainer.

From the age of fifteen, he went out on his own, and it was usually to the theatre. Many productions bound for the West End were tested out on Geordie audiences before going down south, so Philip was able to see people like Vivien Leigh, Laurence Olivier, Richard Burton and Eric Portman, great stars who were applauded and cheered like mad by the Newcastle audience who filled the Theatre Royal each week. Plays, opera and ballet all fascinated the starry-eyed teenager as he sat at the front of the balcony with his head pressed against the brass railings.

Imagine being one of those stars out there on the stage, the very centre of attention, beautifully costumed and dramatically lit, holding those rows and rows of people in the palm of your hand, able to make them laugh or cry or whatever you wanted by the way you moved or sang or changed your tone of voice. Wonderful!

He had never known such a mixture of excitement and relaxation, not even in the cathedral. Sometimes he would send his autograph book round the back to be signed, then wait for the godlike beings to come out of the stage door, and return it to him as they passed. Once he touched Anna Neagle's beaver lamb coat with his hand. It was very soft and beautiful. She was his favourite. He could hardly believe it when she noticed him enough to smile and take his book and sign her name.

He liked to imagine what it would be like if he was part of this glittering world. He was afraid he wouldn't be good enough at learning his lines to be an actor in the theatre, but the cinema – that was different. He'd heard that you only had to learn little bits, because they did each little scene separately when they made a film.

He could be like Van Johnson, very attractive and chased by hordes of beautiful women. One day . . .

The royal family thrilled him too. Just before he left school, he paid for a ticket to go into a shop and watch the coronation of Queen Elizabeth on a huge black and white television set. Philip thought that the new queen was the most wonderful thing he had ever seen. So impressed was he by her beauty and the grandeur of her position, that he began writing letters to Buckingham Palace expressing his appreciation of the monarchy in general and Queen Elizabeth in particular. The letters that he received in reply, signed by the queen's secretary, and passing on Her Majesty's gratitude for his kind comments, were of great value to his self-esteem. He was someone who (very nearly) swopped letters with the Queen of England. You couldn't be much more important than that.

Tragedy struck when Philip was sixteen. His voice broke. No more singing in the choir, no more belonging to the brotherhood of choristers, no more satisfaction through belting out the hymns and the psalms. He still went to the cathedral for Sunday services, and God was still there, just as Alban never ceased to be a close and necessary friend, but it was a great sadness, almost a bereavement.

There was little space for mourning, however, as Philip was approaching his seventeenth birthday, and would have to decide what kind of work to do in the year between leaving school and beginning his National Service. There was some suggestion that he might enter a profession such as architecture, but Philip himself doubted his ability to cope on an academic level, and was in any case more excited about the prospect of leaving home than establishing himself in some kind of career.

In the end his choice of employment was one which absolutely horrified his mother. Perhaps knowing how dreadful she would think it, he decided to apply for the post of assistant at the local Woolworth's store. Unexpected support came from his father who pointed out that it was only a fill-in job, and that Philip would probably come back from the army with a completely different career in mind.

Whatever the true motivation for this provocative choice of employment, Philip had considerable cause for regret on his own account. He hated working in the stockroom, he hated bringing stock up to put on the shelves, and most of all he hated wearing the gruesomely undistinguished overall that he was provided with on his first day at work. So embarrassed did he become by his appearance and his humble occupation that he removed his spectacles whenever he entered the shop so that it was impossible to recognise anyone he knew. His prospects as a stock manager were hardly enhanced by this defensive strategy. Philip was *very* shortsighted. Blundering through the store putting stock on the wrong shelves was unlikely to impress higher management.

Philip discovered one attraction at Woolworth's. Her name was Nellie, and she worked behind the sweet counter. Nellie lived at Sutton Dwellings, known locally as 'the Tenements'. Nellie from the Tenements was a friendly, easy-going sort of girl. She readily agreed to accompany Philip one day on one of his theatregoing trips, and arrived on time outside the Empire Theatre on the following Friday night.

Philip hadn't dared tell his parents that he was taking a girl out. It was only a friendship at the moment, but he was fairly sure that his mother would object to all girls, however suitable, and Nellie particularly, because of her humble 'Tenement' origins. It was very pleasant to have a companion to share his favourite occupation. He had always relished the solitariness of his theatre and cinema visits, but the dreams were beginning to wear a little thin, and Nellie was pleasantly real.

It was just after they had folded their coats and taken their seats that Philip happened to glance back. There,

sitting three or four rows behind, were his mother and
father, their faces rigid with shock and disapproval.
Later, back at the house, the confrontation was loud and
predictable. Philip's mother was furious. Why had he
taken a girl to the theatre without telling them? Who
was she and where had he met her? Woolworth's! She
might have known. Where did she live? Sutton Dwellings! How could he? She threatened to slap him and
forbade him to take that common little person out again.
He had no right to go out with anyone – he was far too
young . . .

Philip did continue to take Nellie out from time to
time, despite his mother's disapproval. She was a friend
and a comfort, but the relationship never became very
serious. The most important and significant person in
his life was still Suzannah, his grandmother, who, now
that he was approaching eighteen and his departure for
National Service, felt free to tell him more about the
background to his troubled childhood.

Philip learned that his mother had spent most of her
life determinedly trying to escape her origins. She was
born into a working-class family that lived close to the
centre of Newcastle on Tyne. As she grew up in the
small flat in the rather shabby terrace where her parents
were to live for the rest of their lives, she became increasingly impatient with the stolid acceptance shown by her
mother and father.

Each day Philip's grandfather arrived home at six
o'clock after a hard day's work at the iron foundry.
Sitting at the heavy wooden kitchen table in his collarless
shirt, a scarf knotted at his throat rather than a tie, he
drank gratefully and noisily from a huge china mug of
tea. As the years went by the noise of the foundry
affected his hearing very badly, so that anyone speaking
to him had to bawl and shout to make him hear.

All these symbols of grinding, ambitionless industry
infuriated Philip's mother. She wanted to be and do

something much grander, and deeply resented the nature of her upbringing.

Eventually she met Philip's father at a pie-and-pea supper held in the local Presbyterian church hall, and, learning that he was hoping to ascend the career ladder in a city solicitor's office, must have decided that she had found a way of leaving her origins behind. However, her husband's lack of dynamism, and the interruption of his career by the war, made her increasingly bitter and disappointed. She could only grip tight the flimsy evidences of advancement that she had managed to accumulate – the house, her clothes, the garden, her pieces of jewellery.

Philip was a shock, an accident. Even worse – he was a boy. If she had to have a child, she wanted it to be a girl; someone she could dress up and use as an extra ornament; something pretty and delicate and suitable for exhibition.

When Philip was born at The Gables private nursing home on 28 May 1936, his mother didn't want to see or hold him. For several weeks he was looked after by a private nurse who performed all the tasks that his mother regarded as too distasteful even to consider. The touch and closeness that commonly form the bond between mother and newborn baby were simply not there. When she did eventually begin to clean and feed and dress him herself, she was still unable to accept his maleness. Looking at early photographs, Philip studied the way he was dressed – the way his hair was done. He could easily have been a little girl.

At last he knew what the very bad thing he'd done to mammy was. He'd been born – and he'd been a boy. She hadn't wanted him at all, except when there was something she needed him for. All those feelings he'd had as he grew up were *because* of her not wanting him; feelings of being weak and mucky and powerless. If it came to that, he still had them. He felt as if he would always be in his mother's power, whatever happened.

Thank goodness – thank God, perhaps – for his granny, and Alban, and the boys in the choir.

Really, he thought, he should have hated his mother. And perhaps he did in a way. There was a fierce, angry resentment burning in him as he looked back over his childhood and growing up. It wasn't fair. Yes, he did hate her – he hated her!

But he loved her too. Whatever she had done, however unfairly she had treated him, he still yearned from the very depths of his heart to make her love him and be proud of him. His greatest dread was still to be finally rejected by her, and now he had to take this bundle of hate and love and fear away with him to wherever the army decided he was to go. Unless something very dramatic and different happened one day, he feared that the burden might handicap him for the rest of his life.

3

Jesus in Germany – The Conversion of Private Ilott (1954–1956)

In 1954 the Newcastle branch of F. W. Woolworth was at last relieved by the Royal Army Pay Corps, when they whisked Philip Ilott away to Devizes to begin his basic training for National Service.

He had never worked so hard in his life, nor risen so abruptly or so early from his bed each morning. The uniform was somewhat less elegant and angelic than the cathedral choir outfit he had loved so much, and he didn't really feel that soldiering was quite his forte, but there were compensations. It was good to be involved in the rough and tumble of life with young men of his own age, and it was especially satisfying to know that every day spent rushing across Salisbury Plain screaming aggressively, or spent drilling endlessly on the parade ground, was a step away from his mother's dominance and a movement towards some kind of genuine adulthood. He often said silently to himself, 'I want to find out what I am.'

Philip's Company Sergeant Major had no doubts on this subject. He thought that Private Ilott was a 'silly bloody little man', largely because of an incident early on in Philip's military career involving a patch of ice.

The CSM in question combined three significant features. First, he happened to be Richard Burton's brother.

He had a strong Welsh accent and a certain reflected glamour, especially in Philip's star-struck eyes. Second, he had a glass eye which seemed to enlarge and almost revolve when he exhibited his third feature, which was a very bad temper. He was able to reduce the young soldiers to jelly within seconds.

His opinion of Philip was formed early one frosty morning when hundreds of men were lined up on the drill square to rehearse a rather special parade due to be inspected by some bigwig or other in a few days' time. It would have been a difficult enough task at the best of times. National Service recruits came in every shape and form. Physical co-ordination and timing could not be issued automatically with boots and berets. The CSM knew he had a job on his hands, and he attacked it with his customary vigour and determination, until the huge body of men seemed to be achieving the 'at ease' and 'attention' positions within a reasonably short time of each other – all except one.

A small, anxious-looking private situated right in the centre of the khaki multitudes seemed to be having a bit of a problem. Each time a new order was barked across the parade ground he executed a wild little dance on the spot, arms waving frantically, his legs performing a strange, alien series of movements. It didn't seem to make any sense at all from the CSM's point of view. He brought the company to 'attention' again, then back to 'at ease', and finally back to 'attention' once more. Each time, the small individualist with the thick glasses embellished with his bizarrely choreographed little war dance what was in theory a very simple movement.

The voice of the CSM, goaded beyond endurance by this apparently deliberate display of exhibitionism, echoed furiously over the heads of the men in front of Philip.

'WHAT IS THE MATTER WITH THAT SILLY LITTLE MAN IN THE MIDDLE?'

Philip quailed and nearly fell over. His problem was

nothing to do with poor co-ordination or lack of timing. He had just picked a bad spot to stand. His voice, thin and high with nervousness, twittered back towards the CSM.

'Please, sir, I'm standing on some ice. I can't keep my –'

'ICE?' bawled CSM Burton. 'WHAT DO YOU MEAN – ICE?'

'I'm standing on a little patch of ice, sir,' continued Philip faintly. 'I can't keep my –'

'WHAT?' screamed the CSM, his glass eye seeming to grow and spin as his rage increased. 'AM I TO UNDER-STAND THAT THIS ENTIRE EXERCISE IS GRINDING TO A HALT BECAUSE ONE SILLY LITTLE MAN HAS MANAGED TO FIND THE ONLY PATCH OF ICE ON THE ENTIRE PARADE GROUND?'

'Yes, sir,' bleated Private Ilott. 'You see, I can't keep my –'

'SHUDDUP!' thundered the CSM.

A few minutes later, under the CSM's irate but expert guidance, the whole parade had been moved several yards to the left to avoid Philip's patch of ice. A profound silence fell as the CSM made his way slowly but heavily through the ranks of uniformed men until he came to the spot where Philip stood.

He said nothing for a moment. He just glared balefully at the private through his huge glass eye and breathed heavily. Philip wondered if some comment was called for.

'I – I couldn't keep my –'

'You,' interrupted the CSM, beginning to speak with deceptive quietness and then suddenly increasing his volume to a terrifying roar, 'ARE A SILLY BLOODY LITTLE MAN!!!'

Despite this excruciatingly embarrassing experience, Philip managed to enjoy his three months in Wilt-shire, not least because he related well to the men who shared his bunk room. And a very mixed bunch they were: Ireland, Scotland, Wales, the north and south of England, all were represented, as well as different backgrounds and classes of society.

During Philip's time in the army, there were two of his fellow National Servicemen who openly declared close allegiance to spiritual or religious systems of belief. Both impressed Philip deeply, and one was responsible for completely changing the direction of his life.

The first, Geoff, a chubby, fair-haired lad with glasses, came from a devout Orthodox Jewish family. He occupied the bed next to Philip's during basic training. On his very first Friday evening in the barrack room, when all the others were feverishly 'bulling up' their boots and belts in preparation for the next day's parade, Geoff sat quietly on his bed doing nothing, in an oddly deliberate sort of way. It wasn't long before people noticed and asked what was going on. Geoff explained that for Jewish believers the sabbath begins on a Friday evening, and finishes on a Saturday evening. During that time it is not permitted to engage in any of the work that you normally do during the week.

Geoff was quite adamant that nothing could be allowed to interfere with the religious practices that were so important to him. He was not arrogant in his insistence, simply determined.

It was the start of a long period of misery for the young Jewish boy. Trouble came from all directions. His fellow soldiers clearly found him ridiculous. They laughed and jeered at his convictions and what they perceived as his foolishness in asking for trouble every week. They hid his clothes, threw his bed coverings around, ridiculed his Jewishness and frequently reduced him to tears with their youthful, mindless bullying. The army was no more sympathetic. Each Friday Geoff was put on a charge and consigned to the glasshouse because of refusal to work. His life became a nightmare.

He had one sympathiser. Philip felt his own heart echoing the misery and rejection that Geoff was experiencing. He knew what it meant to be pushed out and made to feel foolish. His own suffering was too close for him knowingly to impose suffering on anyone else. One night, shortly after Geoff's first passive confrontation with the system, Philip was woken by a stifled sobbing from the next bed. It was the Jewish lad weeping for his family and his faith, and out of sheer loneliness. It was the first of many nights when Philip did his best to comfort his neighbour.

'It's alright, Geoff,' he would say, 'you've got me. Nobody else understands, but at least you've got me. I'm your friend . . .'

He defended Geoff against the other occupants of the barrack room, telling them to lay off their victim and respect what he stood for even if they didn't understand it. Nothing he said made a great deal of difference, but it did help Geoff to feel that he was not totally alone.

Eventually, even the army realised that a weekly charge in such a situation was not a solution to Geoff's dilemma. The padre, the rabbi, and the corporal in charge of the barrack room got together with the CSM and managed to work out a compromise that would enable the young man to find respite. It was a great relief for Philip, who, as well as feeling a great compassion for Geoff, had been very impressed by the strength of his friend's convictions.

It was at Devizes that Philip, anxious to be 'one of the boys', experienced his first pint of beer, in a pub called *The Bull*. Up to that point his acquaintance with pubs had been virtually nil. As a boy, walking home from the cathedral, he had sometimes used a diabolical device made from pieces of steel to alarm the occupants of public houses. When he dropped this small contraption on to a stone pavement it made a noise like a window breaking, and brought the beer-drinkers rushing out to see what had happened. Their subsequent head scratching and puzzlement brought great joy to Philip's mischievous young heart.

Now, actually inside a pub, and faced with a real pint

of beer, he felt a little apprehensive. One or two gulps later he knew what he thought about beer. It was horrible stuff! He poured most of it away without the other lads noticing, and managed to role-play slight intoxication to conceal his disgusted sobriety. He never did take to beer, but those three months of basic training successfully knocked a few undesirable corners off the young man so recently released from the restrictions of a sheltered and somewhat abnormal background.

Philip was hoping that some of the friends he had made in his barrack room in Devizes would be posted to the same part of the world as himself. In fact, most of the people he knew best, including Geoff, were sent to Singapore. Philip was bound for Germany.

The first part of the journey, a sea voyage from Harwich to the Hook of Holland was not good. Down in the bowels of the ship, a portion of the British army, including Private Ilott, threw up frequently and practically in unison. About a decade later, what was left of Philip arrived in Holland and even began to feel some interest in the prospect of seeing foreign countries for the first time. He was so excited during the train journey through Holland and Belgium down into Germany that he spent the whole night awake, talking animatedly, and trying to pick out details in the darkened landscape outside the window.

The Pay Corps was established in German requisitioned property at Lübeck in Westphalia. Here Philip was responsible for assisting in the preparation and payment of wages to British troops stationed in West Germany. So startlingly untalented was Philip in this department that he was very soon transferred to the army post office, where he was not only able to cause less confusion, but also struck up a warm friendship with a colleague called Nigel. Nigel was very generous with his cigarettes, and Philip was still seeking ways to enhance his 'manhood'. Smoking seemed a rather grown-up thing to do until something more substantial came along.

Something much more substantial did come along: Private Ilott discovered Jesus.

Philip shared his room at Lübeck with five or six servicemen. One of them was a red-haired Scotsman called Sandy Morris, who was small like Philip, but, unlike Philip, was quite sure what he believed, and who he believed in. The two young men had been at Devizes at the same time, but they had been in separate barrack rooms and had only a nodding acquaintance. The Scotsman was a tough, hard-grained little character, much tougher than poor Geoff had been. He needed to be. He suffered constantly and intensively at the hands of his roommates. Sandy was a Christian, not in the stolidly traditional British sense, but in a personal, deeply committed way.

Each night before sleeping he would kneel quietly by his bed for a few minutes to say his prayers. This was invariably the signal for a barrage of jokes, boots, belts and anything else handy to be flung at the kneeling Scotsman. He never retaliated once, even when the worst of his oppressors forcibly removed his pyjama trousers and left the small figure half naked, still kneeling by his bed in prayer. That happened more than once.

Philip was very impressed, especially as he was quite sure that Sandy could have dealt with his persecutors swiftly and effectively if he had ever decided to hit back. Philip would never have dared to kneel by his bed to say prayers. Any that he did say were said silently in the darkness as he lay in bed. In any case, religion had stopped being very important to him for a while, ever since he stopped going to the cathedral for services.

After his voice broke when he was sixteen, he did continue to visit the cathedral on Sundays. He hoped that his lost soprano voice might be replaced eventually by a decent tenor voice, but it was not to be. It was heartbreaking to watch the choir filing into their stalls

each Sunday, knowing that he could no longer be part
of a family that had meant so much to him for nearly
seven years. After a few such sad occasions he could
stand it no more, and for the year before his National
Service training he was not a church attender at all.

Philip felt deeply resentful about this loss, but had no
idea where to direct his resentment. He didn't blame
God – he still thought vaguely of God as a father figure
– and he couldn't think of anyone else who might be
held responsible; it was just so rotten!

Now, as he watched Sandy suffering night after night
for the sake of a faith that had nothing to do with being
in a choir or escaping from a difficult family situation,
he realised that being a Christian was, in the Scotsman's
case anyway, something quite different from anything
he had yet experienced. In worship, and at his confirmation, he had known – touched even – the edge of a
great truth or person, but Sandy seemed to have an
insider's knowledge; a calm; a sense of being loved.

Philip decided two things. First, that he found this
faith of Sandy's very attractive; and second, that he
wanted to find out more about it.

Sandy was more than willing to help when Philip
questioned him tentatively. He suggested that they
should both go along to weekly Bible classes run by a
certain Staff Sergeant Philips in an upper room loaned
for the purpose by Padre Storey, who turned out to be
a lovely, gentle man. Philip enjoyed the meetings from
the beginning, but he found some of the language puz-
zling. Everyone talked about Jesus as if he was really
present, not exactly in a casual way, but as though he
were a close and familiar friend. Then there was all the
talk about 'conversion'.

Sandy talked about 'conversion'.

Sergeant Philips talked about 'conversion'.

Padre Storey talked about 'conversion'.

A regular attender called Major Rogerson talked about
'conversion'.

They *all* talked about 'conversion'.

Conversion, it seemed, was something to do with repentance and commitment and accepting the sacrifice of Jesus on the cross as a payment or punishment for your sins. True conversion would involve the establishment of a real and vibrant relationship with the living, risen Jesus, and through him with God the Father.

It was all rather confusing and unlike anything he remembered hearing in the cathedral, but as the weeks passed the carefully planned Bible studies gradually shed more light on the darker areas of confusion, until Philip felt that it really was all beginning to make sense: he was on the verge of finding or doing or becoming – something.

He still didn't kneel by his bed at night like Sandy. Nothing he had heard in the studies so far had offered him anything that made having an army boot thrown at your head seem even remotely worthwhile, and the dogged little Scotsman had certainly never suggested that he should become the second living target in the barrack room.

Then came the weekend at Ostenwalde.

It would be nice to record that Philip sensed salvation awaiting him at this weekend Christian leadership course. In fact he regarded it as a chance for 'a good skive'. Camp food and camp routine and camp personnel all grew rather wearisomely familiar after a few months, and the opportunity for a couple of days away from it all was too good to be missed.

The course was held in a large country house on the edge of the village of Ostenwalde. It was a lovely house with its own private chapel and enough rooms for Philip to be able to sleep on his own for the first time in months in a building that was separate from the main house. That evening, the first evening of the course, everyone gathered together in the largest room of the house to be formally welcomed to the weekend by the army padre who was leading the course.

Geoffrey Groebecker was a very impressive-looking man. Tall and quietly elegant in dress, he had an air of stillness about him that Philip had never before seen in anyone. His eyes, especially, fascinated the young man as he sat near the front of the room waiting for the talks to begin. The course leader's eyes were large, deep-set pools of perfect peace. For some reason it occurred to Philip that Jesus might have looked a little like this.

A hush descended as he stepped forward to speak. 'This weekend', he announced in a warm, even voice, 'is going to introduce you to Jesus as a real person . . .'

From that second the event ceased to be 'a good skive'. This man with the untroubled eyes had got what Sandy had, only more so. Now he was suggesting that others could have the same, and suddenly Philip knew that he wanted that meeting with Jesus more than anything else in the world; only it must be real – it *must* be real.

The next evening a film was shown. Its aim was to show the beauty and precision of God's created world. There were marvellous sequences demonstrating the mystery and complexity of the solar system, as well as film of creatures in the wild, and the natural cycles by which their species were maintained. It was awe-inspiring, moving stuff. Philip was entranced. It was the climax to a day of learning, discussion and challenge.

As the film ended, Geoffrey Groebecker stood up. It never occurred to Philip to doubt the next words he said. He regarded the padre as a fire at which to warm his faith and emotions. That was why he was sitting right in the middle of the front row this evening, to be as close as possible to where he felt Jesus was.

'The God, who created the universe, and his Son, Jesus, can be as real to you as you want them to be.'

He paused for a moment, his eyes scanning the rows of expectant faces before him.

'I'd like you to go back to your own rooms now and speak to Jesus in your own words. Make him as real and personal for you as you possibly can.'

Philip stood with the others, his heart thumping with excitement – something was going to happen! The combination of certainty and gentleness in Geoffrey Groebecker was irresistible. There was no question of not doing what he suggested. Without speaking to anyone, Philip picked up his notebook and pen from the chair where he had been sitting and made his way down the side of the lecture room towards the door. Others were lingering and chatting quietly. Philip wanted none of that. He had an appointment with Jesus, and that was all that mattered at the moment.

Almost shaking with excitement, he made his way along the corridor to the refectory room, where he drank a hasty cup of cocoa before leaving the building. Along a narrow gravel path, across a stone-flagged courtyard, and there he was, back in his own room at last.

He stood irresolutely by his bed for a moment, debating inwardly what his next move should be. Still pent up with excitement, he asked himself what one normally did when expecting an important visitor. The voice of his upbringing answered immediately: 'Have a good wash . . .' Yes, that was the polite thing to do; you ought to be more or less clean to welcome Jesus. He had a bath to make absolutely sure.

Then there was the whole question of pyjamas. Should you be fully dressed for an occasion like this? Or was it alright to present yourself in blue-striped nightwear? He decided that, all things considered, pyjamas were probably okay as long as you kept tops *and* bottoms on. After all, Sandy always knelt to pray in his pyjamas, and Jesus was real to him. Yes, pyjamas were quite suitable.

Clean and pyjamaed for the Lord, Philip knelt by the bed at last and picked up his Bible, vaguely thinking that it might be right to read an appropriate passage. It was no good. He was so strung up with anticipation that the words ran into each other and became meaningless. Tonight was a night for meeting the writer, not for reading his book. Laying his Bible aside on the bed, he closed his eyes, took a deep breath, and spoke like a hopeful child.

'Jesus, I saw in that film tonight the wonderful things you've done in creation, and I've seen so much of you in people like Sandy and especially in Geoffrey Groebecker. Now he's asked us to come back to our rooms and talk to you so that you become real to us. Would you please be real to me?'

There was a pause. Philip didn't know what he was waiting for, but the response, when it came, was more than anything he could ever have imagined.

It was as though a vast container of peace, happiness and sheer presence was upturned above his head, showering and drenching him with a sensation that was completely new. He felt that he was truly falling in love for the first time, as his spirit opened like a flower to receive a rain of joyful acknowledgement.

This love seemed to go deeper and further than any he had known previously: further than his feelings for parents or friends or Nellie from the Tenements; further than the secret friendship he had known and still knew with Alban; further and deeper even than the love he felt for his grandmother. Jesus was there – holding, cuddling, supporting, reaching down into him to comfort the little boy who had wanted so much to be loved and wanted by his mammy.

It felt like starting all over again, but with someone who wanted you – all of you, including the messy parts – right from the beginning.

It was almost like being born again . . .

Philip stayed on his knees for hours, lost in the sparkling novelty of this undreamed-of relationship with Jesus that had become his. In the early hours of the morning he finally got into bed and slept a deep contented sleep. Next day, it seemed only right to ask for a private interview with Padre Groebecker. In the course leader's peaceful, book-lined study, he explained what had happened to him. The padre's response was one of joy and affectionate congratulation.

'I am so very happy for you,' he said, his eyes alight with pleasure. 'I will let the padre at your camp know what has happened, and you must tell him in your own words as well. Will you promise to do that?'

'Yes, of course I will,' replied the happy young man. 'As soon as I get back.'

After lunch that day Philip went for a walk through the woods surrounding the house. It was one of those jewel-like autumn days. Sunshine and leaves fell softly around him as he strolled between the friendly, light-stippled trees, savouring his new-found joy and speaking softly to Jesus, the Son of God, who, incredibly, was not too proud to be his brother. It was a moment of eternity, of pure unalloyed happiness, and it was a necessary prelude to the immediate future. Going back to camp – and to the barrack room in particular – as a converted believer was not going to be easy, to say the least.

The easiest and most pleasant part of returning was telling Sandy. They went for a walk at Philip's suggestion. Sandy was thrilled with the news. It was a prayer answered. Later in the day Philip also sought out Bill Storey, his own padre, anxious to keep his promise to Geoffrey Groebecker. Padre Storey, who together with his wife offered untiring hospitality to Christian soldiers in the camp, was warmly enthusiastic and understanding.

It was wonderful to receive such a welcome from these two Christian folk, but the real test was to come at bedtime on that first night back in the barrack room. Philip knew what he had to do, and, despite an almost paralysing fear, the power of feeling loved enabled him to do it.

That night two National Servicemen knelt by their beds to pray. The response was predictable. Any faint hopes Philip might have nurtured that a minority of two would be less liable to persecution were dashed immediately; Sandy and Philip's roommates were over-joyed to discover a new target for their attentions. Objects of various kinds, and obscenities of every kind, were flung mercilessly at the brothers in Christ. Philip marvelled at the patience with which Sandy had endured it all for so long.

He himself underwent a variety of ingenious but highly crude and unpleasant attempts on the part of his fellow soldiers to make him swear or lose his temper, but his resolve was not shaken. The climax came a few nights later when two or three of them filled a huge balloon with icy-cold water, and, waiting until Philip had finished his prayers and got into bed, punctured it directly above him, just as he was snuggling down for the night. The sensation was dreadful beyond belief, but in a strange, absurd way it felt like an aggressive baptism into the kind of grittily committed way of faith that Sandy had been displaying since his first night in the barrack room. The two believers became very close friends, and Philip never lost his respect for the tough little Scot whose example had paved the way to his own experience of meeting Jesus.

Philip settled down over the next few days to write some important letters. The first was to his parents, explaining in detail what had happened, and trying to communicate some of the intense joy and excitement that still bubbled up in him days after his conversion.

When the next letter with his mother's handwriting on the envelope arrived, he tore it open eagerly, and scanned the pages hurriedly, searching for her reaction. There was not a reference to his conversion; not a single word in that letter, nor in the next. It was as if he had never mentioned it.

Though heartbreaking, it was not the same as before. Philip had hoped that his rebirth experience would take away the crippling emotional dependence that still bound him to his mother; the old aching need to secure her approval and love. To some extent this had happened. There was a new attachment. His mother's lack of response hurt deeply, but the 'pit' was no longer bottomless, nor was it empty.

The letter to his grandmother was a joy to write. He pictured her picking up the envelope from her front-door mat before carrying it back along the dark-painted hall and into the warm kitchen, there to nod and smile fondly over every word.

This time the reply to his letter was everything he could have hoped for. Full of love and warmth, it affirmed and rejoiced over Philip's vivid encounter with God. 'Since the day you were born,' she wrote, 'I have prayed for this. Now you have discovered his love for the first time and my prayer is answered . . .'

Not all of Philip's fellow believers at Lübeck were impressed by what had happened to him. One of them, a man whose churchmanship was solidly in the Anglo-Catholic tradition, was clearly worried that this kind of conversion might, at its best, result in a short-lived and superficial kind of faith, or at its worst simply be self-delusion fuelled by wishful thinking. He persuaded Philip to write yet another letter, this time to a lady whose name was Dorothy Needham.

Mrs Needham was a committed Anglo-Catholic. On receiving Philip's letter she wrote back to say how worried she was about the whole concept of sudden conversion in the evangelical tradition, and how she would like to help Philip to maintain a right balance in his faith. It was a kind letter, and Philip did continue to write to her with questions and problems. He had, after all, asked himself why there seemed to be no tie-up between what had happened at Ostenwalde, and the things he had heard and been taught during his time as a chorister in the cathedral at Newcastle. On the other hand, it didn't make any difference what people said about traditions or balance or theology, because the experience of that wonderful night in Ostenwalde had not been a theological one, nor had it been an Anglo-Catholic or an evangelical one.

Whatever anyone called it – wishful thinking, mystical experience, or conversion – didn't really make any difference. Philip knew what had happened. He had met Jesus. The question of where he was to house and express his faith was another matter altogether. In the meantime he was quite happy to take communion at the garrison chapel on Sunday mornings and to join others for the 'breaking of bread' at Major Rogerson's house on Sunday afternoons.

The evangelical way of looking at things had a very bright and immediate attraction about it, especially after a visit paid to Hamelin, the famous 'Pied Piper' city. As well as touring the streets and noting with amusement how much of the bread in bakers' shops was baked in the shape of rats, Philip paid a visit to the Church Army Club, which was engaged in evangelism, prison visiting, forces welfare and other areas of social outreach.

It was a surprise to learn that this body of trained, uniformed men and women existed within the Anglican Church. He had heard of the Salvation Army, of course, but this was something new. It inspired him to think seriously about full-time Christian service. He was not convinced that the priesthood would be right. Lacking academic confidence, and feeling that he still needed a broader experience of the world, it seemed to Philip that the Church Army, predominantly but not exclusively evangelical in character, would offer all that he needed. Learning from Captain Wilson, who ran the Church Army Club, that training lasted two years and took place at a special college in London, he wrote to Church Army Headquarters and arranged to attend a selection weekend during one of his leave periods. It was very exciting.

Full of his new faith and plans for the future, Philip arrived back in England for his first home leave with a letter in his pocket written by Major Rogerson commending the young man to the local Brethren group across the Tyne at Gateshead.

Ever optimistic, Philip hoped that, once they actually met, his mother might react positively to his new way of looking at things. His hopes were quickly dashed. The whole of his spiritual experience was a phase, according to his mother. It would pass, as phases tend to. Strange things happened, she said, when you were young and impressionable. 'Getting religious' was one of them. Philip's meeting with Jesus was put to one side, tidied away, and disposed of. So was the Church Army – definitely the 'Woolworth's' end of the church in her view. As for the idea of breaking bread with some tin-pot little group of nonconformist weirdos in Gateshead – she was furious at the very idea. It was improper and unthinkable. 'If you go there,' she said finally, 'then you needn't come home, and that is that!'

In vain, Philip waited for his father to say something, to defend him, or at least to mediate somehow, but there was to be no help from that source. Philip had brought home the most precious thing he had ever found to show the people who should have cared most, even if they didn't agree with him, only to find it mocked and belittled and counted as nothing.

'That is that!' his mother had said, and such was the power of her personality when she fired with all guns that she must have fully believed that *was* that. But she had reckoned without one vitally important fact. Philip really had met Jesus, and that meeting had shifted the dynamics of his relationship with his mother and father. Her dismissal of his conversion and his father's inability to offer support were still deeply hurtful. The pain, the memories, the yearning – they hadn't gone away, but they had lost some of their power.

'Well, I'm sorry,' he said to his mother on the first Sunday of his leave, 'I'm going just the same. I'm going now.'

Greatly upset, but determined to do what he believed

to be right, Philip set off across the city to make his way to Gateshead. There he tracked down the Brethren church whose address he had been given and joined them for the breaking of bread. He was welcomed very warmly by the Christians there, who prayed over him before he left, knowing that he was likely to have a battle on his hands when he returned home.

As it turned out, the battle was over before he had a chance to take part. Arriving back at his parents' house he discovered his suitcase lying in the front garden, packed with the things he had brought back on leave with him. The front door was locked, so was the back door. Philip panicked suddenly, his stomach cold with uncertainty and dread. Surely his mother couldn't have meant it when she said he needn't come home. She couldn't have! This was where he lived. Surely his father would have . . .

He banged on the door a few times. Nobody came. Kneeling down, he pushed the letterbox open with his fingers and shouted into the house: 'Aren't you going to let me in?' Still nobody came. Philip walked down the path with his suitcase, and stood on the pavement, his eyes filling with tears of abject loneliness and abandonment. It was, he thought, just as he imagined hell – to be finally thrust out and rejected like this. What on earth was he to do? Where would he sleep?

There was only one place he could go, and he remembered it with a warm rush of relief. Granny's! Of course! Granny would never turn him away. A bus ride later, he was standing at the top of the two steps outside granny's flat, banging the knocker that was so easy to reach nowadays. Granny was marvellous, warm and welcoming, sympathetic and hospitable. He almost cried all over again.

Unwilling to widen the rift between his grandmother and his parents, Philip didn't stay long at the little flat. There was a Church Army hostel in the Benwell area of Newcastle, run by Captain Luke Aylott and his wife.

Here Philip found a refuge, and a very welcoming one, for the remainder of his leave.

During the rest of his service in Germany he continued to write regularly to his parents, longing for reconciliation, but they never wrote back, neither jointly nor separately. His fantasy was to hear his mother say, or to read in a letter she had written, the words: 'I'm sorry for the things that were my fault – I love you, Philip.' Those words might have transformed his life. But there were no letters and there was no contact. Philip was not to meet his parents again for almost two years.

* * *

National Service continued to reveal that Philip's contribution to the armed services would most appropriately be a temporary one. But there was now a future to look forward to in a different kind of army.

After attending a selection weekend in London during one of his leaves, a letter arrived by post in Lübeck, inviting Philip to spend two years training at the Church Army College when his National Service was completed. It was a great comfort to know that he was wanted and had a place reserved especially for him.

People had been very kind in accommodating him since the split with his parents, but there was still a gnawing insecurity about having no real base or home. Now he knew where he was going, where he would eat and sleep and brush his teeth. He was going there to learn how the love he had experienced at Ostenwalde and was still experiencing daily could be expressed clearly and practically for the benefit of others, and he couldn't wait for his training to begin. In the meantime, he had a very curious dream.

In his dream, Philip was travelling through Germany in a train, just as he had done many times in reality. The carriage was crowded with passengers, but he was the only one dressed in uniform – the only soldier. The others were in shabby, ill-fitting clothes, and their faces seemed dull and depressed. They looked like very poor peasants or refugees.

As the train rattled along between flat green fields, Philip gradually became aware that the rhythmic sleepiness of the atmosphere was being disturbed by voices and other noises further up the train.

A sense of doom enveloped him as the sounds came nearer and nearer. They were the sounds of German soldiers hunting for someone. Their voices were loud and harsh as they stomped down the corridor of the now stationary train, pulling open the door of each compartment and firing questions that he did not understand.

The train stopped. Suddenly, with a spasm of horror, Philip knew with absolute certainty that they were searching for *him*. There was no way to escape. They were outside the adjoining compartment now. If he went into the corridor they would see him and catch him immediately. Here in his own compartment there was nowhere to hide. Dressed in his uniform, he stood out a mile from his fellow travellers.

Sick with the gut-fear of a nightmare, he cowered down in a corner by the window, praying that he might become invisible. The sliding door crashed open and hard-faced men in German uniforms grunted with satisfaction on seeing the terrified figure in the corner. Rough hands gripped his arms and pulled him out into the corridor.

He tried to shout for help, but no sounds could squeeze through his fear-constricted throat. The other passengers said and did nothing, just stared hopelessly and helplessly as a train door was opened and Philip's captors hauled him from the carriage and started to drag him swiftly across a grassy, uneven field.

Jerking his head rapidly from side to side, trying to see where he was being taken, Philip caught a glimpse of some wooden construction lying on the grass behind him. Then there was an abrupt halt and he was pushed brutally on to his back, with something hard pressing into his head and spine, and behind his outstretched arms.

Pinned fast by the weight of several soldiers, he only began to realise what was happening as the first monumental pain exploded in his right hand precisely in time with the sound of a hammer striking metal: he was being crucified.

Finally, lost in a sea of silently screaming pain, he felt the cross being raised by juddering degrees to the vertical, until he was able to see the train again, with the white faces of the refugee passengers staring expressionlessly from behind the glass of the windows. Then he woke up, sweating profusely and weeping uncontrollably.

It was such a strange, vivid dream that Philip decided to write to Dorothy Needham (who by now had become a sort of unofficial godmother to him) and ask her what she thought it might mean. She wrote back at once, suggesting that Philip's past difficulties, when combined with the recent conflict with his parents and subsequent separation from them, might easily have produced such a result. It was a perfectly reasonable interpretation of the dream, and probably true to an extent, but Philip couldn't help feeling that there was more. He seemed, ever since waking from that nightmare, to be in possession of a sure knowledge that one day the events of the dream would become a reality in his life, though whether actually or symbolically he had no clear idea. He connected the experience with the story of Alban and Amphibalus. Because of his new-found faith, Alban had given his life for a man he hardly knew. Philip believed that one day something would be asked of him in the same way, but he couldn't have said why he believed that. He wondered if it could be something to do with his parents and the things he might have to tell them in the future, but he wasn't sure.

Later in his life he was to realise the mercy of God in

not letting him know the real meaning of that dream until the right time came.

Philip was allowed an early release from his term of National Service duty so that he could start his Church Army training in the autumn of 1956. Although glad to leave the army, he was conscious that through it he had gained something more precious than gold. He was very keen to begin his new life, and determined that he would do well. Perhaps his evangelicalism was overtaking his faith a little, but no doubt God was used to that, and would put him straight in time.

4

London – Another Army
(1956–1958)

Philip's first encounter with the Church Army College was charged with excitement. For the first time in his life he was about to undertake something that he really wanted to do. Twenty years old, and a 'raving evangelical', as he was to describe himself in retrospect, he could hardly wait to find out how prayer and the Bible and evangelistic outreach might be used to change the world.

Standing for the first time before the institutional-looking Victorian building in Cosway Street, just off the Marylebone Road, he mentally set aside the cold weight of his parents' rejection and determined that, here, he would do well.

As Philip picked up his bags, he noted the two separate frontages, each with its own main portal, one for the men, and one for the women. Gratified by the simplicity of this, his first decision as a Church Army student, he entered through the correct door.

Inside, the decor and furnishings were simple to the point of sparseness. The little single bedrooms were hardly more than cubicles, and were lined up on each floor like pigeon-holes in a desk, with one bathroom for each landing.

The churchmanship of those who entered the college in Philip's year was on the whole very similar; neatly pigeon-holed and militantly undecorated. In this atmosphere of fiercely evangelical simplicity, Philip felt obliged to leave his Anglo-Catholic origins at the bottom of his trunk, as it were, and strive for excellence within the ethos of the college. And he did not strive in vain. Before the first term was more than a few weeks under way, Brother Ilott had established himself as one of the most competent, moral, energetic and holy individuals in his year. Much later Philip was able to chuckle when he reflected on how insufferable he must have been at times, especially when he was earning his reputation for 'holiness'.

This was acquired in a variety of ways. First, there was the early morning routine. This was strict enough in itself. In Philip's army barracks only Sandy had knelt by his bed to pray in the early morning; here in the college every student was expected to have his Quiet Time of prayer and Bible reading at some time between the rising bell at 7.00 a.m. and 7.30, when the college met for corporate morning prayer. God must have looked on with a mixture of exasperation and fond amusement as these young men engaged in a deadly serious competition to see who could awake first, and therefore be in the bathroom first, and consequently be starting his Quiet Time or 'QTs' before anyone else. Quite often it would be Brother Ilott, shining with soap and saintliness, who could be spotted through his open bedroom door, kneeling in prayer even before the rising bell had sounded.

Then there was the question of 'pleasure'. Each student was allowed only twelve shillings and sixpence per week. Uniforms were provided, but such items as underwear, socks, hair-cuts, holidays and anything else had somehow to be covered by that sum. There was little left for such recreational activities as the cinema, or going to hear music. This was not a problem for Philip, who denounced nearly all occupations of this kind as ungodly and very dangerous. On one occasion, he stood up during a discussion following a lecture on 'social life' and heatedly harangued his fellow students for even contemplating the possibility of going to a dance.

'What if the Lord should return in the middle of a dance?' he cried. 'What would become of you then?'

He went on to tell them that, in his opinion, they would end up, like all pleasure-loving sinners, in hell.

Philip relished nearly every aspect of his Church Army training, excelling in the study of the Old and New Testaments, church history, Christian doctrine, the Prayer Book and moral theology. In addition there was practical experience: hospital visiting, prison work, forces welfare and all the other areas that made up the sixty-seven departments of Church Army work. Very early on in his training, Philip discovered in himself a particular talent for preaching, and this has remained one of his greatest pleasures to the present day.

There was one area of outreach, however, where the young Ilott found his evangelical zeal wearing rather thin. It was in that activity known as 'Pubbing'. In the same way as the Salvationists do, Church Army students were expected to visit pubs with a collection box and copies of the organisation's official magazine, the *Church Army Gazette*.

Philip, allotted a very rough area around Paddington, found the prospect of trying to sell his wares in these centres of alcoholic confusion, loud voices, smoke, and potential violence, frankly terrifying. Of course, all the inhabitants of these sin-ridden establishments were most assuredly on their way to hell, and therefore needed to be contacted and saved, but it was all so unpleasant and so frightening. It really was a very rough area, and Philip's sole experience of imbibing was that single pint of beer he had only partially consumed at Devizes during his time in the army. Moreover, 'Pubbing' always happened on a Friday evening, when the pubs were at their busiest and customers were most likely to be drunk and aggressive.

It was with a heavy heart that Philip set out one Friday night for his second visit to the local hostelries. The students were only allowed to pursue this activity in pairs, and on this particular night Brother Philip, small and slight in stature at that time, was accompanied by Brother Ronnie, a tall softly spoken Irishman, as thin as a rake. As the two smartly uniformed figures set off along the pavement, carrying their wooden collecting boxes and their bundles of *Gazettes*, Philip looked up nervously at his lanky colleague's face and spoke.

'Ronnie?'

'Yes, Philip?'

'Do you enjoy going in the pubs, Ronnie?'

'No, Philip, I do not at all.'

'It's frightening, isn't it?'

'Yes, Philip, it is very frightening, it is that.'

'Ronnie, I don't think I can do it tonight.'

'Nor me, Philip.'

'So how about if we just put all the money from our pockets into the collecting boxes, hang about for a bit, then, well – just go home?'

'That is an attractive idea you have there, Philip.'

The couple continued their walk in silence for a time, relief and guilt chasing each other round and round their minds. At last they found themselves standing outside the first public house on their itinerary. Sounds of raucous enjoyment were audible from the other side of the heavily ornate Edwardian doors. The two evangelists looked at each other. Right triumphed.

'I think we should be going in there, Philip. I think we should.'

'I agree, Ronnie, but let's pray before we do it.'

'Well, we don't want to look like Pharisees, praying publicly outside a pub, do we . . . ?'

'We do not, Ronnie.'

'So let's go in that telephone box, Philip.'

'Very well, Ronnie.'

If there was one thing those two knew about, it was prayer. Wedged solemnly into the nearby telephone box, Ronnie prayed towards the light bulb, and Philip spoke earnestly into Ronnie's midriff. They knew that prayer wasn't just a game. God always did something. He would do something now.

He did do something. As they requested holy protection of their entry into the devil's stronghold, the doors of the pub flew open with a crash, there was a loud and energetic oath, and a drunk was thrown out on to the pavement just in front of the telephone kiosk. As the pub doors slammed shut again, the inebriated one made a last feeble attempt to lift himself from the ground, then subsided into total unconsciousness.

Philip peered out and down through one of the little square windows of the kiosk. The drunk was lying right against the door. He gave the door a tentative little push. It wouldn't move. He pushed it harder. It still wouldn't move. They both pushed it as hard as they could, but it wouldn't budge more than a fraction of an inch.

'Philip,' said Ronnie thoughtfully. 'I think we are trapped in this kiosk.'

It was true. The two Church Army students were sealed into their telephone box by a deeply slumbering member of their wider congregation.

There are many ways of learning humility. Few can compare with having to ring the police station to ask for a constable to come and roll a drunk aside so that you can escape from a telephone kiosk. Philip could only guess at the inner response of the police officer who finally arrived to find what must at first sight have seemed like several Church Army cadets of various sizes jammed, inexplicably, into the same phone box.

Philip never did develop any great enthusiasm for 'Pubbing', but many other enjoyable and exciting activities more than compensated for the hollow dread of

Friday nights. One of his particular favourites was something that the Church Army called 'Trekking'.

Seven or eight of the trainee brothers, together with an experienced captain or two, would load a cart with clothes, Bibles, teaching material and other necessities, throw a tarpaulin over everything, rope it down, and fix a shield on the top announcing, for example: 'Church Army Trek From Bristol to Cleethorpes.' Using ropes attached to the front, the uniformed trekkers would pull the cart by hand through towns and villages on a pre-planned route. Their mission was to preach in churches and halls in the parishes they visited, sometimes visiting people in their homes, and usually organising meetings for families during the morning and afternoon.

Everywhere they went, especially in the country areas, people would stop and stare at the colourful little procession, frequently running indoors to fetch a camera so that they could record the event. Usually, the trek would be scheduled to end in a seaside town, culminating there in a beach mission, aimed at attracting holiday-makers as well as locals.

Sleeping arrangements for the trekkers varied considerably. At best there might be camp beds available; more often it would be the cold floor of a church hall, or even some corner of the church itself. The discomfort didn't matter – indeed, it added to the sense that one was sacrificing normal comforts for the sake of the gospel.

Philip loved every moment of it, and in later life came to cherish the memory of those warm companionable little safaris, punctuated every other day or so by the stimulation of arrival at a fresh and quite unpredictable preaching venue. He was much in demand for his preaching skills on these occasions, the high expectations of his fellows causing him to agonise over the preparation of his sermons, especially as there was no question of cheating by using 'repeats'.

Evening services followed an unvarying pattern. After the sermon had been preached, a beckoning hymn would be sung – something like 'Just as I am, without one plea . . . O, Lamb of God, I come' – and then the service leader would extend his hands in invitation, call people to the front, and pray with them about their decision to seek a new relationship with God. Many people were converted, including, during the beach missions, a number of rather surprised holiday-makers whose comment was generally, 'I never expected this to happen!'

Back in London there was the occupation known as 'Fishing'. This meant stopping people on the street and engaging them in conversation about the Christian faith. Philip used to do his 'Fishing' on the Edgware Road, just next to the tiny chapel of Saint Paul's, where a film would sometimes be shown for the benefit of passers-by who had been 'fished' in by Brother Ilott or one of his colleagues.

Once, Philip was loudly confronted by a Buddhist who was not only unwilling to be reeled in on to a strange bank, but vigorously contested this Christian upstart's right to be throwing his hook into the Edgware river at all. Philip, as dogmatically sure of himself as only a twenty year old can be, stood his ground and argued the point out nose to nose and toe to toe. It was only when a huge crowd gathered and the police had to come and clear the pavement that the two representatives of their respective religions of peace agreed to suspend the disagreement. The Buddhist stalked off – on his way, as Brother Ilott doubtless believed – to hell, while Philip straightened his glasses and rebaited his hook.

Not too far from these fishing grounds, in Hyde Park, the students were able to practise the slightly more traditional soap-box variety of preaching. Hecklers were plentiful and vociferous, but for Philip there was a tremendous sense of exhilaration about taking his place on a platform between the Communist Party on one side and the Salvation Army on the other, not to mention the inimitable Donald Soper preaching the gospel in his own special way a little further along the row.

There was no doubt in Philip's mind that God had led him into the Church Army in order to learn how to pass on the truth he had found on the night of his conversion. At first this leading seemed to be amply confirmed by his success as a brother in training. Apart from his rather dismal experiences on the 'Pubbing' scene, he crackled with energy and rectitude in every other department.

The most evangelical of evangelicals, he had the least decorated room, spent the most time in prayer and Bible study, and led the least indulgent lifestyle of all the men in his year. His preaching was first-class and his personal appearance was immaculate. His mother (if she had been a more normal parent) would have been proud of him. Perhaps, on some deep level, Philip knew that a large part of his constant striving for excellence as a student was yet another attempt on his part to earn the maternal approval that he had so achingly yearned for all his life.

Conversion, a real experience of falling in love with Jesus, had allowed him to achieve a measure of independence from the inner demands that his mother still made on him, but he was by no means free yet. He knew, for instance, that there was no question of him loving a woman properly until some of the most fundamental hurts in him had been uncovered and healed. In the end it was through a change of direction in his churchmanship that Philip began to find the healing he needed in that part of his life.

'Churchmanship' was one of the 'three "C"'s' that underpinned Church Army life and practice. The other two were 'conversion' and 'consecration'. At first Philip had no problem with the business of churchmanship. There was a very small number of students in his year who were from a high church background. These attended Anglo-Catholic churches on their free Sundays, and were regarded with some suspicion and scepticism by their evangelical fellows, who felt that even the placing of a crucifix on a bedroom wall came very close to idolatry. The little group that used to meet in Philip's room for regular prayer would have been very reluctant to admit such misguided individuals to their holy sessions, and Philip himself, of course, was the leading exponent of low-church living.

It was therefore with great consternation that, as the first year progressed, Philip began to be uncomfortably aware that his own church background simply would not stay at the bottom of the trunk. Those days, far in the past now, when a lonely little boy had discovered warmth and companionship for the first time among his friends and adopted brothers in the choir of Newcastle cathedral, had left a much deeper and more abiding mark than he had realised.

Coupled with this very human feeling was a growing sense that there was something superficial about his uncompromisingly evangelical approach. The in-built mechanism that drove him blindly towards being 'the best' had taken no account of the fact that Philip, by his very nature, needed and wanted to be able to express his faith visually and dramatically.

All of the things he had been so energetically involved in – prayer, Bible study and evangelism – were no less important. On the contrary, they would have a deeper and much more meaningful role in a form of churchmanship that allowed the whole of Philip Ilott to be used in God's service, instead of the part of him that constantly sought approval.

Philip's faith needed to find a home, and he decided to seek it in the Anglo-Catholic church.

On free Sundays he began to explore the part of London where he lived, looking for churches that might give him a clue about what was missing, and where it might be found. Two churches in particular became great favourites. The first, St Mark's, Marylebone Road, was very Anglo-Catholic. Six candles on the altar, holy water at the door, and the scent of incense; Philip enjoyed every aspect of it, feeling, paradoxically, that he was both coming home, and experiencing something he had missed as a child. The other church, a beautifully designed and decorated building, was St Cyprian's, Clarence Gate.

Now feeling closer to the God he had met at his conversion than he had at any other time, Philip visited St Cyprian's regularly to pray on his own about his future, wondering whether God might be leading him ultimately towards the religious life of a monk. He often noticed one of the Church Army sisters from the college praying in another part of the Little Lady Chapel at the side of the building. He knew that her name was Sister Margaret Puddicombe. If it hadn't been for this new-found vocation for the religious life, and if he could have been freed sufficiently within himself seriously to consider marriage, she would be the kind of girl who would make a wonderful wife . . .

Philip still had not mentioned his change of heart to anyone else, but now, as the end of his first college year drew near, he knew that he would have to do something or burst. Nowadays his Quiet Time was conducted behind a closed bedroom door, and as he began to feel an increasing closeness to God through prayer and meditation, so he was overwhelmed daily by a sense of his own sin. He confessed it always in the normal course of his devotions, but for some reason that didn't seem enough. He wanted, as the Bible puts it, to confess his sin 'one to another'.

Eventually, when the burden of his confusion and guilt was truly weighing down his spirit, he decided to speak privately to one of the few Anglo-Catholic brothers in his year, one of those whom Philip and his evangelical fraternity had inwardly castigated for leaning too heavily on the 'props' of their faith. The brother in question was, remarkably, as sympathetic as any low-churchman. He listened carefully to Philip's explanation that he felt the need to make a formal confession, and suggested that the principal – Prebendary Donald Lynch – would be the man to talk to.

It was good advice. The college head, much later to become godfather to Philip's daughter and a close family friend, was very understanding. He nodded, smiling a little, when the worried young man spoke of his fear that those students who had been closest to him until now would never understand the change of direction that he was contemplating. They might laugh, or criticise him, or worst of all ignore him altogether. Donald Lynch made a practical suggestion: 'On your next free Sunday, don't just go and pray in one of these churches between services. Go to a morning service – listen to the sermon and see how you feel. Why not try St Mark's?'

The following Sunday, Philip sat gingerly at the end of one of the pews in the highly decorated interior of St Mark's, almost holding his breath as the service began. Further along the pew, a little line of people wearing the familiar uniform indicated that this was a favourite place for worship for the Anglo-Catholic minority from the college. Their eyes rested on the slightly nervous figure of Brother Ilott with some speculation and no little surprise.

Philip relaxed within minutes. 'Smells and bells' there were in abundance, and a rich, deeply satisfying sense of the presence of God in the visual urgency and drama of the mass.

'Here,' breathed Philip to himself, 'I can be me, for God.'

It was a pity the sermon had to go and spoil everything. The preacher was speaking about Mary, the mother of Jesus.

'Our Lady,' he said, 'is an important and necessary part of our lives. Just as she was and is the mother of Our

Lord, so she would like to be in a motherly relationship to us . . .'

That was enough – in fact it was too much for Philip. Propelled quite spontaneously to his feet, he turned and almost ran down the centre aisle, desperate to escape from those awful words and the confusion of anger and painful misery that they had caused. Like a grenade lobbed from the pulpit, the concept of Mary as the mother of all men had exploded in his mind on all three levels – emotional, intellectual and spiritual. As he walked rapidly along the pavement, away from St Mark's and the heresy that it enshrined, the super-evangelical stormed and raged at the front of his mind about the dreadful, unscriptural nature of the message that was presumably still continuing in that heathen edifice whose dust he had just shaken from the soles of his Church Army boots.

'No man comes to the Father except through me . . .'

'There is no other name given . . .'

'At the name of Jesus . . .'

His mind produced verses and fragments of verses with Pavlovian ease. That was the point of learning them, of course. So that, on occasions such as this, when the devil sought to pollute the clear stream of doctrine, you were armed with weapons to drive him back and protect the purity of the gospel. How could anyone be so blind – so wicked! God would punish those who deliberately misled the innocent followers of Christ in this blatant manner! Philip clamped his lips grimly together, trying to feel nothing but righteous anger.

It didn't work. His steps slowed almost against his will, as a different and more distant voice spoke from the back of his mind. The voice was more desperate than angry, and it was the voice of a tearful child.

'I don't want Mary! I don't want another mother – I don't want the one I've got, because she hurt me and she doesn't love me and she *won't* love me whatever I do! I don't want to hear about mothers or wives or women or girls, because they're all nasty, horrible people who shouldn't be allowed . . .'

Philip stopped dead as the tears in his heart threatened to rise to the surface and leave him sobbing in the street. That reaction just now, back in the church, it hadn't really been about theology at all, it had been about the block in him that wouldn't move enough to allow the thought of physical or emotional closeness to women. At an even deeper level he was unable to accept the maternal side of God himself, personified or symbolised, he wasn't sure which yet, by the person of Mary, the mother of Jesus. Something had to be done – something needed to happen.

He walked slowly and miserably back towards St Mark's, arriving at the door just in time to meet the other brothers as they emerged at the end of the service. They were not pleased. One in particular, an assistant training officer, was furious. He was scandalised by the very idea that a Church Army representative in full uniform should have walked out of a service in the middle of the sermon. He made it quite clear that he intended to report the matter to the principal at the earliest opportunity. It was a very dejected Brother Ilott who sat down to his cold Sunday lunch a little later that day. Almost certainly Donald Lynch had already learned that he was a 'disgrace to the Church Army'.

The next day, Philip, who had always rather relished his role as a model student within the college, took himself with dragging steps to the principal's office and tapped gently on the door. He *was* a disgrace, he told himself as he waited; he deserved everything he was about to get.

Wise people are always kind when they need to be. Prebendary Donald Lynch saw far more as he studied the embarrassed young man before him than Philip could have realised. Gently, he suggested that an apology might be in order to Father John Crisp, the priest who had delivered the sermon at St Mark's on the previous day.

Greatly relieved by the principal's response, Philip visited the priest as soon as it could be arranged, to express his contrition. It was something of an anti-climax to learn from an amused John Crisp that the disgraceful walk-out had not even been noticed from the pulpit.

Emboldened by the warmth of this encounter, Philip went on to describe his longing to make a confession that would allow him to feel truly absolved. The priest agreed to prepare him for his first formal confession, sending him back to college with instructions to think back through his life and pick out all the important and significant occasions on which he had hurt, or been hurt by, other people.

Much of Philip's enthusiasm for confession drained away as he obeyed this instruction and surveyed the wrecked landscape of his childhood. Could he really sit in the darkness of the confessional box and reveal to someone he hardly knew the wounds that still crippled him in early manhood? How would he find the words to describe such things? Suppose he broke down and made a fool of himself? What would Father John think of him? What would his mother say or think or do if she knew that her unsatisfactory son was about to make a vulgar display of things that were better kept hidden and forgotten for ever? He shrank inwardly at the thought of her voice, full of scorn and contempt for his latest ludicrous exploit. For a moment he thought of Mary, caring for *her* little boy with such gentleness and devotion. The old anger flooded him again. He thought of those nights, the rows, the shed . . .

On the day appointed for his first confession, Philip was in a state of fragile readiness. It had been tempting to back out. Most of the other students were still unaware of the radical changes that were happening in him. He could have dismissed recent events as products of a passing mania, but somehow he had resisted the temptation and now he was quietly, though nervously, determined.

Always a smart dresser, Philip spent even longer than usual that morning polishing the buttons of his uniform and brushing the grey serge until not a single unwanted speck was visible. At breakfast, which was always taken in silence, he prayed with fearful simplicity to the God who loved him, for help and protection in the unfamiliar experience that was to come.

It seemed that God had answered his prayer in a completely unexpected way when, later that morning, the principal appeared and drew him confidentially to one side.

'Philip,' he said quietly, 'I'm afraid I have some bad news for you. Father Crisp has had a most unfortunate accident involving a slipped disc, and is likely to be in hospital for some considerable time. I don't have to tell you what that means, do I?'

Drawing on whatever thespian skills he had, Philip gave a very fair impression of a deeply disappointed man. He sighed convincingly. 'Yes, Principal,' he said, 'it means that my confession will have to be postponed.'

Donald Lynch patted the young man's shoulder sympathetically as he walked away, clearly feeling genuinely upset by this development.

Philip's spirit skipped and sang like that of a man who has avoided dental treatment. No confession today! No delving into the past and getting upset and feeling embarrassed. He didn't have to go, and it wasn't his fault! Of course, he felt sorry about poor John Crisp, but how wonderful that . . .

'Ah, Philip. Good news, my boy!'

The principal had reappeared, a satisfied smile illuminating his face.

'Father Crisp has telephoned from the hospital, Philip.

He tells me that he is more than happy to conduct your confession from his hospital bed. Happy news!'

'Yes, indeed!' responded Philip hoarsely, his acting skills stretched much further now by the need to appear enthusiastic and thrilled. 'That's wonderful!'

Later that day he arrived at the information desk of St Luke's Hospital for the Clergy, in Fitzroy Square, slightly perspiring and still very apprehensive. A nurse led him to a small private room, showed him in, and closed the door behind him. John Crisp was lying on his back, in bed, with one leg suspended in the air.

All through Philip's life, he was to see God playing this kind of game with him. Yes, Brother Ilott, and later Father Ilott, would be allowed to express himself through the ritual and elaborate practices of the Anglo-Catholic church, but again and again the deeply significant moments in his spiritual journey seemed to happen in the most homely circumstances.

Philip had certainly been dreading the fulfilment of his desire to make confession, but at least it would have had an aura of ceremony and sacrament about it. The darkness of the wooden confessional box, the mysterious grill, the sense that God's agent was invisible but present in the neighbouring compartment; it all added up to an experience that promised to resound with a bass spiritual note. There was something mildly hysterical about the idea of making your first confession to a man lying flat on his back with his leg stuck in the air in a hospital room. It was bizarre.

But God knew best. A sick and vulnerable man is much easier to open up to than someone who is healthy and vertical. Later in his life Philip was to learn this lesson from the other side of the confessional relationship.

Kneeling by that hospital bed the child in Philip was allowed to pour out his sadness and pain for the first time. The floodgates were opened and the past flowed like a torrent into the present. It was a marvellous re-

lease. Years and years of anger and hurt escaped and
evaporated. In particular, the hate he felt for his mother,
subdued and repressed for so long by her invisible,
grimly judgemental presence, was articulated for the
first time.

It was, he reflected much later, like a clearance sale.
Everything that could go at that time went. In return,
John Crisp offered the young man kneeling by his bed
wise counsel and gentle encouragement, finally absolv-
ing him from his sins in the name of Jesus Christ, whom
Philip already knew and loved.

If it hadn't been for the dignity due to his uniform,
Brother Ilott would have liked to dance and somersault
and skip all the way home. There were still deep layers
of doubt and difficulty that lay untouched, but God and
the passing years would deal with them. For now, he
knew only joy – the joy of forgiveness and freedom –
together with the rare and precious knowledge that
repentance is a happy thing.

Back at the college, Philip slipped quietly up to his
room, closed the door behind him and, kneeling by the
bed, opened his Bible. John Crisp had given him a
penance. He was to read the Beatitudes. As his eyes
followed the familiar words, something seemed to melt
in him. Never before had they made sense as they did
now in connection with his confession. These words of
Christ were not the words of a man whose interest lay
in consigning sinners to hell, but the words of someone
who would have been ready to suffer the agonies of the
cross even if Philip Ilott had been the only sinner in the
world who needed salvation. His eyes were misting over
a little as he laid the Bible down and softly repeated the
words that had spoken to him most clearly:

Blessed are those who mourn, for they shall be
    comforted . . .
Blessed are the merciful, for they shall obtain
    mercy . . .

Blessed are the peacemakers, for they shall be called
    sons of God . . .

As a result of this experience – almost a second conversion – Philip came to two conclusions.

First, he decided the time had come to 'go public' with
his return to the Anglo-Catholic church. He hung a
plain wooden cross up on the wall of his room, and he
determined that when the creed was said at college
services he would kneel at the words: '. . . and was
incarnate by the Holy Ghost of the Virgin Mary, and was
made man . . .' This was a sure indication of Anglo-
Catholic orientation. The rest of the brothers couldn't
fail to notice that.

Nor did they. They noticed everything, including of
course that Philip was now attending high Anglican
church services on his free Sundays.

The response was as strong in some quarters as Philip
had feared. God and the principal of the college may
have been happy enough with the way things were
going, but many of Philip's erstwhile evangelical associ-
ates were not. They recoiled from the cross on his wall
like vampires from garlic. Many of the group that had
been accustomed to meet for prayer in that room decided
that the Lord would have them do so no longer. Some,
and this was *deeply* hurtful, refused to speak to Brother
Ilott at all.

It was painful, but in no way did the hostile response
deflect him from his course. He felt no inclination to
persuade others against their form of churchmanship,
but he had now found a home for the expression of *his*
faith, and that was that. Philip's prayer and devotional
life began to grow, in depth now as well as in competition
with others. His desire to take communion and make
confession had become a longing, a yearning, a real
need. In the old phrase, he was 'on fire for God' – and
the fire warmed him wonderfully.

The second conclusion that Philip came to was evidence that something little short of a miracle had happened when he knelt and made his confession at John Crisp's bedside. He concluded, though with some uncertainty, since he had never known such an emotion before, that he was in love with Sister Margaret Puddicombe.

5

The Wooing of Margaret Puddicombe

It was one of those times, rare enough in most people's lives, when you experience nothing but compassion for all those people who are not fortunate enough to be you.

Seated by a window in the packed railway compartment, Philip, immaculate as ever in his Church Army uniform, turned his eyes away from the dirty, rain-streaked window for a moment to glance at the other occupants of the carriage. Most of them had settled into that semi-hypnotised, trancelike state that long train journeys always seem to induce. The camaraderie that arises among the English in bad weather and war had lasted for only a few miles after their departure from Chester, and now the only sound, apart from the train itself, and an angry rattle of rain on the window, was an occasional creak from a waterproof as bodies shifted in the cramped conditions, or the rustle of a newspaper or magazine.

None of these people, thought Philip, could possibly be as excited or as happy as I feel at this moment. It was almost impossible to contain the surging current of longing and anticipation. He felt as if it must burst the carefully polished buttons of his tunic at any second. Not for anything in the world – not for riches or worldly success, not even for the love of his mother – would he consider changing places with anyone in this carriage, or this train, or this country, or this entire earth. For Philip was on his way to secure the third love of his life. The first had been his grandmother, the second was Jesus, and now there was a girl called Margaret.

Philip had turned towards the window once more, leaning his elbow on the sill and cupping his chin in his hand. Outside, the rain and wind seemed furious with the earth, whipping and lashing and beating with such intensity that the countryside was almost completely obscured. It was rather cosy being inside while the weather stormed impotently outside; cosy and soporific.

Letting his body sway with the rhythm of the train, Philip thought about Margaret, and a smile spread automatically across his face. Tomorrow, if his vicar in Chester had really heard God speaking, and if Margaret had received his telegram, and if by some miracle she had a free day, and if she wanted to of course, she would meet him in that special church in London, and he would tell her that he was in love with her. She was even more beautiful than the queen – and that was saying something.

As the steam monster at the front of the train powered its way through the ever-worsening conditions, Philip said a sincere 'Thank you' to God for leading him into the Church Army; for it was there that he had first met Sister Margaret Puddicombe, more than two years ago now, when they began their training on the same day in the same college, not far from Madame Tussaud's and the Florence Nightingale Hospital.

Could it really have been that long ago? Those two years, the happiest of his life so far, seemed to have passed like a flash.

Half dozing, warm and protected from the elements as he journeyed, he smiled again as he pictured Margaret in his mind.

He certainly hadn't been looking for a wife – or even a girlfriend. Since 'Nellie from the Tenements' there had been no one. His only other close encounter with a member of the female sex had not been an encouraging one.

There was a girl he had met during National Service. She was the daughter of an officer and her name was Jean. Jean was very correctly behaved, very well turned out, most prim and proper, just the sort of girl that Philip might have taken an interest in at that stage in his life.

When he left the army she gave him her address and asked him to visit her if he was ever in London. Prompted by curiosity and other equally natural but probably unconscious motives, he arrived at the front door of her flat one day and rang the bell. The vision who answered the door was certainly Jean, but a markedly different and, to Philip, quite horrifying version of the same girl. She was dressed in a *very* tight black top and tight leopard-skin trousers. Her face was heavily made up and, worst of all for the little boy who lived in Philip, the nails on her fingers and toes were painted bright red. She would want to master him and hurt him and use him, just like . . .

Like many young Christians before and since, Philip escaped fear by taking refuge in judgement. She was a harlot! She was a whore! He must resist the devil.

Asked in, he advanced, but stood rigidly on his guard, and lost no time in announcing to the bewildered Jean that she was 'on her way to hell'. Perhaps not surprisingly, this put an end to the relationship before it had a chance to begin. Telling girls they are bound for eternal damnation is hardly the basis for a prolonged courtship. Philip left the flat with his heart pounding and his lips muttering thanks for a mighty deliverance.

At the college, however, there was absolutely no question of contact, inappropriate or otherwise, between male and female students.

The brothers and sisters were very strictly segregated, meeting formally in only two situations. In chapel services (matins, morning prayer and communion three times a week), the sisters sat in a block on the left, the brothers on the right. In lectures the girls occupied the front seats, while the boys paid attention from the back.

So concerned were the authorities about the possible effects of 'mingling' that students of a different sex were forbidden to speak to each other even if they met in the street outside. Infringements of this rule meant almost instant dismissal.

Sister Margaret Puddicombe was perfectly happy with this arrangement. From the age of eleven she had felt she wanted to do something for God, and the call to full-time Christian work had been a part of her since she was a girl of sixteen. College life was simply a means of identifying the specific task awaiting her. She found something very special in the corporate worship each morning, but generally speaking she regarded the men as having no great relevance to her life. Like Philip, but with much more humility and no self-advertisement, she very soon became the 'star of the show' on the girls' side, very highly thought of and inclined to emphasise the love of God in her preaching, as opposed to the salvation and judgement theme that characterised Philip's earlier sermons.

She was also extremely pretty.

Philip first noticed Margaret one day when she was on sacristan duty. This involved practical preparation for services in the chapel. His eye was caught by the care and devotion she put into the simple act of unravelling the altar, that is, removing an outer covering-sheet from the altar cloths themselves. There was something about the loving precision with which she performed this humble task that appealed to him in a way he found hard to define. Also, ironically, he found the content of her preaching attractive and reassuring, despite the very different nature of his own. Margaret (a woman!) invited people, with great gentleness, to come and be loved by God.

Philip found himself responding on a personal level to this female personality who managed to combine self-effacing humility with achievement and popularity. It was not a sexual attraction at that time; Philip was not yet sufficiently in touch with his feelings to acknowledge fully his own sexuality, but if there is a spiritual equivalent to sex-appeal, Margaret had it – and Philip fell for it. Physical attraction followed very quickly.

Following his first confession, Philip was able to recognise for the first time the strength of these growing feelings, and to enjoy the sense of a special significance in the fact that both he and Margaret used the beautiful Lady Chapel of St Cyprian's for private prayer, although not a word passed between them. There is often a delicious piquancy about the ways of God with humankind. There in that chapel, at least once a week, two Church Army students prayed separately and earnestly about whether they should join celibate religious orders at the end of their training, little suspecting that within a few years they would be married to each other.

It was Philip who was the first to realise that celibacy was not for him. He found himself doing less and less praying at St Cyprian's and more and more covert glancing at Margaret's attractive profile as she knelt devotedly and obliviously at the other side of the chapel.

Unable to contain his feelings any longer, he mentioned to Terry Crolley, a fellow student, that he was falling in love with Sister Margaret Puddicombe. Terry, one of those resourceful types who have a genius for side-stepping rules without suffering retribution, managed somehow to convey this information to one of the sisters on the girls' side, and she in turn lost no time in finding Margaret.

'Margaret,' she said in hushed, excited tones, 'guess what I've just found out. Philip Ilott is really over the moon about you! Did you know?'

'No,' said Margaret coolly, and then in a masterpiece of brevity and conciseness: 'He can stop that for a start! I'm not interested!'

'Ooh, Margaret,' persisted her informant in a squealed whisper, 'he is! He really is, Margaret!'

But Margaret was adamant. Her sole reason for attending this college was to be commissioned into the Church Army, so that she could go out and be a full-time servant of God in whichever place she was best suited; and, whatever her specific expectations might have been, that is exactly what happened.

Not very long after learning of Philip's 'over-the-moonness' Margaret broke her leg and was in plaster for several weeks. For the first two days she was obliged to rest, and it was then that Philip first managed to communicate with her in person.

Terry Crolley's intelligence service was not the only means of contact between one side of college and the other. The most popular and least risky means of passing news on was that which utilised the corporate time of prayer held each morning in the chapel. Suitably phrased spontaneous prayer could convey any message you liked.

'We pray for Brother Bernard as he travels to Doncaster today to visit the parish in which he might be taking up a post . . .'

'Lord, bless Sister Jane, who received bad news in the mail this morning . . .'

'We bring before you, Heavenly Father, dear Sister Margaret, who has broken her leg by banging it against a piece of furniture, and will be in plaster for six weeks at least, and resting without moving for the next day or two . . .'

Why those in authority should have believed that God and his angels needed all this detailed information is an intriguing question, but no one ever queried or commented on these strange prayers. God himself may have felt a little left out of the process, but he is infinitely forgiving, and it *was* a very efficient information exchange.

Philip found an opportunity that day to hurry out to

the nearest newsagent's shop. He spent a few pence out of his precious twelve and sixpence on the nicest 'Get Well' card he could find, then hurried back to the college to write an appropriate message. Somehow he managed to persuade one of the staff sisters to allow him to deliver the card in person.

'It isn't the thing at all,' she said sternly, 'but if you're very quick . . .'

Sister Puddicombe, sitting in the girls' lounge with her plastered leg resting on a chair, was quite flabbergasted when Philip walked in with the unsmiling staff sister, who had insisted on being present in the role of chaperone. There was no question of speaking. Philip, who must have wondered if he was destined for ever to share important moments with people whose legs were out of action, was allowed only to hand the card to Margaret, give her one of his sweetest smiles, and leave.

Alone again, the invalid opened her card and read: 'All my love, Philip.'

'Oh, glory!' she said faintly to the empty lounge.

It was a dramatic move, but it didn't change Margaret's mind. Even if she had been interested in 'that sort' of relationship, it was highly unlikely that she would be drawn towards someone like Philip, whose narrow and loudly expressed views on dancing and other evils were all she knew of him from lectures and sermons during the past year. But Philip was remarkably persistent. Just as he had made up his mind to steer back towards the Anglo-Catholic church, whatever the opposition might be, so he now determined that Margaret would one day be his wife. It was just a matter of time.

One day Margaret was busy in the first-floor laundry-room that was used by the sisters. To her alarm, the door which gave access to the fire escape suddenly crashed open and one of the brothers appeared, breathless but excited, waving an envelope in his hand.

'Quick!' he cried. 'Take this!' With a swift parting wave he dashed back across the top of the fire escape to a door which opened into the brothers' side of the building. The bewildered Sister Puddicombe looked blankly at the envelope. Closer examination revealed that it contained a letter from that annoying Philip Ilott, this time stating in sentimental but quite unequivocal terms that he was in love with her.

Margaret remained determinedly unmoved by these and other courtship ploys, though by the time her two years of training were finally completed she must have been aware that Philip was in deadly earnest.

Amazingly, by the time both of them had been commissioned and the day for leaving college had arrived, there still had not been a single word exchanged between them. Philip was desperate to know what Margaret's new address would be, and a tip-off from the ubiquitous Terry, that her trunk, neatly labelled, was standing in the front hall awaiting her departure, seemed a heaven-sent opportunity. Making some excuse to go to the chapel, he grabbed a pen and a scrap of paper, flew down to the hall and hastily scribbled down the address from the luggage label.

With college ended, the brothers and sisters, now full-fledged officers in the Church Army, went their separate ways, some to work in parishes, others to become attached to caravans (the mobile equivalent of trekking carts), a few, such as Margaret, to be assigned as children's missioners.

It was after just a few weeks engaged in this kind of work in Clapham that Margaret received the longest letter she had ever seen in her life. Philip (now *Captain*) Ilott, writing from the Chester caravan where he was now based, took thirty-two closely written pages to explain his feelings in every detail, concluding with the expression of his burning desire to marry Margaret as soon as it could possibly be arranged. Interspersed with the more romantic sentiments were statements intended to convey Philip's conviction that the Ilott–Puddicombe union was divinely inspired and approved, and therefore difficult to argue with. For someone who had found it almost impossible to convey his feelings to women all his life, it really wasn't a bad effort at all.

Margaret, shaken but not stirred, was still not very happy. Her calling to serve God remained the most important thing in her life. Like the man who searches for his spectacles without realising he has pushed them up on to his forehead, it never occurred to her that, through Philip, God was calling her to a more testing full-time service than she could ever have imagined.

By the end of October that year, Philip could think of nothing but Margaret. Supposedly fully involved in mission work in Cheshire, he was finding it more and more difficult to concentrate on the task in hand. Over and over again, the mental image of her gently beautiful profile, her warm brown, shoulder-length hair and her pretty smile, filled his mind and monopolised his attention. Finding that his longing to be with Margaret was amounting to an almost physical pain, Philip wrote once more, begging her to agree to a meeting in London. Sister Puddicombe wrote back. She would have none of it. She was 'too busy'.

Agitated beyond words, Philip went to his senior officer on the Chester caravan, Brian Tompkins, and stumblingly explained about the mental distraction that was making his missionary work so hard to focus on.

Captain Tompkins was displeased, to say the least. The last thing he needed was something as powerful as true love interfering with the total commitment of his smart young junior officer. Fortunately, he was wise enough to realise that Philip would never relax until some solution to his problem had been found. He suggested that the parish priest should be consulted.

Philip was very fond of his priest in Chester. In his early sixties, and going progressively blind, Father Cross was one of those rare people who seem to walk so closely and humbly with God that they are able to hear the voice of the Spirit in ways that can be startlingly explicit. Sitting at his study desk on that rainy October day, he listened quietly as Philip poured out his longing and frustration, then sat silently for a moment before speaking.

'Philip,' he said, 'let me pray about this.'

It was a strange moment. Certainly, Philip was beginning to learn that there really was a God, who really was present, and really did care, but there was still a great deal of Philip Ilott at the centre of it all. This was somehow different, and it puzzled him.

The priest turned his failing physical eyes towards the window; as if by using some other kind of sight altogether, he had located a friend standing just behind his chair. Philip wasn't sure what to do. Should he pray? Should he go? Father Cross was still facing away from him, very still, as if he was listening. At last he turned back, his face completely at peace.

'You are to send a telegram today, Philip. You will travel to London this evening, stay at the Church Army hostel tonight, and meet Margaret at eleven o'clock tomorrow morning.'

Philip was dumbfounded. The authority in the voice of the priest was absolute. It never occurred to him at that moment to doubt that God had spoken through Father Cross. He was going to see Margaret tomorrow – no question. Pausing only to thank his adviser, he set off through the rain towards the post office. The message he sent was short. It had to be. Telegrams were terribly expensive.

MEET ST CYPRIAN'S ELEVEN TOMORROW – PHILIP

He had no idea if Margaret would be at the address to which he had directed the telegram. She might have been sent away on a mission to some other part of London, or even some other part of the country. Even if she were there, there was no reason to suppose that the next day would be a free one, or that she would want to meet him if it was. But a fizzing mixture of trust and excitement made it impossible to dwell on improbabilities. He *must* go!

The rain was still pouring as he went back to the caravan, explained to the long-suffering Brian, packed a bag, and later boarded the London train that came hissing and thundering in not long after his ticket was bought and safely stowed away in his tunic pocket.

For some people a train journey in the rain offers enjoyment so edible that its flavour tingles on the tongue. Add the ingredient of a crucial encounter with someone you are in love with at the end of the journey, and you have a veritable feast of immediate and anticipated pleasure.

Wedged into his seat by the window, Philip found that the long journey took on a dreamlike quality. Sleeping, waking, dreaming and praying, it was difficult to believe that there ever had been or ever would be anything but this carriage, and these people, and the endless rhythm of the wheels clattering through the rainswept darkness.

Arrival at a cold, wet Euston Station dispelled this illusion very effectively, but nothing could dampen Captain Ilott's inner excitement as he made his way to the Livingstone House hostel in North London. There, he did his best to settle and sleep; but with his fiercely active imagination raging incessantly, it was impossible to do more than doze for a few minutes every now and then. The rest of the time he spent either in prayer for a successful outcome from tomorrow's adventure or in the elaborate construction of mental images involving himself and Margaret meeting and melting into each other's arms and lives. Towards dawn he slept a little, and on waking drew back a corner of the curtain behind his bed to find that the rain was falling with unabated vigour. He must get ready.

First, brush the grey uniform over and over again to make sure it looked absolutely perfect. Then the shoes, buffed until they shone. Philip had learned all about 'bull' during National Service and Church Army training, not to mention his mother's impossibly high demands for perfection in all outward appearances. But this wasn't for his mother. It was for Margaret. He gave his shoes an extra, slightly defiant brush to prove it. There! Finally, and very importantly, there was the little mother-of-pearl cross attached to a red ribbon (red for the blood of Christ) that hung in a loop on the pocket button of his uniform jacket. All the students had been given one when they were commissioned. He polished the tiny object with infinite care, a symbol of his first real achievement since leaving home. Finally, with another glance at the downpour outside, he donned his light grey mackintosh, only just dry after yesterday's soaking, placed his peaked cap neatly on his head, and stepped through the front door of the hostel, his heart beating with at least as much insistency as the driving rain on the shining pavement outside.

St Cyprian's Church, Clarence Gate, is just on the edge of Regent's Park, a short walk from Baker Street tube station. Coming out of the station entrance and walking up Baker Street gave Philip an extra sense of warmth and exhilaration. Being here in the vicinity of the college was like coming back home. If only – if only she would be there when he walked into the church, it would be perfect!

The dry stillness of the church porch was in dramatic contrast to the turbulence of the outside world. Philip closed the outer door carefully behind him, removed his cap, and paused for a moment as he realised that he had forgotten to breathe for some time. Passing a hand over his wet forehead and damp hair, he swallowed hard and pushed open the inner door.

Slowly his eyes travelled in an arc from left to right across the interior of the building, picking out the familiar features almost unconsciously: the simple oak pulpit; the beautiful, elaborately carved chancel screen with its fourteen saints depicted on figure panels; the massive High Altar, an enormous stone slab more than

a yard wide and twelve inches thick, bearing six pewter
candlesticks; and, to his right, the Lady Chapel, where
he and Margaret had knelt in silent, solitary prayer on
so many Sunday afternoons. Today there was only one
person visible in the church. In the Lady Chapel, kneeling in the place that Margaret had always used, was a
slight figure in a green coat. For a moment he wasn't
quite sure, then she moved very slightly, and all doubt
disappeared.

She was there.

Between them, God, Father Cross, Margaret, the
General Post Office, British Rail and Philip Ilott had got
it right.

Margaret was there, and as Philip walked quietly up
the length of the church, his heart seemed to swell to
bursting-point. She was there – she was there, waiting
for him. Reaching the Lady Chapel, he genuflected to
the reserved sacrament on the altar, then knelt without
speaking, next to Margaret. For a few moments they
prayed silently, then sat back side by side on the pew
and looked at each other for the first time. Philip laid his
hand gently on hers and spoke with a little tremor in his
voice.

'I'm so glad you're able to be here, Margaret.'

He paused, searching briefly for a form of words he
had never needed to use before.

'You realise that I *do* love you?'

'I – I believe so.'

Margaret's answering smile was a little nervous.

Philip studied the slight form of the girl he had come
so far to see. An impartial observer might have noted
the limply saturated green mohair coat, the soaked
shoulder-length hair hanging in rat's tails, the flushed
and slightly troubled face. Philip was not an impartial
observer. He saw only radiance. The time had come to
pay her the greatest compliment that he could think of.

'Darling,' he said, 'you look so beautiful – you look
like the queen.'

Later, over lunch, Margaret described how on receiving Philip's telegram she had been advised by the senior sister to meet her young suitor at the suggested time and place. Clearly, Father Cross had been closely tuned in to the voice of God. This particular Thursday was the day after Margaret returned from one mission, and the day before she departed for the next. It was her only free day in weeks.

She was still concerned that her response failed to match Philip's ardour and certainty, and arriving at the church looking and feeling like a drowned rat had not increased her confidence. Now, though, a little drier, sitting in a nearby café, listening to her companion's further protestations of love, she began to feel rather different. It was obvious that he genuinely cared for her, and if God was placing them together – well . . .

Philip wanted an immediate engagement. Margaret, still cautious, suggested that they should write to each other, and meet when they could – after all, because of the vows they had made at the beginning of the course, they were both committed to three years' work with the Church Army before marriage was possible.

Talking and planning, the couple made their way to Euston Station for the first of many painful partings.

Margaret walked along the platform, still holding Philip's hand as the train slowly pulled out, suddenly realising, with a little flurry of inner panic, that today she had given part of herself away. She sensed, for the first time, the strange combination of pain and joy that constitutes love, and, standing on the platform of Euston Station watching Philip's train recede into the distance, prayed in fear and hope that all would be well.

Philip, once again overcoming the temptation to perform double somersaults in an inappropriate place, hugged the success of his journey to himself all the way up to Chester. The next day he threw himself back into his missionary work with such zeal and single-mindedness that Brian Tompkins felt amply justified in the decision he had made to allow the love-sick Ilott to pursue his passion.

When Margaret told her parents that she would be seeing Philip on a fairly serious basis from now on, they extended a warm invitation to the young Church Army captain to join the Puddicombes for their annual festivities.

For Philip it was something new and quite wonderful to be part of a bustling family that behaved more or less normally in a large house at such a special time of year. He loved them all: Margaret's father and stepmother, her sister Heather, half-sister Monica, and half-brother Alan. For an unhappy only child, it was heaven.

An extra heavenly bonus involved the putting up of the Christmas decorations. Margaret and Philip were supplied with a huge box of materials, collected over years of Christmases, and instructed to take responsibility for decorating the entire house. Using a stepladder, the pair began work in the hall, but were delayed very early on in the proceedings by the happy discovery that kissing was a far more enjoyable occupation than fastening paper-chains to the wall. Happily ensconced on the top rungs with Philip, Margaret began to feel that there might be something in this 'love business' after all. There was a satisfyingly large number of rooms in the house, all of which could be worked on for hours. The breakfast-room, the dining-room, the sitting-room, all received the lingering attentions of the two conscientious decorators. Often the puzzled cry of Margaret's stepmother could be heard from another part of the house: 'Haven't you two finished yet?'

It was the best Christmas ever, and to Philip and Margaret it must have seemed that they were at the beginning of the good times. They both belonged to God, and because God loved them he had given them each other. In a little under three years they would be free to marry and continue to serve in a joint full-time Christian role of some kind.

God must have smiled to see these two young people of his caught up so completely in their enjoyment of each other and their surroundings. But the heart of God is a mixture of joy and sorrow as well. One day in the distant future Philip was to discover the meaning of his strange dream of crucifixion, and when that time came he would need Margaret in ways he had never dreamed of; and understand fully, for the first time, the depth of divine kindness that had given her to him.

6

Cornwall – Personalities
and a Poltergeist
(1958–1959)

Margaret's first encounter with Philip's parents was a
nightmare.

The reconciliation between Philip and his family happened half-way through his training at Cosway Street.
His mother and father had written to say that, as he
was approaching twenty-one, they would meet him in
London on his birthday. The venue for this occasion
was to be London Zoo. For some reason Mrs Ilott was
convinced that a zoo trip was the ideal 'treat' for a young
man attaining his majority.

Philip was very nervous about the meeting, still afraid
of rejection, and hurting inside about the two years of
silence that was now to end. They greeted each other
with great politeness, then trailed slowly around, gazing
vacantly at the animals. Philip desperately wanted his
mother to ask him how things were going, what his
training was like, how it felt to be at college. He wanted
her to comment on the uniform that he wore with such
pride, to say something – anything – to show his life
was of interest to her. He was disappointed. She wanted
to know nothing about any aspect of his life that was
not directly connected with *her*. His father made feeble
attempts to fill the gap, but it was not his respect and

interest that Philip wanted; not any more. It was too late
for that.

As their tour of the zoo ended, Philip was presented
with his twenty-first birthday gift, a pair of brown suede
shoes which he hated on sight, and a cake. It was all
rather bizarre, but at least they were back on speaking
terms again.

Now, nearly a year later, he was bringing the girl he
intended to marry home to Newcastle to meet and stay
with his parents. It was a great risk – perhaps even
greater than taking home his new-found Christian faith
– but he hoped and prayed that Margaret's natural charm
would overcome any obstacles.

In fact, the visit proceeded along the disastrous lines
that he had instinctively known it would. Only a few
hours after meeting Margaret, Philip's mother lost all
interest in her future daughter-in-law. The flowers Margaret had shyly presented to her never actually reached
the inside of the house. They were dumped in a bucket
outside the back door. There was nothing right about
Margaret. She was the daughter of a typewriter mechanic
for a start, and then she was a Church Army sister, a
member of that shabby little body who did unspeakable
things on street corners and had lured Philip away from
the pursuit of a 'proper' profession. Then, to cap it all,
Margaret happened to mention that her stepmother's
name was Edith. That was Philip's mother's own Christian name. For some reason this annoyed her intensely.
She hardly spoke to Margaret after the first morning,
communicating with her in a pointedly indirect way
through Philip. Margaret was very hurt and bewildered.
She had tried so hard.

That night, as Philip tried to rest in the room that had
once been called his 'bedroom', his mother came in to
tell him in hissed whispers that he had chosen the wrong
girl, and to ask him what he thought he was doing
bringing that sort of person back to the house. He was
in torment, inwardly raging with anger, but emotionally

devastated by this vicious withholding of approval at a time when it was most needed.

Next morning the process of eclipsing Margaret began. Edith Ilott selected from her wardrobe the most elegant and expensive clothes that she possessed. This dowdy little rival of hers was going to learn what a real woman looked like. There was no question of Margaret competing, even if she'd wanted to. On a Church Army sister's stipend you didn't buy many clothes. It was a miserable, humiliating situation. Philip's father was unexpectedly sweet in his attitude to Margaret, but it didn't make up for the barely concealed hostility of his wife.

It was a relief to set off into Newcastle on the following day with the exciting object of buying an engagement ring. Funds were low, but it didn't matter a jot. With her heart beating as though she had a thousand pounds to spend, Margaret selected a ring with a little solitaire, and Philip handed over sixteen pounds and ten shillings to the man behind the counter. Returning happily to the house, they met Philip's mother, dressed to kill as usual. She asked them what they had been doing. Surely, thought Philip, nothing can go wrong with this. He smiled at his mother, trying to convey to her the special happiness of their small adventure.

'We've been out and bought the engagement ring,' he said.

Suddenly animated, Edith Ilott leaned forward, holding out a crimson-nailed, beautifully manicured hand.

'Ooh!' she said. 'Let me see it.'

Flushing prettily with the pride of possession, Margaret smiled and put her ring in the older woman's hand.

'Oh, goodness,' she cried scornfully, eyebrows arched in disdain, 'it's cheaper than a dress ring!'

Badly hurt, Margaret muttered something about the cost not being the important thing, but those few words of derision had cut into her, deepening the fear and foolishness that she was already feeling in the presence of this strange, threatening woman. The visit was supposed to last a week, but Philip decided to cut it short. His mother's cruel treatment of Margaret and her nightly visits to his room to criticise his choice of a wife were too much to bear. Visiting his father the next day in the city office where he worked, he explained that as the visit was simply not working, and as Margaret was becoming more and more upset, they had decided to leave earlier than intended. His father's reaction was one of rueful understanding, and they left that day to stay with Margaret's family in Kent.

Here, a few days later, after the Christmas midnight mass, Philip took Margaret into the Lady Chapel of Holy Trinity Church, Beckenham, and proposed formally and sentimentally before slipping the little band of metal with a solitaire on to the third finger of her left hand. In the light of the flickering Christmas candles her eyes shone like the diamonds on a thousand pound ring.

*   *   *

Philip was very happy working on the Chester caravan, especially after his trip to London. Brian Tompkins was as evangelical in his churchmanship as Philip was Anglo-Catholic, but there was no doubt that they were following the same Jesus, and temperamentally the two men were well suited. It was illness that brought the working relationship to a premature end.

Philip had suffered two bouts of a rather mysterious illness during his college course. The doctor had put it down to overwork, which seemed reasonable, but Philip had been quite unnerved on each occasion. Illness smacked somehow of imperfection or failure. He had dreaded his mother learning that he was unwell. No son of Edith Ilott could possibly be anything but healthy.

This time it was more serious. Philip collapsed completely one day, and was unconscious for thirty minutes or more. When he woke he remembered nothing prior to the attack and had no idea how long he had been dead to the world. The second collapse was even more serious. Philip was forced to stay in bed for some time, and was clearly extremely ill. Brian Tompkins, advised by the local doctor that strain was the probable cause, decided that the pressure of working on the Chester caravan was too great, and that his recently commissioned assistant would be better off in a more leisurely environment. He arranged Philip's transfer to a different caravan, this time the one based at Truro in Cornwall.

In theory, it was the perfect placement. The Cornish caravan was the newest and most modern one in the whole of the Church Army, and Cornwall itself was as beautiful as ever. But Philip's senior officer at Truro, a flamboyant young man called Barry Newman, was much more difficult to live and work with than Brian Tompkins had been.

Like Philip, Barry was a high-churchman, but his approach to the work was very different. Philip had broadened out dramatically since his early days at training college, but he still wrestled inwardly with the concepts of right and wrong. It wasn't always easy for him to see what was acceptable and what was not. Barry Newman, on the other hand, was one of those outgoing, confident types who seem to leap blithely and safely over the chasms of doubt or uncertainty that cause others to hover worriedly on the brink.

It was a considerable shock for Philip, on the first occasion when he returned from a mission service, to find Barry sitting in the caravan with two girls, one on each knee. Not that there was any question of impropriety. It was just that the other man's personality had a magnetic quality – and he liked girls! Philip couldn't help feeling that this kind of thing was a little over the limit. Showmanship and flirtatiousness seemed to him to be in conflict with the general nature of their mission.

In his more honest moments, however, Philip had to admit to himself that some of these negative attitudes towards Barry were due to a feeling of being eclipsed

and overshadowed by the other man's extravagant
nature and flashing smile. Throughout the year in Cornwall, this sense of being diminished, a feeling that he
was unable to achieve recognition, never left Philip. At
college he had been a leading light, a star pupil, now he
was playing Silas to someone else's Paul, or feeling like
a little doggy who trails behind his master. Always
nervous about his own ministry, he found it doubly
difficult in this situation, as well as feeling genuinely
embarrassed by some of his colleague's more blatant
excesses.

The relationship survived, as it had to in the limited
space of a Church Army caravan, and there was always
plenty to do. Every few days it would be time to move
on to a different parish. This involved finding someone
with a car or a Land Rover who would be willing, with
or without payment, to haul the caravan to its new site,
while the two Church Army captains followed on Barry's
motorbike, a machine which gloried in the name of
Georgina.

From Portscatho on the Roseland peninsula they travelled to St Just, and then on to St Mawes. Everywhere,
they relished the beauty of the countryside around them,
and looked forward to discovering what the new parking
site would be at the next placement. It might be a church-
yard or a vicarage garden, or even the middle of a field.

In each new parish the routine was similar. First, a
commissioning service at which they were welcomed by
the vicar, then a week or more of home or school visiting,
with special evening services to follow up the work of
the day. It could have been a very pleasant and fulfilling
way of life if Philip had felt happier about his senior
officer. He began particularly to enjoy his free days,
when it was possible to go for solitary walks and just
pray, or think about Margaret.

It was during one of these days off that Philip had his
first experience of a poltergeist.

After walking happily for an afternoon, he happened

to pop into a typical dumpy little Cornish church to say his prayers. There was always something very attractive about being on his own in the cool interior of an empty church. Just God and Philip. It was refreshing, especially when things weren't going as well as they might otherwise.

Finding a pew in the centre of the nave, he knelt contentedly on one of the row of embroidered cushions and opened his Prayer Book. At that moment the silence was broken by footsteps, and an elderly grey-haired man dressed in full priestly robes appeared through a doorway at the side of the chancel and made his way across to the vicar's stall.

As Philip watched and waited, the old man, presumably the local parish priest, opened a book on the desk in front of him and began to sing the office of Evensong. Philip was taken aback – he hadn't realised that the time for Evensong had arrived – but he was pleased rather than anything else. It was terribly touching to know that this faithful old servant of God felt it worthwhile to come in here every day, dressed in full robes, to sing his office to a church that must almost invariably be empty. He decided to say the Prayer Book responses at the appropriate places.

'O Lord, open thou our lips,' sang the priest.

'And our mouth shall show forth thy praise,' said Philip in response.

'O God, make speed to save us.'

'O Lord, make haste to help us . . .'

Suddenly the big church Bible on the lectern opposite the vicar's side of the church fell to the floor with a slam and a flutter of thin paper pages. Philip jumped in his seat. The Bible must have been balancing on the extreme edge of the lectern, he supposed. How else could it have fallen when the nearest person was yards away? Perhaps vibration from a passing vehicle had dislodged it and just tipped it over the edge?

'Glory be to the Father, and to the Son: and to the Holy Ghost.'

'As it was in the beginning, is now, and ever shall be: world without end. Amen,' Philip responded mechanically.

'Praise ye the Lord.'

'The Lord's Name be praised.'

The priest was continuing as though nothing had happened. Now he walked slowly across the front of the chancel, picked the Bible up, and replaced it on the lectern. Leafing through the heavy book, he found the Old Testament lesson, read it out aloud, and, after marking the New Testament lesson, walked back to his stall to read the Magnificat.

'My soul doth magnify the Lord: and my spirit hath rejoiced in God my Saviour. For he hath regarded . . .'

Crash!

This time Philip was watching the Bible. Not only had it fallen over the edge of the lectern, but he had seen it *slide* along the smooth wooden surface before plummeting to the stone floor below.

A cold sweat broke out on the young Church Army captain's brow as he tried to mentally accommodate this strange happening. How could the Bible have moved on its own? How could it? Could the whole building be on a slant, so that with a highly polished lectern the Bible would . . . No, that was silly! But why hadn't the vicar turned a hair? Suddenly Philip wanted very much to get out of this strange church, only he seemed to be stuck in his position, far too frightened to move.

'. . . is now, and ever shall be: world without end. Amen.'

The priest had completed his reading of the Magnificat and was moving towards the lectern again. Patiently, without any visible signs of annoyance or puzzlement, he descended heavily on to one knee, picked up the Bible for the second time, and put it gently back on the lectern. Finding the New Testament lesson once more, he read the words in an unwavering voice, then crossed the chancel again to begin the Nunc Dimittis.

'Lord, now lettest thou thy servant depart in peace . . .'

If only he would, thought Philip with total sincerity. By now he was badly frightened, and was willing the service to end so that he could leave. As the Nunc Dimittis proceeded, his eyes were locked on to the church Bible, closed now, lying peacefully in its place on the lectern.

'. . . mine eyes have seen thy salvation . . .'

The Bible didn't move.

'. . . To be a light to lighten the Gentiles . . .'

It still didn't move.

'Glory be to the Father, and to the Son . . .'

Perhaps nothing else would happen.

'. . . world without end. Amen.'

Time for the creed. The priest rose to his feet.

'I believe in God the Father Almighty, Maker of heaven and earth: and in Jesus Christ . . .'

Then it happened.

Philip stared in dumb horror as the Bible raised itself slowly into the air above the lectern and began to float down the centre aisle at about head height, increasing speed rapidly until it hit the west wall at the back with a loud crash. There was a brief chorus of rustling and slapping noises from other books somewhere at the back of the church, then a deep and resounding silence.

'Surely,' whispered Philip to himself through bone-dry, trembling lips, 'surely he must stop and say something now.'

But, amazingly, the old man continued imperturbably through the creed and the remainder of the service without an eyelid's flicker or a moment's pause. Nothing could have induced Philip to leave now. It would mean going out through the door at the back, past – past whatever it was. At the end of Evensong the priest made his way down the church to greet the pale young man in the grey uniform who appeared to be rooted to the pew he was sitting on.

'You must be a visitor to the area,' said the priest kindly. 'I was so pleased to see that I had a congregation this evening. You must have wondered why I trouble to read the lessons to an empty church. Well, you never know if someone might be hiding in a pew, or perhaps' – he chuckled – 'a courting couple. They might catch something of the word of God, and besides . . .'

'E-e-excuse me,' interrupted Philip at last. 'About the Bible. W-what was . . . I mean, why did it . . . ?'

'Oh, you mean our poltergeist,' said the vicar mildly. 'We often get this during the week. On Sundays as well sometimes.'

Clearly the man was not the least bit troubled by this strange phenomenon that was a regular occurrence in his church. Philip knew nothing about exorcism or deliverance, but it did seem to him that if the poltergeist, or whatever it was, was some kind of unhappy or trapped spirit, then someone ought to say or do something to release it. There had been something about the nature and sequence of events just now that suggested the actions of a sulky, very unhappy child, determined to draw attention to himself at the most significant moments of the service. As Philip bade farewell to the elderly priest, and made his way nervously and rather hurriedly out through the back of the church, he wondered why the situation had been allowed to continue for so long without anything being done.

Walking briskly back towards the village where the caravan was presently based, he remembered the gentleness with which the priest had replaced the Bible on its lectern. He pictured the old man coming into the church, day in and day out, to say his office and read the lessons to an empty church, and suddenly he knew why things had been left as they were. That thing in the church – that spirit, or poltergeist, or whatever it was – may have been a nuisance, but it was also company . . .

Philip's stay on the Truro caravan might have continued for two or more years if he hadn't been struck down yet again by the illness that had dogged him for the last few years of his life. This time he collapsed in the middle of a mission service, and was put to bed in the spare room of a little cottage owned by an elderly couple named Ball. The doctor who visited was no more specific in his diagnosis than Philip's previous physicians had been.

'Overwork' was once more the only suggestion put forward, but although there was something almost heroic about the idea of 'ill health through overzealousness', it was all rather worrying. What if Philip was suffering from some serious, progressive malady? The thought produced an odd mixture of embarrassment and fear in him.

Though vague about diagnosis, the doctor was quite definite about treatment. Philip was to stay in bed for a couple of weeks and rest until he felt fully fit again. Mr and Mrs Ball were more than happy to offer their spare bed for as long as the 'poor young captain' needed it, so Philip settled down to begin his period of enforced immobility, rather relieved that he wouldn't have to be incarcerated in the caravan. The old couple looked after him well, Mr Ball in particular showing considerable ingenuity on the first day of his young guest's stay.

He appeared in the doorway of Philip's room clutching a large green flower vase, and after glancing significantly from Philip to the vase and back to Philip again, said in a broad Cornish accent, 'Yew may foind this yewsful!'

Philip stared intently at the vessel, trying hard to interpret what had sounded like some kind of coded message. Failing to discover any cryptic significance at all in the vase or the message, he decided to respond to Mr Ball's words according to their face value.

'Has someone sent me some flowers?' he asked brightly. It was only later, when no flowers appeared and the vase still stood beside his bed, that he realised what it was for. He was still a very naive young man.

An unexpected joy: after writing to Margaret in Clapham to tell her of his illness, she was released from her duties to come down on the train and be with Philip for several days, staying in another cottage nearby. They were blissful days, all the sweeter for being so unexpected, but her eventual departure cast a gloomy shadow over the immediate future. It was time to rejoin Barry Newman in the caravan, and the prospect was not an inviting one.

Philip soldiered on for a time, missing Margaret terribly now, until the combination of worry about his still unidentified illness and the unsatisfactory feel of the working situation became too much for him. In addition, and this was a much more acceptable argument to offer the Church Army when applying for a transfer, there was a growing sense of frustration about the business of arriving in a parish, working with people and even seeing them converted, then leaving without being able to get involved in the follow-up process. Whatever the dominant motive really was, Philip managed to persuade those in authority over him that a more permanent, residential placement would be a good idea.

In 1959, towards the end of the year, he received the offer of a placement at the mission church of St Francis of Assisi in Ashford. It sounded ideal, a place to settle down and do some really useful work. Even better, in comparison with Truro, it was really quite close to Clapham.

7

Ashford –
A Bike, a Bride, and
a Baby (1959–1962)

Philip's new parish priest was a frightening man.

Father Peter Goldsmid was a passionate character, full of love and anger. Adopted as a child, some deep-seated fury or frustration had been exacerbated by his experiences as a prisoner of war. From the beginning he shouted at Philip a great deal, terrifying him frequently, until time revealed that there was a burning, apparently non-expressible love beneath the crashing words. That was fine for those who knew the man well, but Philip didn't, and he could no more have argued with the priest at the beginning of his placement than he could have defied Company Sergeant Major Burton during his National Service training.

Father Goldsmid, a tall, dark man with piercing eyes, explained that Philip would be responsible for building up the work of St Francis of Assisi, the little daughter mission church which stood on the edge of a local council estate. He was to live on the estate with a couple who were near retirement age called Bert and Claire Pay. It was expected that he would be particularly concerned with the development of youth work.

Was that clear?

Yes, it was!

The priest's next words threw Philip into a panic that he hastily concealed.

'The first thing we need to do is get you on wheels!'

Wheels? thought Philip frenziedly. What kind of wheels? Did this uncompromisingly forceful man think that he had a driving licence? He had never sat behind the wheel of a car in his life, let alone taken a driving test. What sort of explosion might such a revelation provoke? He knew he ought to confess this deficiency, but the words just crouched inside his mouth, too terrified to come out.

'Fortunately,' went on the priest, 'I know of a deceased postman.'

Philip stared uncomprehendingly.

'I mean, of course, that his decease is fortunate for you and your transport needs. I have arranged to purchase his bicycle for your use.'

The relief that flooded Philip's mind on hearing this news was short-lived. He had never ridden a bicycle either. Now was the time to make this clear.

'Thank you very much,' he said feebly.

'Well, no time like the present,' said Father Goldsmid. 'We'll go up there in the car now and see if it's the right size. If it fits, you can ride it back. Let's go!'

Throughout the short trip from the vicarage to the home of the deceased postman, Philip tried hard to pluck up the courage to tell his fierce companion that he had never balanced on two wheels, but every time he opened his mouth the sight of the choleric priest's grim profile was too threatening, and he shut it again.

Arriving at the house in question, the priest pointed at a sturdy-looking bicycle leaning against the garden fence.

'There you are,' he announced firmly, 'a good bike! Get yourself on and see if it's the right size.'

Gingerly, Philip took hold of the handlebars and wheeled the machine into the centre of the garden path. Hopping slightly on one foot to keep his balance, he swung his other leg over the crossbar, and after one wild moment of near collapse and frantic adjustment, managed to achieve a fairly convincing stationary stability.

'Fits like a glove!' barked Father Goldsmid. 'I'll go and pay for it.'

As he disappeared into the little house, Philip felt quite relieved. The priest would go on ahead by car, and he'd be able to push his new bicycle back to the lodgings and practise riding it in private when he had time. It wasn't working out too badly after all. If he just stayed here, straddling his bicycle without moving, as if relishing the moment when he *would* be able to set off, then all should be well.

'Right! Off you go, and I'll follow you down the road in the car.'

Father Goldsmid's words shattered Philip's frail little edifice of relief.

'Oh, can't I err . . . couldn't I just walk down with it and . . . ?'

'Come on! Off you go. I'll follow. What are you waiting for?'

There was no arguing allowed, and it was too late to reveal the truth now. Feeling pale, both inside and out, he paddled the bicycle out on to the edge of the busy main road and balanced precariously for a moment by resting one foot on the kerb. Behind him a car door slammed and a motor coughed into life as the priest prepared to follow. Philip's whispered prayer was a deeply fervent one: 'Please, Lord, help me to stay on this bicycle! Help me – please help me!'

His prayer was answered right up to the point when he fell off. He had to fall off because he knew no other way of dismounting. The ride to the vicarage had been a hair-raising experience, an erratic, wobbling nightmare of a trip, during which Philip had been aware of great waves of annoyance and puzzlement emanating from the slowly moving vehicle behind him. Lying on the kerb outside the vicarage, entangled in his new bicycle, he heard the car door slam once more, and then Father Goldsmid was standing over him, breathing heavily through his nostrils.

'My goodness me, man!' he said with furious restraint, 'you haven't ridden a bicycle for a very long time, have you?'

'No, Father,' replied Philip faintly, 'I haven't.'

Over the next couple of weeks Philip spent many spare hours cycling round and round a local children's playground until he became reasonably proficient on two wheels. He even managed to cycle back to thank the deceased postman's widow for providing the vehicle, narrowly escaping a private display of the site of her gall bladder operation when the milkman arrived at the back door for his money. It was nearly a very nasty moment.

The lodgings worked out well. At the Pays' council house in Poncia Road, Philip was provided with a comfortable bedroom upstairs, and a study on the ground floor. Bert and Claire were a charming couple, but they were very different. Bert's interest in religion was obsessional. It was all he talked about, morning, noon and night, and although Philip was quite happy to indulge the old chap in this, Claire got very fed up sometimes. Often, when Bert was out, she would turn on the radio and tune into some dance music – Victor Sylvester was her favourite – then invite her young lodger to dance around the little living-room, until Bert's creaky bicycle warned of its owner's imminent return and the dancing had to stop. Claire was old enough to be Philip's grandmother, and the dances were nothing but innocent fun, but she did hold him very close sometimes.

Philip toiled very hard at his youth work, and was gratified to discover that he had a real talent for enthusing and energising young people. A very large Sunday school became even larger under his leadership, while the youth club, initiated by him and named 'The Young

Franciscans', went from strength to strength as modern music and dancing were introduced for the entertainment of the teenagers of the parish.

It was the age of Adam Faith, a very young Cliff Richard, Screaming Lord Sutch, and rather 'doubtful' types of music such as jazz. Much more released now from his fierce anti-enjoyment phase of a few years ago, Philip introduced a jazz band into the youth service that was held once every month, and often joined in with the dancing at the Young Franciscans' club nights.

He was frantically busy for most of every day, partly because he was by nature a highly active type, and partly because Peter Goldsmid demanded constant, detailed accounts of everything he had done, everyone he had spoken to or encountered, and anything he was planning for the future. The priest's bad temper was liable to erupt at any time, and for the smallest reason. Work and the proper documentation of work was, on the surface at any rate, the only thing of any importance. Illness he seemed to regard as a deliberate personal insult to himself.

During Philip's three years in Ashford he suffered three attacks of his mysterious illness, diagnosed this time as 'nervous exhaustion resulting from hyperactivity'. Each time Father Goldsmid was furious; he wasted no gentle words on this namby-pamby youngster pretending to be afflicted by some airy-fairy nonsense of a modern illness that probably didn't exist at all! Philip, who was actually very poorly indeed on these occasions, had to endure not only the illness, but a great deal of guilt induced by his priest's annoyance and scorn.

Sensing, as time went by, that Father Goldsmid's aggression concealed a quite different spirit altogether, Philip never became vindictive or deeply resentful about being made to look like a frightened rabbit so often, but it was hard not to feel considerable satisfaction on one particular day when the priest lost his dignity quite dramatically.

It happened at a crowded Annual General Meeting of the Parish Church Council, when Father Goldsmid was chairing the meeting from the position of power at one end of a long trestle table. Seeking to force his irascible point of view on the assembled company, he began to shout loudly and bang his fist on the table. If he had not leaned his chair back on two legs at the same time, he would have been perfectly alright. As it was, the sheer physical energy of his verbal attack sent him flying over backwards. He ended up on his back, with his feet waving wildly in the air, and with only a muffled but furious spluttering audible to the shocked assembly. Nancy Goldsmid, the incumbent's contrastingly charming wife, leaned her head close to Philip, who was choking desperately beside her, and whispered dryly, 'Serves him right!'

On 16 September 1961 Philip and Margaret were married at the Puddicombes' home church in Beckenham, Peter Goldsmid having reluctantly conceded that a slight break in routine might be necessary.

It wasn't until a week before the wedding that Philip's mother and father announced that they were definitely coming to the service. Since Margaret's unnerving first encounter with Philip's mother, relationships had been strained and variable, although Philip continued to write regularly, in the rather plaintively hopeful vein that had always characterised his contact with home. Margaret couldn't understand why he was so very persistent, and it was difficult for him to explain that, despite his experiences of conversion and confession, there was still an important part of him that cried out for his mother's love and approval.

On the night before the wedding, Philip's parents met Margaret's father and stepmother for the first time. It was a shock for Edith Ilott. Margaret's father, a very direct and forceful man, was determined that his daughter's wedding day would not be spoiled by the kind of tantrums that had hurt Margaret so much at that first meeting. He expressed his point of view very clearly to the couple from Newcastle: 'Now look! You really have got to behave yourselves tomorrow. We want no scenes . . .'

Quelled presumably by this unaccustomed male dominance, Philip's mother did behave herself, and the wedding proceeded without any problems. The best man was Terry Crolley, Philip's ingenious friend from Church Army training days, while Barry Newman acted as usher; this was a happy way for Philip to set a peaceful seal on a relationship that had never been an ornament to his spiritual self-image.

Philip himself was bursting with elation and nervousness as he took his place next to Margaret at the front of the church, jumping slightly as she discreetly reached over to turn his service sheet up the right way. Philip was not yet aware of Mr Puddicombe's stern warning to his mother, and still felt worried that something untoward might happen in the middle of the service. He felt particularly tense at that point when the vicar said: '. . . if any man can show any just cause, why they may not lawfully be joined together, let him now speak . . .' He wondered if his mother's response might be to faint or collapse – something designed to call attention to her instead of the two young people at the front. It wouldn't have surprised him at all, but it didn't happen.

When Philip walked his bride back down the aisle towards the main doors after signing the register, he caught a glimpse of his mother's face, strained but controlled, and suddenly felt sorry for her. Before the service he had presented her with a brooch, a sign that despite his marriage she was not forgotten. She had been unexpectedly delighted, and was wearing it now as he passed her. It had cost considerably more than the five pound note that his father had furtively pressed into Philip's hand when they met earlier. 'This is for your wedding,' he said. Philip had felt so upset and disappointed that he nearly tore it up. Five pounds was five pounds though, and the honeymoon would be expensive.

The reception was an opportunity to greet friends and relatives whom Philip had not seen for a long time. His grandmother was there, smiling and happy for him. So was Donald Lynch, the college principal, together with a strong contingent of the married couple's Church Army contemporaries, all smartly dressed in the familiar grey uniform. Philip enjoyed it all – meeting everybody, being one of the stars of the day, the speeches and the cake-cutting. It all caused a warm glow inside him, but most of all he enjoyed the fact that Margaret and he belonged to each other now, and that as long as they both lived he would never be alone again.

En route to Devonshire, the newly-weds spent the first night of their honeymoon at the Strand Palace Hotel in London. There probably never was a more transparently obvious honeymooning couple than Philip and Margaret. They did their best to appear casually experienced, but their high colour and nervous stiffness proclaimed the truth with silent eloquence from the moment they entered the reception area at the hotel. Reaching the safety of their room at last, Philip opened one of the cases, only to discover that it was awash with confetti. The action of lifting the lid sent a shower of multicoloured fragments all over the bed and the carpet. Hastily they both dropped on to hands and knees, anxious to remove all evidence of their newly married state before someone came in. Not until the very last piece had been picked up off the bed and placed carefully in a waste-bin by the door did the young couple feel able to sit side by side on the edge of the bed and breathe a joint sigh of relief. At that precise moment fate elected to send a young chambermaid barging through the door, upsetting the waste-bin as she entered, and sending the newly gathered confetti flying all over the bedroom carpet once more. The girl looked from the colourful mess on the floor to the beetroot-hued faces of the young couple perched on the end of the bed and giggled squeakily. You could have fried a pound of bacon on Philip's face.

The next morning, at a *very* early hour, while Philip and Margaret were still fast asleep, there was a loud ring on the door bell, and a waiter entered bearing a heavily laden silver breakfast tray. Battling his way back into consciousness, Philip stared with bleary, unbelieving eyes at the clock beside his bed. What on earth was this god-like being doing in their room in the early hours with a huge unordered breakfast? The waiter was far too magnificent to be argued with; and what would he say if he came back later for the tray and found the food not eaten? Croaking out a word of thanks to the departing aristocrat, Philip woke the still-slumbering Margaret, and together they ate their way sleepily through the contents of the tray. At last it was finished. Philip leaned over to slide the tray under the bed, and the couple snuggled back under their covers to resume a night's sleep that had been so unexpectedly interrupted. It wasn't difficult to drift back into the world of dreams.

Philip was very nearly there when a loud ringing noise jerked him back into wakefulness. It was the door again. Sitting up in bed with a little moan, he stared incredu- lously as a different waiter entered bearing another mountainous breakfast on yet another silver tray. This man, too, looked as if he was probably a duke or an earl who had fallen on hard times and been forced to seek humble employment in the hotel industry. You couldn't tell an earl that you didn't want the breakfast he'd just humped up a couple of staircases.

'Thank you very much,' mumbled Philip to the earl's back, as he leaned over to nudge his wife awake. Mar- garet was more than a little bewildered to learn that it was breakfast time again. What a strange hotel! Courageously, the tired pair attacked their second early morning meal, collapsing eventually, bloated and exhausted back on to the pillows, in the hope that it might still be possible to snatch an hour's sleep before it was time to be up and away.

It wasn't quite so easy to slide off into unconsciousness this time, but Philip was just beginning to manage it when his nerves were shredded by the sound of the door bell ringing *again*. Shooting bolt upright in bed, he just managed to suppress a little scream as a third waiter sailed majestically into the room, balancing a crowded tray on one hand as he pushed the door open with the other. This time the breakfast-bearer was truly regal, a recently exiled monarch from some mid-European country, at the very least. Not a man accustomed to having his breakfasts rejected by mere commoners. Philip smiled a ghastly smile as His Majesty deposited the tray and swept elegantly from the room. Margaret didn't need to be woken up this time. She was staring over the edge of the coverlet, with bulging eyes, at this third massive instalment of fruit juice, fried food, toast, marmalade and coffee. She and Philip looked at each other. Keen as they were to keep the peace in this singular establishment whose catering arrangements appeared to be completely out of hand, there was nothing on this earth that would make it possible for them to accommodate a third breakfast. Later, when the newly-weds had paid their bill and departed hastily before anyone could offer them several lunches, a puzzled chambermaid discovered three breakfast trays under their bed, one of them completely untouched.

The rest of the honeymoon was pleasant and relatively uneventful.

* * *

Philip and Margaret were very much in love, but the early days of their marriage were not without problems, especially for Philip. He experienced great difficulty in disentangling his perceptions of Margaret as a wife from his tendency to expect motherlike responses from her, a problem that would not be properly solved for many years. It affected their early married life in a number of areas.

Quite apart from their physical relationship, which released twenty-year-old memories and brought them flooding back into Philip's mind at the worst possible moments, there were such things as needlessly asking for permission to go out, and covering up accidents or mistakes in a very childlike way, as if Margaret was likely to be as condemning and unforgiving as his mother had been.

Very early on in their marriage, Philip spilt some gravy on the tablecloth at lunchtime, and completely bewildered his new wife by apologising to her as if he had battered her half to death with the poker. 'But, darling,' she said lightly, 'we'll just wash it. It's not a problem.'

It was some time before Philip learned to accept that the new woman in his life had qualities of acceptance and loving tolerance that were not going to disappear now that their lives were lived in intimate closeness. Perseverance and the passage of time helped a little. So did contact with Margaret's family, which was traditionally patriarchal. Mr Puddicombe always welcomed Philip into his house as though he was a son. There was a sense of order and safety in that home. Philip loved and benefited from it; especially he loved the moment before mealtimes when Margaret's father said a solemn and ceremonial grace. It was so exactly right.

Margaret's problems tended to be more practical ones. Philip's income as a Church Army captain was a mere five pounds a week. Out of this it was possible to set aside only one pound and ten shillings for ordinary housekeeping purposes. Philip arrived home one day to find his pretty young wife in tears because she just couldn't seem to manage on that amount. She had said nothing for some time, knowing that there was no more money available after the bills were paid, and that Philip would be very upset by her unhappiness. In fact, it was helpful just to share such difficulties, even if a solution wasn't immediately possible and Peter Goldsmid was not a man who was easy to approach with problems.

The spiritual bond between Philip and Margaret was probably their greatest support in those early days. Each day they set aside a time to be quiet and pray together, and at the close of most evenings it became their habit to say Compline, the short service designed to bring a spiritual full-stop to the waking day.

'Visit, O Lord, we beseech thee, this our home, and drive far from it all the snares of the enemy . . .'

These comforting words were an ideal prelude to sleep at the end of a busy or difficult day.

Soon there was a new distraction for Margaret. In the spring following the wedding she discovered that she was pregnant. It was a great joy to both Philip and Margaret, except for one thing. Philip dreaded telling his mother the news, guessing instinctively that she would see it as a final confirmation of her son's 'lack of faithfulness' to her. He was absolutely right. She flew into a passionate rage, telling Philip that he was a sex maniac, and that he had only married to feed his insatiable lusts. This hurtful episode resulted in another period of non-communication, which lasted until Margaret was very heavily pregnant. Philip and Margaret never did sleep in the Newcastle house as a married couple. Philip would have found it impossible, and Margaret not only agreed and understood, but still found it difficult to understand why, in the circumstances, he made *any* efforts to keep the peace.

Margaret had a very difficult labour with Paul. He was quite a long time overdue, and by the time of his birth she had spent ten rather lonely and unhappy days in hospital while her stepmother looked after Philip at home.

As usual the arrival of a real live baby seemed to eclipse the drabness and monotony of waiting. Paul was a beautiful, healthy child, and Margaret was exhausted but triumphant. Philip didn't actually see his son until the day after the birth. When he did, he was ecstatic, unable to stop gazing at the perfect miniature mirror image of himself that lay gently blinking in the hospital cot. A little later, unable to contain his exhilaration, he rode wildly through the parish on his bicycle (he was an expert on two wheels by now) shouting at the top of his voice, 'It's a boy! It's a boy!' Even Peter Goldsmid managed to contort his irascible features into something resembling a smile and grunt a word or two of congratulation.

The day of Margaret's return home was an occasion for great celebration. Philip arranged bunting and flowers all around the front of the little house they had lived in since getting married, and hung a big sign over the front door, saying WELCOME HOME. It was like a royal event. Now they were three.

Edith Ilott's initial response to the birth of a boy was much more positive than Philip had expected. She sent a telegram of congratulation on Paul's arrival, and, as time went by, brought him little gifts in an attempt to cement her reconciliation with the family. This did not, however, prevent her from stating her view that Philip and Margaret were 'obsessive' about their son. She found it hard to accept the constant discussion about Paul's general welfare, and the way in which things such as mealtimes were arranged to suit the baby. She may also have experienced some resentment over the fact that she was never allowed to look after her grandson when no one else was present. Philip was simply not able to rid himself of the fear that his mother might harm Paul if she was left alone with him.

After Paul's birth, Philip's parish work continued even more busily than before. The youth work went on growing, while the congregation in the mission church doubled and trebled under his energetic ministry as young people brought parents and friends to witness and take part in the church life that they were enjoying so much. It was rewarding and exciting to see so much happening.

It was also extremely time-consuming. The combination of Philip's in-built need to be the best he possibly could, and Peter Goldsmid's constant pressure, was responsible for setting a pattern of ceaseless work that was to have a very negative effect on some aspects of Philip's family life as the years went by.

For now, though, it was a very satisfying way of life. Margaret was also busy in the parish, running a women's fellowship, opening bazaars and other events, and, of course, looking after Paul. There were few clouds on the horizon, and, apart from Philip's illnesses, only one really dark moment during the remainder of the Ilotts' stay in Ashford.

Philip went into the church one day to find that vandals had viciously attacked everything that could be damaged. Books were torn up and smothered in tomato sauce, the altar cloth was ripped from end to end, and statues of St Francis and the Virgin Mary had been decapitated. The destruction was so comprehensive that the church had to be closed while repairs and replacements were carried out, then reconsecrated before being used again. It was an alarmingly unpleasant incident, and the culprits were never caught or identified.

Other than that, the Ashford days were very happy ones. Philip was even more committed to Anglo-Catholic churchmanship than he had been before, often slipping into an empty Roman Catholic church to light a candle and say his prayers. Westminster Cathedral became a place of mini-pilgrimage. It was seductively easy to believe that an unrelieved diet of furiously energetic work with an appropriate seasoning of prayer was the invariable recipe for happiness.

After three years, and with entirely predictable fury, Peter Goldsmid received the news that Philip and Margaret were contemplating a move. Why on earth, with a young baby who was just under a year old, and with a decent house in a thriving parish, did they want to go rushing off to some other place they knew nothing about? Madness! Complete and utter madness!

But Philip was developing a rather good line in quiet stubbornness. He had decided it was time to go, and nothing was going to deflect him. Letting the boiling priest's protests pass over his head, he applied for a post as assistant to the chaplain who worked with the Royal Signal's Junior Leaders regiment at Denbury, on the edge of Dartmoor. The prospect of using his recently acquired skills in an environment that might seem very familiar after National Service days was an attractive one. Forces welfare work might offer opportunities to support lonely believers like Sandy, and introduce Jesus to those who had no faith. Philip and Margaret left Ashford with great sadness, but with bright optimism about the future. Peter Goldsmid, who was little Paul's godfather, was still muttering irritably as they left. Philip was a great loss to him.

*　　*　　*

Denbury was a total disaster.

Philip had been led to believe that he would be involved in the running of confirmation classes and Bible-study groups, as well as staffing a canteen for the young soldiers. In fact, it was the catering work that demanded all the energy and time available to the young couple.

Philip welcomed the baker at six o'clock each morning, then prepared enormous quantities of rolls, sandwiches and cakes in preparation for the endless queues of ravenous fifteen and sixteen year olds who descended on the canteen whenever they had a break from the day's activities. So brisk was the trade that little Paul spent hour after hour in his pram, as Margaret joined the battle to feed the masses.

It wouldn't have been so bad if they had been good at what they were doing. The long lines of hungry youngsters seemed to flood the counter. They came from all parts of the British Isles, some with accents so thick that it was impossible to understand what they were saying. Many an outraged customer pointed indignantly at a vast trayful of some article that Philip had just denied any knowledge of. The next customer in the queue might well ask for the same thing in a different but equally unintelligible accent. And there were so many of them. Philip felt like Charlie Chaplin in some crazy slapstick comedy – except that it wasn't funny.

Margaret fared little better. Her first excursion into the mystical world of milk-shakes was profoundly depressing. Her very first customer reappeared thirty seconds after making his purchase, and turned his full glass upside down. Nothing fell out. The strawberry milk-shake mixture had set solid.

They lasted six weeks. No guidance was needed to suggest a radical change of plan. Philip wrote to the head of the Forces Welfare department of the Church Army, who travelled down to Devon to investigate. He soon agreed with Philip's complaint. It was a caterer they needed at Denbury, not an evangelist. He suggested that a return to parish work would be much more appropriate.

Immensely relieved that he hadn't been told to pull himself together and get on with it, Philip stitched up his tattered self-image and applied for a post in the parish of Leavesden in Hertfordshire, greatly attracted by the fact that it lay in the diocese of St Albans. The 'shed-companion' of his childhood had continued to be a secret, brotherlike reality in Philip's life. The very name of Alban had a warm and welcoming ring about it. It would be marvellous to face the challenge of a new and complex parish again; another opportunity to work hard and shine.

The future contained only one shadow: the fear of further illness. The cause of the mysterious collapses that had dogged his life since early Church Army days, and had so infuriated the parish priest at Ashford, still had not been properly identified. There was a nagging dread in Philip's heart that the old 'overwork' label was completely incorrect, and that one day he would be faced with a much more alarming diagnosis.

8

Leavesden – A Call, a Dark Secret, and a Gift from God (1962–1971)

'We've done all the tests we need to do.'

Doctor Parson-Smith's expression as he sat at the end of Philip's hospital bed was not an encouraging one. The little semi-circle of medical students standing behind the eminent neurologist leaned forward a little, earnestly attentive, as he continued to speak.

'Everything points the same way, I'm afraid. There's only one possible answer.'

Philip felt every muscle in his body grow tense as he waited for the doctor's next words. Ever since entering the Charing Cross Hospital for tests, he had feared this moment. At last he was going to discover the nature of the illness that had troubled him for so long and was now interrupting his work in Leavesden. It had all been going so well . . .

Philip's new vicar was another Peter, but a very different one. Peter Smith was a smartly dressed, good-looking man, solidly Anglo-Catholic by tradition, and a genuinely compassionate Christian. From the moment Philip saw him striding down the platform to meet them from the train, he felt a tremendous sense of security and rightness about his future in Leavesden. The priest took to the Ilott family straight away. Later, as he helped them to unload their belongings from the boot of his car, he noticed a little tin box, black with red and yellow stripes and with a key stuck to the top.

'Whatever do you keep in here, Philip?' he asked.

'All the money that we have,' said Philip simply, 'in little envelopes.'

'It makes me want to cry,' said Father Peter with a little smile. 'All the money you have – in little envelopes . . .'

The Ilott family settled very quickly into their council bungalow. Peter Smith and his wife Mary couldn't have been more supportive, and the parish was complex and busy enough to absorb even Philip's energy.

The parish priest was a highly organised man who carried out his duties with style and expertise. Every sermon contained three solid main points, so that – as Philip put it – you always knew when he was going to finish. His efficiency was not without grace, however. People from all kinds and levels of society had reason to be thankful that they had encountered this servant of God.

There was old Tommy the tramp, for instance, who spent every Christmas at Leavesden, sleeping in the church boiler-room at night, and spending most of each day apparently reading avidly, until closer investigation revealed that his books or newspapers were invariably held upside down. Tommy got Philip into trouble during his first Christmas at Leavesden by turning off the boiler on Christmas Eve because it had got so 'bloody hot' down there. Peter Smith, who had entrusted Philip with the task of ensuring that the church was warm for midnight mass, was not at all pleased. Tommy remained unrepentant. As long as he was brought meals by the parishioners and he managed to cadge enough money for the odd drink, nothing else really mattered. He appreciated his Christmas 'lodgings', though.

Then there was Fred, the church caretaker, who was also a resident at the local mental hospital. Fred was entirely safe and reliable, but Mrs Flowers, the Irish lady who cleaned the vicarage, lived in mortal terror of falling victim to a maniacal attack by the mild, hardworking caretaker.

All Saints', Leavesden, also played host to a local gypsy family who had found other churches less than welcoming. Once, while Peter Smith was away overseas, they arrived at the church with a very young baby, asking for a baptism to be performed.

'We've come to have the baby done,' they said.

The church was packed with family, and friends of the family, as the usual ritual question was asked.

'Dost thou, in the name of this Child, renounce the devil and all his works, the vain pomp and glory of the world, with all covetous desires of the same, and the carnal desires of the flesh . . . ?'

'I thoroughly recommend them all!' replied the father loudly, provoking loud roars of laughter from the rest of the congregation, many of whom were considerably the worse for drink. It was a kind of folk-religion that brought them to the church, but at least they came and were welcomed.

Philip's duties were many and varied. Visiting and youth work took up much of his time, but his new vicar encouraged him to experience as wide a range of parish work as possible. The parish priest was a very good, unobtrusive teacher, thorough and meticulous in all he did, and anxious that proper training should be given whenever appropriate. The new parish was everything that Philip had hoped it would be.

Both Philip and Margaret were very keen that Paul should have a brother or sister as soon as he or she cared to come along, but the bitter disappointment of two miscarriages seemed to rule this out. Finally, they considered the possibility of adoption, and after much discussion decided that they would put their names forward for consideration via the moral welfare department of the diocese.

The process of assessment was a long and, for Margaret particularly, a very difficult one. She was obliged to submit to physical tests to establish that she was unable to bear children of her own, a painful experience on all levels after the misery of her miscarriages. Finally the tests confirmed what Philip and Margaret already knew. Now, it was just a matter of waiting. They knew exactly what they wanted. It must be a girl; a special, different, chosen little girl who would never be compared with her brother Paul. There was a deep well of love and care in Margaret and Philip, just waiting to be poured out on the fourth member of the family when she came.

At last, one morning, a white envelope plopped on to the Ilotts' front-door mat just after Philip had returned from the Eucharist that was held early every morning at All Saints'. The letter informed them that a little girl had come up for adoption, and might be right for their family. Her name was Melanie.

Philip's parents were due to come and stay over the following weekend, and agreed, when they came, to take Philip, Margaret and Paul in their car to meet baby Melanie. Not that they approved of course.

'You must be mad!' said Edith Ilott. 'You don't know what you're taking on.'

Filled with fear and trepidation, but undeterred by this typically gloomy forecast, Philip led his wife and son into the Cambridge nursing home where the baby's mother had given birth just over a month earlier. To Margaret's great relief her parents-in-law decided to stay in the car. After a short wait one of the nurses arrived carrying what at first sight seemed an impossibly small baby, dressed in an absurdly long woollen striped shirt. Gazing down at the tiny figure in her footballer's shirt, Philip and Margaret laughed as they saw how Melanie's minute tongue curled up pinkly just outside her lips. It was a sweet little face.

'Is this my sister?' asked three year old Paul in great excitement.

'Well, it might be, darling,' said Margaret quietly,

sitting down so that Paul could see the baby's face. 'What do you think?'

'Well,' replied the little boy, '*you* kiss her, mummy.'

Margaret kissed Melanie gently.

'Now you kiss her, daddy,' instructed Paul.

Philip lowered his face obediently.

'Now me.'

Paul placed his lips carefully on one of the rosy cheeks, then sat back and looked at his mother and father, his eyes bright and confident.

'Now she's ours,' he pronounced definitely, before running across to the window to see if he could spot his nana and grandpa outside.

Somehow, Paul's assurance was a seal on the decision that Philip and Margaret were already on the verge of making. If Melanie's mother was willing to release her, then this was the child they wanted to adopt, and as soon as possible. They left the nursing home in a state of quivering excitement, sorry that they were unable to take the baby home in the back of the car there and then. It was to be more than a fortnight before the fourth member of the family joined them, a fortnight during which Paul stood by the window of their bungalow for a part of every day, gazing anxiously down the street and asking the same insistent question again and again: 'When is my sister coming? Oh, *when* is my sister coming?'

Eventually, Melanie arrived, and a period of nail-biting uncertainty followed as the Ilotts' ability to cope was assessed, and the young mother of the baby battled with her very understandable reluctance to sign the document of adoption. It was a huge relief when the matter was finally settled and the Ilotts became four.

Philip's practical involvement with his new daughter was far greater than he had anticipated. During a one-night visit by the family to the Puddicombes' home in Beckenham, Margaret became very ill. The local doctor, diagnosing meningitis, rushed her off to hospital, where she stayed in isolation for a number of weeks. Her mother and father would gladly have cared for Melanie and Paul for as long as necessary, but Philip was adamant. This little girl of his had already had a rough start, with her natural father disappearing before she was even born, and her mother being forced to part with her because of difficult circumstances. He was quite determined that Margaret's disappearance from Melanie's life so soon after they had come together should cause as little damage as possible. His new daughter was not going to be passed around like a parcel. He would look after her.

Margaret's family were a little put out by this display of stubborn independence, but there was no arguing with Philip. He did everything for Melanie, changing her, feeding her, and taking her for walks. Particularly, he loved bathing the tiny form, marvelling at her exquisitely miniature hands and feet, and slightly fearful that he might easily damage arms and legs that seemed so thin and fragile.

He was deeply and transparently proud of his two children. Almost every afternoon he would take them to the Zoo Gardens at Crystal Palace, Melanie in her pram, and Paul trotting alongside as they strolled through the gardens looking at the big dinosaur models and trying to decide if, out of the corner of his eye, Paul really had seen one of them move an inch or two.

All three of them slept in the same room at the Beckenham house each night, a tightly bound little family unit, waiting for their missing one to return. Margaret continued to be very unwell indeed for some weeks, and for a long time, because of the danger of infection, she could only be seen by Philip and Paul through a glass door. When she did finally return home she was still very pale and thin, but the first thing she did was to hold and hug the little girl she had gained and temporarily lost so soon afterwards.

Two weeks later the Ilotts travelled back to Leavesden

and Philip resumed his work, much to the relief of Peter Smith, who had been extremely patient during his assistant's long period of enforced absence. Margaret was still not able to cope with children and housework on her own, so Philip rather shortsightedly accepted his mother's offer to come and stay for a while to help with the work. Predictably, her self-absorption resulted in a variety of problems. Philip would return from a trying day's work to discover her sitting on the back doorstep in tears because she 'couldn't cope', especially with Margaret's illness, any more than she had been able to cope with anyone else's illness over the years.

'Margaret's no better, and whatever I do doesn't seem to be right,' she complained.

She also found it very difficult to accept the variety and general unpredictability of Philip's day. If he was five minutes late for a meal, explosions and acrimony followed. Margaret's health was not improved by constant worrying about the tension between her husband and her mother-in-law, and in the end, by mutual agreement, Edith Ilott returned to Newcastle and Margaret moved into the vicarage, where Mary Smith provided warm and sympathetic care.

It was a long time before Margaret fully recovered from her illness, but in later years Philip was to value enormously the bond that was formed between himself and baby Mel in those first few weeks when he was all she had.

Settled in a parish like Leavesden, his family complete, and with a man like Peter Smith to work with and learn from, Philip knew that he had every reason to feel content. But, as the months passed, a new desire began to grow and develop in him, until, at last, he simply had to tell Peter Smith what was on his mind.

Together, the two men drove out into the countryside in the vicar's blue Ford Cortina, and, finding a suitable place, parked the car and set off to walk among the fields and hedgerows while Philip unburdened himself.

It wasn't, he explained, that he was any less proud of the kind of job he had been doing. On the contrary, his whole experience of the Church Army had been a very positive one, and it still meant a great deal to him to have the right to wear the distinctive grey uniform, even if people didn't always know what it signified. Peter Smith smiled gently to himself as Philip described how on one occasion he had been taken for a member of the Canadian army, and on another how someone had decided he must be a cemetery attendant. It had all been good and worthwhile, and he'd learned a lot, and he thanked God for it, but now, and especially after working at Leavesden under such a competent vicar, he felt that he was being called to something more.

He was beginning to long to be able to officiate at the sacraments himself, to hold the bread and the wine in his own hands and communicate the essence of those potent symbols to the people in the pews. That moment, the heart of the Eucharist, seemed to him the valve through which the lifeblood of the church flowed out to nourish its members. He wanted to take hold of the grape himself, crush it in his own palm, and see it flow over. At the moment, every time he assisted at the mass, he felt that he was only touching the hem of the garment of a new vocation.

'Father Peter,' he concluded, 'I feel sure that I have a call to the priesthood. Every day – each time I walk into the church – it grows a little stronger. I would very much like to put myself forward for testing. I really would!'

For a few moments, the two men walked on side by side in silence as Philip waited rather apprehensively for the older man's response. It was a great relief when the words finally came.

'Philip, I couldn't agree with you more. In fact, I've sensed this desire in you for some time – I think you ought to contact the Bishop of St Albans and ask him to send you before a selection committee.'

After that the selection process itself went very

smoothly. The bishop was very encouraging, and the people of All Saints' were just as supportive as the vicar had been when they learned Philip's plans.

Only two obstacles presented themselves. The first was lack of money. Philip was interviewed by a somewhat officious lady who made it clear that, as a trainee ordinand, he would be expected to find a large percentage of his own funding to cover college fees and housekeeping. Could he guarantee, she wanted to know, that Margaret would not become pregnant again during the two-year course? It was a question that offended Philip deeply. It seemed a highly inappropriate response to a serious vocation. He explained that Margaret had already suffered two miscarriages, and that they had decided to adopt Mel for that reason.

It had been a hurtful conversation, but the central problem remained: how was he to raise the money to supply his family's needs over the next two years?

With characteristic thoroughness Philip wrote more than a hundred letters to organisations and societies, asking for financial assistance. Eventually, with a particularly helpful grant from the British Legion (an organisation he had joined during his time in the Royal Army Pay Corps), he managed to get together enough cash and promises to cover his fees, plus a little extra.

Then the parish stepped in. A list of people, inspired and co-ordinated by a very energetic and generous lady called Mary Rawlings, made a firm commitment to supply a weekly sum of housekeeping money for as long as Philip's course lasted. It was an offer born out of genuine affection, and the Ilotts accepted it with gratitude.

The second and more worrying obstacle was Philip's poor health. The attacks that had so infuriated Peter Goldsmid in Ashford had continued to lay Philip low during his early years in Leavesden, and eventually the doctor, as puzzled as his colleagues had been in the past, arranged for Philip to enter the Charing Cross Hospital for neurological tests.

The month that followed seemed to last for ever. For much of his stay Philip was situated between an alcoholic tramp on one side and a man who spoke not a single word of English on the other. The ward had a depressing, workhouse-like atmosphere, and Philip was in no mood to offer support or comfort to other people. On the contrary, he dreaded the prospect of his fellow patients discovering the nature of his occupation. In his present state – frightened, vulnerable and seriously underweight because of worry – he felt quite incapable of dealing with his own problems, let alone those of anyone else. He dreaded the outcome of the tests, not just because he feared illness, but because his complaint, whatever it was, might prevent his progress towards the ordination that was beginning to glow like a beacon in his future.

Miserably he waited, the long days broken only by Margaret's regular visits. Most of the things she brought him were annexed by a very plausible Glaswegian in the bed opposite, and Philip had little or no will to resist.

Now, as he waited for Doctor Parson-Smith's final verdict, he could hardly breathe.

'The results of your tests have led us to the inescapable conclusion that you are suffering from epilepsy.'

It was as bad or worse than anything he had imagined. Almost automatically his thoughts flew to his mother. Imagine how shocked and disgusted Edith Ilott would be if she found out that her son suffered from this awful wrong-in-the-head thing called epilepsy. Philip felt demoralised, embarrassed and deeply ashamed that he suffered from an affliction that was beyond his control. In the past there had at least been a dignified feeling about the presumption that his collapses were due to overwork.

'Nervous exhaustion, old boy. You've worked yourself into the ground.'

Comments like that from the doctor were much more

acceptable, suggesting, as they did, a respectable and almost commendable reason for collapsing so totally. This was different – horribly different. He had visions of himself writhing on the floor and frothing at the mouth, despite the fact that these had never been features of his condition, and he loathed the idea of having to take phenobarbitone to control the illness. It was, he thought, like becoming a leper. He was unclean and unfit to mix with normal people. No one must know about this terrible thing. When Margaret arrived he shared his terror-stricken, tumultuous feelings about the doctor's pronouncement. Together they agreed that no one other than doctors should learn about the true nature of the illness, Philip's fear being so palpable that Margaret saw no point in trying to argue.

As far as the parish was concerned, the diagnosis was 'nervous exhaustion'. They saw nothing strange in that. Philip had talked in the past about how, from right back at the beginning of his Church Army days, it had been said that God could only get Brother Ilott to rest by getting him into bed. Philip had almost come to believe it himself over the years. In any case, he *was* suffering from nervous exhaustion, brought on by worry about the outcome of the tests, so there was a stratum of truth running through the deception.

Thus Philip comforted himself and tried to push his condition to the back of his mind as he awaited final acceptance by the college in Rochester where he had applied for training. Christmas was almost upon them, and as he passed a group of carol singers outside the Leavesden Post Office one chilly afternoon, Philip pleaded with God to make it possible for him to train for the ministry. God seemed to have heard his prayer, because on Christmas Eve morning, a very special present in a blue envelope came in the morning post. Trembling with anticipation, Philip tore the envelope open and scanned its contents. A whoop of joy alerted everyone who was around to the fact that Philip Ilott had been offered a definite place on the course that began in the following year. In two years' time he would come back to Leavesden as a curate, and shortly after that, he would be a priest.

Training was very hard work. Philip found it quite difficult to regain the discipline for study, and had to retake his paper on church history, although he did well in other subjects. He was by no means alone, however. Fellow students who had abandoned careers in law, banking and other professions were equally rusty from the academic point of view. Much rueful sympathy was exchanged. When it came to preaching, the sympathy stopped. Sermon post-mortems could be cruel and devastating, but everyone suffered in the same way, and there is little doubt that many congregations of the future benefited directly from these exercises in mutual criticism.

Occasionally Philip relaxed and enjoyed a game of croquet or bowls, but the dominant theme of those two years was hard work. Most of his time was spent studying in a small room with four or five other students, attending lectures, or taking part in cathedral worship. It was a means to an end, and the only way to attain that end was through a fairly sacrificial industriousness. Philip saw very little of his family during those two years of study.

One dark event during this period was the death of Philip's granny in a Newcastle rest home. Aged eighty-eight, she died of a heart attack, leaving two hundred pounds to Philip and Margaret. Philip and his father attended the funeral. Edith Ilott refused to go. It was a sad day.

The day of Philip's ordination was the most wonderful day of his life so far, second only to his marriage day. He woke that morning, still in retreat, as all candidates are in the week immediately before ordination, full of excitement, but desperately wishing that Margaret could be there to help him get the stud through the hole in the back of his collar. Suppose he broke his first clerical collar? Horrors! Suppose he was late arriving at St Paul's Cathedral? Double horrors!

None of the horrors materialised. The stud went in, the journey was uneventful, and the service itself proceeded without a hitch. Rehearsals had been held earlier that day in St Alban's Abbey, a moving occasion for Philip, who, after the rehearsal was over, knelt at the shrine of Alban and said his last prayers before setting off for the cathedral. Kneeling there, next to the place where his lifelong friend lay buried, was an electrifying experience.

Later, during the service of ordination itself, Philip was in tears. The sense of coming home to the place where God wanted him to be was quite overwhelming. Through the grace of holy orders, through the power of the Holy Spirit in the laying on of hands by the bishop, he felt that a special extra help was being given to him, something beyond anything he had experienced as a Church Army officer. And sitting among the congregation to witness this great event were Margaret and Paul (Mel was too little), Margaret's parents, and even Philip's mother and father, who had accepted the invitation to be among the strictly limited number of special guests allowed to each ordinand.

As Philip stood after receiving the laying on of hands, it was as if Alban whispered in his ear: 'We've waited for this a long time, haven't we, Philip?'

'We have, yes. This is such a happy day!'

'Do you know what God is saying, Philip?'

'What is he saying?'

'He's saying: "Philip, you think this is a happy day for *you* – if only you knew what it was like for me!"'

Philip's return to Leavesden as curate of the parish was an occasion of great rejoicing. At a specially organised welcoming party, the church hall was packed with people from the parish who had supported and prayed and waited for Philip with great faithfulness over the past two years. Suddenly he was Father Philip with a dog-collar, instead of Captain Ilott in a uniform. The Church Army uniform and commissioning papers had to be handed in at headquarters, just as Margaret's had been when she married.

There was a slight sadness for Philip in thus marking the end of such an important era of his life. On the other hand, he was now embarking on a new and exciting area of ministry. It was a time for looking forward. As a deacon under holy orders, he was allowed to conduct funerals and baptisms while he served his apprentice-ship, or 'title' as it is called.

In the following year Philip was priested, together with a number of his fellow deacons. Now he was licensed to conduct marriages and, most important of all from Philip's point of view, he could preside over the Eucharist, consecrating the symbols of the body and blood of Jesus, and offering them with his own hands to the people who knelt at the altar rail each week.

His first communion service was a crowded, buzzing, celebratory affair, like a wedding reception or a night at the Proms. The family of All Saints' was there in force to see their new priest initiated into his intimate engage-ment with the mystery of mysteries. Together with him they rose to the emotional and spiritual crescendo of the mass, that moment when Philip, filled to the brim with a strangely mixed sense of humility and power, turned to the congregation and, holding the host high in both hands, offered them the body of Christ.

*   *   *

There was something Philip had to do in private that had only become possible since his priesting. Often, since Margaret had suffered her two miscarriages, his mind had been troubled by the fate of those two little lives that had been lost before they had a chance to know what living really is. One day, without letting anyone know what he was doing, he slipped into the church, locking the doors securely behind him. In full robes he celebrated a Requiem Eucharist to lay to rest the souls of the two unborn children who had neither sex nor names in his mind. He prayed quietly that they might be at rest, and then spoke to them aloud, as though they were sitting side by side in front of him.

'. . . so sorry that your mother wasn't able to carry you through to birth. We both feel such sorrow for you and about you. We miss you very much . . .'

The peace that Philip felt as he left the church and closed the door behind him a little later was immense. He was rather taken aback by his own initiative in holding the service, but deeply relieved in his spirit as a result of it. As the years went by his concern and compassion for miscarried or aborted babies was to grow and intensify. Whenever he passed an abortion clinic, or visited the gynaecological ward of a hospital, a sense of sadness and dread filled him at the thought of children lost before their time. Always he hoped and prayed that whichever priest was concerned would do something for the souls of these little human beings who had once had life in them.

Philip's three years as a curate in Leavesden were of great benefit to the parish and himself. During this relatively peaceful period he learned his 'trade' and threw all his considerable talent and energy into developing the life at the church, particularly among the young people. It must have become very difficult for Peter Smith and the congregation to imagine All Saints' without their vigorous young curate. When the time came to leave, Philip was not at all sure how his vicar would receive the news.

Peter Goldsmid and Peter Smith were very different men, but they had one thing in common. They were both furious on hearing about Philip's plans to move on. In the case of Peter Smith the fury was probably justified. With his deep-seated fear of rejection by authority figures, Philip had once again played his cards very close to his chest, postponing the moment when he communicated his intentions until the whole thing was more or less signed and sealed.

He had started to experience itchy feet just after his priesting. He began to relish the idea of having a church of his own, with all the responsibilities that it would involve. To be a real vicar, doing all the things real vicars did – that would be wonderful. It would somehow set the seal on his personal achievements and allow him to explore and develop a ministry that seemed to be growing daily in the Leavesden community.

When some months later a member of the congregation happened to mention that he knew of a church named St Alban's, Ventnor, that would shortly need a priest-in-charge, Philip's ears pricked up. Through an acquaintance, he managed to inform the priest whose responsibility included the appointment of a man to look after St Alban's that he would be interested in applying, and he received an encouraging letter in return. Without mentioning his plans to anyone but Margaret, he travelled to the Isle of Wight on a day off and was met at Shanklin railway station by Father Peter Hewitt (another Peter!), to be shown around the church and parish that was about to fall vacant.

The Ilotts had spent a summer holiday on the island, and they already loved it. Now Philip was enchanted by Ventnor, which he had not seen before, and particularly by the setting of the church and vicarage that would be his if his application was successful. They were situated on opposite sides of a long flight of stone steps leading down from a main road on the higher level to a smaller coast road far below. The view from the two buildings on that sunny day was an eternity of sea and sky, unutterably peaceful and still.

In the cool dark interior of the church, Peter Hewitt pointed out a consecration stone in the centre of the altar. It had been transported all the way from St Alban's Abbey, the scene of Philip's ordination. It seemed, at that moment, to have a special significance.

After a good lunch and an escorted stroll around the rest of the parish, Philip returned excitedly to Leavesden and much animated discussion and prayer with Margaret. They soon made a decision. If Peter Hewitt invited Philip to take the post of priest-in-charge of St Alban's, they would go.

A week or so later a letter arrived from the Isle of Wight. In bad blue type, altered in pen where the keys had jumped, Father Hewitt formally invited Father Ilott to become priest-in-charge of St Alban's, Ventnor.

The family were ecstatic, but one hurdle remained. Peter Smith would have to be told.

Although recent events had moved with such swiftness, it had been a year or more since Philip first heard about the Ventnor vacancy. The parish priest wasn't even aware of his curate's desire to leave. Philip felt quite apprehensive about telling him. Not that Peter Smith was generally an irascible type like Peter Goldsmid, but he could be very stern at times. The third member of the Leavesden clergy team, William Smith, the senior curate, and, incidentally, Peter Smith's father, occasionally made silly mistakes in his work. More than once Philip had overheard the older man being roundly disciplined by his son in the privacy of the latter's study. If he had no compunction about telling his own father what he thought about mere procedural errors, what would he say to a junior curate who had been secretly planning to move for the last twelve months? Perhaps he would feel that Philip was being terribly ungrateful after the parish had supported him through two years at college and frequent periods of illness. But then, it had been eight years since Philip and Margaret came to Leavesden with little Paul; three years as a Church Army captain, two years in college, and three years back in the parish as a curate. Surely he had paid his dues by now?

Staff meetings at All Saints' were held on Tuesday mornings. Philip decided to break the news of his departure at the following week's meeting, after normal business was concluded and William Smith had gone. When the time came he didn't find the words easy to say.

'Oh, by the way, Father Peter,' he began, trying to inject a quality of casual brightness into his tone, 'I've got something to tell you about my future . . .'

He went on to explain about his growing feeling that he wanted more independence and responsibility, how attracted he had been by the sound of St Alban's on the Isle of Wight, and how meaningful it had seemed that part of the very fabric of the church had once rested in the place of his ordination. Finally, and not without a tremor, he confessed that he had already been offered the vacant post and was about to accept it.

At first he thought the parish priest couldn't have heard what he was saying. Peter Smith sat motionless beside the big roll-top desk which beautifully graced his study, staring into the distance and saying nothing. For a long, unnerving period, there was complete silence in the room. Then, slowly and with studied care, the priest placed on the desk the pen he had been holding, and spoke with grim determination: 'Well, we shall have to see about that, shan't we?'

'What do you mean, Father?' asked Philip nervously.

'I mean exactly what I say,' replied the other man, still not looking in Philip's direction. 'We shall have to see about you going elsewhere. I may not let you go!'

The child in Philip screamed silently. His stomach lurched. To release something from inside himself and have it rejected was still a nightmarish experience. In eight years of contact with Peter Smith he had never earned so much as a hard word. Now the atmosphere in the study was heavy with anger and disapproval.

'I may write to the Bishop of Portsmouth and inform him that you will not be moving,' continued the priest icily, 'and also to the patron of the Ventnor parish. I shall simply point out that your appointment to that place has been negotiated with neither my knowledge nor my approval.'

A further long silence ensued. Storms continued to rage inside the two still figures. One was a storm of outright anger and disappointment that one who had seemed so close could plan and pursue his departure without consultation. The storm in Philip combined elements of panic and despair. The panic was his habitual response to disapproval; the despair was a product of his fear that he was eternally condemned to suffer as a refugee from his own childhood. When would he finally and properly grow up to be his own man? All he wanted now was the chance to run away. It came.

'You may go now,' said Peter Smith tonelessly, still staring into the distance.

Philip left without another word, hurrying straight back to Margaret to lay the outcome of this encounter in her lap.

Like all loving couples since time immemorial, they set about the task of comforting each other with a list of passionate justifications. Hadn't they discussed the question of moving many times and at great length? Of course they had! Hadn't they prayed together and separately about the Ventnor parish? They certainly had! And then there was the question of the children's schooling. Paul was now nine years old. Wasn't it crucial to consider the adverse effect of moving schools at some later date? As a responsible parent, didn't one have to think in practical terms like that? Naturally one did! Hadn't Peter Smith been unnecessarily aggressive in his response to Philip's news? Yes, agreed Margaret, with reassuring anger, he jolly well had! If Father Peter thought Philip was a fixture at Leavesden for the rest of his life, he'd better think again! They carefully avoided any mention of the fact that Philip could have almost completely avoided conflict with his parish priest if he had taken him into his confidence from the beginning.

Sadly the conflict was locked away in that study for

ever. Philip and Peter never did discuss the matter heart
to heart. Philip was, in any case, not yet capable of
discussing anything that lay in his heart of hearts, except
with Margaret. Matters of work and ministry were open
to debate, of course, but the dark and desperate parts of
his personality were still too unstable and tender to be
inspected or touched by anyone else.

The next few days were very difficult indeed. The two
men were forced to meet in the course of their duties,
but the relationship was uncomfortably strained, and
communication tended to be monosyllabic. Philip woke
each morning with a sense of overwhelming dread at
the prospect of having to say mass with the senior priest
yet again.

In the end it was Mary Smith who eased the situation
by acting as a conveyor of her husband's feelings and
thoughts. His first reaction, she said, was the result of
shock. The idea of Philip leaving had never occurred to
him. He was as much upset as angry. She told Philip
and Margaret how sad she and Peter were to lose them,
and how much they would be missed by everyone. All
in all, she did a marvellous job of invisible mending, as
wives so often do, but the bond between the two priests
was never quite the same again.

Perhaps the most healing occasion between that first
encounter and Philip's departure was William Smith's
funeral service. Peter Smith didn't feel able to preach the
sermon, and he asked Philip to do it, realising perhaps
that this gesture would be rightly interpreted as a profoundly conciliatory one.

At last the date of the Ilotts' departure drew very near.
At a farewell party, held in the vicarage garden, Philip
and Margaret were presented with personal gifts and a
sum of money, followed by a farewell speech from Father
Peter that must have been very costly to deliver. Philip
found it a beautiful, sad occasion. Eight years is a long
time, and he had made many friends. If only the un-
pleasantness over leaving had never happened. It was

quite a relief actually to depart when the time came.

Philip, Margaret, Paul and Mel set off by train from Victoria Station, carrying only hand luggage and, in a bottle, a goldfish called Margaret, who got spilt on the train floor at one point and had to be hastily scooped up and returned to her travelling container.

Their first night on the island was spent at the house of Richard Dawes, the church treasurer, a man who impressed his dominant personality on Philip's newly arrived sensibilities from the first moment of their meeting. In the course of their first evening's conversation, he made it quite clear that he kept a firm grip on every significant aspect of the parish, and that Philip would do well to understand his relative unimportance in the scheme of things. Obviously there were new and different storms ahead.

The following day, however, shone with novelty, excitement and sunshine. Dropped off at Ventnor in the morning by Richard Dawes, the Ilotts gleefully explored the big airy vicarage just below the upper street level, and then the Church of St Alban's further down the steps. Paul and Mel could hardly believe it was true. Just down there, not far from the bottom of the steps that began near their new house, was the sea! They were going to live by the sea! Wonderful!

Later, the removal lorry, driven by an ancient local character named Mr Mew, arrived on the upper road and was unloaded by Mr Mew and some underlings, while the family stood and watched. It became rather nerve-racking. Although very confident and cheerful, the elderly Mr Mew looked as though a breeze could have blown him off the steps and wafted him down into the sea, yet he insisted on carrying large heavy objects from lorry to vicarage with much panting and gasping.

'He'll give himself a hernia if he's not careful,' said Philip at one point to one of the underlings.

''E's already 'ad one o' them,' grinned the man. 'You try an' stop 'im – I can't, an' 'e's my dad!'

It was when the old man spat on his hands and started dragging the upright piano from the back of the lorry that the Ilotts finally lost their nerve and decided to walk down to the seafront.

'I've told them where to put the rest of the things,' Philip told Margaret. 'Let's take the children down to the beach.'

The walk down the cliff steps was a blissful one. As they went, Margaret enthused about the vicarage. They'd never had a house like it – four bedrooms, a big sitting-room, and a lovely kitchen facing out towards the sea. For Philip there was a study – also with a sea view – and a special back entrance so that visitors coming on church business would not have to use the family's part of the house. There was also quite a large garden. It needed a lot of hard work, but it could be made beautiful. Altogether, St Alban's Church House, or Presbytery, as Philip preferred to call it, could not have been more ideal.

The period that Philip, Margaret, Mel and Paul spent on the beach at Ventnor that day was one of those rare, special times when the present is full of peace and the future beckons warmly. As the children played happily on the sand, Philip and Margaret relaxed in deckchairs, enjoying the sunshine.

'I really think we might be very happy here, darling,' said Philip.

Just then the deckchair attendant arrived. After collecting his money, he stood for a moment, eyeing Philip's clerical collar.

'Are you the new priest?' he enquired.

'Yes,' said Philip, 'I am.'

The man pushed his peaked cap to the back of his head.

'You'll be seeing a lot of me, then,' he said.

'I don't really think so,' smiled Philip. 'I shan't have much time to sit on the beach, I'm afraid.'

'You'll still see a lot of me,' said the man. 'I'm not just a deckchair attendant.'

'Oh, you're not just . . .'

'I'm the undertaker as well!'

9

Isle of Wight – Hardship and Healing (1971–1978)

'Have you asked Richard Dawes what he thinks?'

Philip gritted his teeth as he heard that infuriating question for the umpteenth time. Every time he suggested change or innovation, or anything that involved expenditure, he seemed to be referred back rather nervously to the church treasurer, as though the priest-in-charge had no power to make decisions at all.

Philip's very early fears were well-founded. Richard Dawes, a tall, slim man with a rather impressive scar on one side of his face, was setting out to overwhelm the new priest as thoroughly as he had his predecessor, and he was very good at it. Apart from his naturally commanding presence and an all-important grip on church finances, he had very effective ways of signalling disapproval and disagreement to a congregation far more in awe of the treasurer they knew than of any man with a white dog-collar who'd only been there five minutes.

Dawes was not Anglo-Catholic in his churchmanship. Decorating the inside of the church, for instance, one of Philip's early priorities, was considered to be a waste of money. It was only through specific gifts and practical assistance from the congregation that anything of that kind was achieved in the early days. Richard Dawes believed that money was best spent on charitable works, especially (and very commendably, in Philip's eyes) on projects connected with young people and on social needs of various kinds. The idea of 'tarting the church up', as he put it, was quite unacceptable, and he simply refused to release funds for that purpose. Money spent on candles or incense should actually go to Christian Aid or Oxfam, and, bearing that in mind, said the treasurer, would it not be better for Philip to preach far less about the sacraments and far more about the parables?

Services became almost intolerable. As a member of the choir, Richard Dawes took his place each Sunday up in the organ loft, dominating the situation with his elevated presence, and acting as a constant reminder to Philip that the most important person in the church heavily disapproved of most things that he did and said.

His response to incense upset Philip particularly. As the fumes started wafting up towards the high ceiling, the treasurer would ostentatiously fan the air beneath his nose with a service-sheet or hymnbook. The gesture was an unmistakably negative one, and usually succeeded in provoking an impotent and distracting rage in the priest down below at the front.

Philip endured his deteriorating relationship with Richard Dawes for nearly eighteen months. It soured and spoiled what was otherwise a very fulfilling start to his Ventnor ministry. He was quite independent of Peter Hewitt, the patron of the parish, whose church was a good five miles to the west, and it was an interesting, mixed parish. There was a council estate, quite a lot of terraced housing, and a number of large expensive private properties. There was also a comprehensive school and a Church of England primary school, the latter attended very happily by Mel and Paul.

Contrary to what the church treasurer seemed to believe, Philip was as interested in real people and real problems as he was in making the fabric of the church beautiful enough to house the worship of God's people. Through his usual blend of enthusiasm and energy he brought new life to St Alban's, attracting both adults and

young people in numbers that were quite unprecedented. His visiting and involvement with the folk of
the parish was genuinely committed and persistent, but
the shadow of this one man's antagonism was casting
gloom over everything. It was to be nearly two years
before that particular conflict was resolved. In the meantime two very significant events occurred. The first was
the death of Philip's mother.

Edith Ilott had always hated hospitals. She wasn't
even able to visit members of her family when they went
in for treatment. The time she had been forced to spend
in a nursing home when Philip was born nearly destroyed her. The physical vulnerability of that kind of
situation was quite unbearable to one so neurotically
unable to tolerate imperfection. In 1972 she became
seriously ill and was taken into hospital in Newcastle for
tests to be carried out. For some time the doctors were
not able to diagnose her complaint, but after a succession
of medical explorations and X-rays a malignant growth
was discovered in her windpipe and an emergency operation was performed very shortly afterwards. It was
not successful. Finally, in 1973, the unhappy woman
returned home to die in the house where Philip had
grown up.

Shortly before the end, Philip travelled to Newcastle
by train to visit his mother for the last time. Lying in bed
in the house that had once meant so much to her, she
was a pathetic sight. Philip almost flinched on seeing
how painfully thin and weak she had become. All the
power and dominance, the ability and will to hurt, was
gone, wasted away by this thing that was making her
breathing almost impossible. Sitting beside her, Philip
felt a sigh shudder through his body as he remembered
how many times he had tried to please his mother with
presents as a child, and with achievements as an adult.
The presents had been barely acknowledged, deliberately broken on one occasion, and the achievements
minimalised or openly scorned. Was there anything he

could offer this frail remnant of a person that, even at this late date, she might think worth accepting? He had only one thing to offer, one last gift that could be received or rejected. The risk of hurt was no less now than it had ever been.

'Mother . . .'

Philip leaned forward to speak, barely able to control the fear and passion that lay behind his words.

'Mother, I can give you Holy Communion and anoint you with oil for healing if you want me to. As a priest I can do that . . .'

Edith Ilott's pain-laden eyes looked into her son's anxious ones for a moment, then she spoke with all the enthusiasm she could muster.

'Oh, yes, please!'

Calmly and professionally, Philip administered the sacrament, anointed his mother's head with oil in the sign of the cross, and prayed for her healing. Then he put his arms around the emaciated figure and kissed her gently on the forehead.

Suddenly all calmness and professionalism deserted him. Overwhelmed by the knowledge that, for the first time, he had been able to give his mother something she really wanted, Philip broke down and wept like a child. They wept together for a very long time, the first emotion they had shared in more than thirty-five years.

The next day Philip kissed his mother once more and returned to the Isle of Wight, deeply thankful that he had been allowed to experience those few minutes of real communication. His father remained in Newcastle to nurse his dying wife. He too was in an emotionally turbulent state, and had felt unable to be present when Philip administered Holy Communion. Now that his wife was dying, he seemed a strangely isolated figure, waiting for pain and relief.

A fortnight later, as Philip was about to disrobe in the vestry after celebrating the mass, Margaret appeared at the door, her eyes full of dark news and compassion.

She took one of his hands softly into both of hers and looked straight at him. Margaret was always able to be direct when it was necessary.

'Darling, your mother has died.'

Philip had half thought he might be prepared for this moment. Perhaps part of him was. Father Philip, the priest, husband and parent, might have received the news with reasonable equanimity; but little Philip Ilott, the small desperate boy who had been hurt by his mammy in ways he didn't even understand, and who had tried so hard for so many years to earn the love and admiration that only she could give him, was completely devastated.

Mammy was dead! There was nothing else to be hoped for from mammy, because she was dead and gone for ever.

Philip collapsed across the vestment chest at the side of the vestry, crying out his loss in great racking sobs. Mammy had never really said she was sorry for what she'd done, and he'd never actually forgiven her, and now it was too late.

Margaret and Philip travelled to Newcastle for the cremation. Mel and Paul were left with two friends called Joan and Wilf Philpott, who lived in a big castle-shaped house in Ventnor. The Ilotts did not much enjoy the chilly October atmosphere as they travelled northward on the train. Philip was preoccupied with planning what he would say at the committal, and Margaret had never ceased to experience a feeling of dread about being anywhere near her mother-in-law's house.

For once Philip was not very proud of his speech. The only positive thing he could find to say was that his mother had given birth to him so that a priest could be created. He said a little about his father, then pressed a button to consign the coffin to its fiery furnace.

The journey back to Ventnor was no more pleasant than the outward one had been, and a new complication had arisen. Philip's father, without any discussion or consultation, had announced that he would be winding up his work as a legal executor, selling the house in Newcastle, and moving down to live with his son's family. Margaret and Philip had been too taken aback to argue. They simply agreed, and now it was a fact.

Philip tried to feel generous about accommodating his long-suffering parent, but it was very difficult. He despised his father and still felt a deeply ingrained, barely acknowledged anger towards him because of his weakness in the past. More, he had to give up his study in the vicarage, so that his father could use it as a bed-sitting room, and move down into a room under the house that until now had been used as a storage space.

The whole situation produced strange, uncomfortable echoes in Philip's heart. Moving down into this ex-junk room that could only be entered from outside the house was just a little too much like being consigned to the shed of his childhood, especially as his father was constantly present to provoke memories and feelings related to that part of his life.

Sometimes, sitting in his new study in the early days, the whole emotional experience flooded through him. He was pushed out, while upstairs the important ones lived important lives in the really important parts of the house. It was ridiculous, of course – he knew that. He and Margaret were very devoted to each other, and his father was very generous and no trouble at all. It was just a feeling that the past had invaded the present, and he didn't like it at all. It took away his peace.

The second significant happening in Philip's life before the resolution of the Ilott–Dawes conflict was the occasion when, in the same moment, he was healed of epilepsy *and* baptised in the Spirit.

Philip had managed to convince himself that the epilepsy was a thing of the past. For five whole years before coming to the Isle of Wight (the period of theological training, and his curacy in Leavesden) there had not been a single attack. Perhaps it had just gone away.

Perhaps God had healed it. Philip knew nothing about such things, but he supposed vaguely that it must be possible.

His only previous experience of the healing ministry had been a wholly negative one. During his time at Church Army training college, Philip once fell prey to a very virulent strain of influenza. As he lay in bed, sweating and shivering by turns, he was visited by a young fellow student who had a zealous and virtually unquenchable belief that God *always* healed *all* illnesses. After praying loudly and confidently for Philip, he claimed that recovery must now have taken place, and that if the invalid left his bed and returned to work he would receive his healing. Nothing loath, Philip dragged his aching body out of bed and attempted to resume his duties. Having to be carried back to bed half an hour later, feeling even worse than before, did nothing to encourage his belief in miracles of physical healing.

Not that he would have asked for prayer even if he *had* felt a cure was possible. When they arrived on the Isle of Wight, Margaret was still the only other person, apart from the doctors, who knew about his epilepsy. He certainly had no intention of sharing such a shameful secret with anyone in the Ventnor parish. Anyway, if it had gone for good, by whatever means, it was best forgotten.

The attacks began again after Philip's mother went into hospital for tests in 1972. Six years had passed since the last collapse, but there was a greater tension in him now than there had been for a long period. At the time he didn't associate it with his mother's illness. It seemed to Philip that the sensation of strain that was building in him was solely attributable to the problems he was having with Richard Dawes. The stress involved in conducting services Sunday after Sunday under the disapproving eye of the treasurer had become almost unbearable.

Perhaps it was no coincidence that the first collapse

happened in church at the conclusion of the mass. As Philip was about to give the blessing he experienced the inward lurching that had always preceded attacks in the past. A desperate panic seized him. He was going to collapse here at the altar in front of Richard Dawes and all these other people in the congregation. Gritting his teeth, he forced himself to pronounce the words of the blessing.

'The peace of God, which passeth all understanding, keep your hearts and minds in the knowledge and love of God, and of his Son Jesus Christ our Lord . . .'

Philip could feel consciousness slipping away from him as he went on.

'. . . and the blessing of God Almighty, the Father, the Son, and the Holy Ghost, be amongst you and remain with you always.'

As he completed the final sentence everything went dark, and in a last instant of awareness he knew that he was falling backwards over the altar, like a rag doll. Little Mel, dressed in her red and white choir uniform, watched with wide-eyed horror as the shocked servers picked up her daddy's limp body and carried it through to the sacristy. Was daddy dead? Where were they taking him? She turned to look at her brother's face, but he looked as frightened as she felt. Down below, in the body of the church, a concerned murmur indicated that the members of the congregation were hardly less dismayed. Philip had crumpled and fallen so suddenly, and at such a dramatic moment, that it almost seemed like the climactic scene in some film.

Philip awoke to find himself back in the vicarage. They must have carried him up the steps to the house. How horribly embarrassing! Someone was saying something. One of the people standing in the mist around his bed was talking to the others.

'. . . almost dying. I'm not sure precisely what it is, but he's suffered some kind of acute attack.'

It was the local doctor who was speaking. He obviously had no idea that epilepsy was responsible for the collapse.

As the mist cleared, Philip recognised the other two people who were gazing down at him, their brows creased with worry. One was Margaret. (Dear Margaret! She would be so worried.) The other person was a lady called Brenda Wright, who had been in the congregation when he keeled over. Brenda was the local district nurse, a profoundly caring person and a good friend. She was to become one of the few people in the parish who knew the true nature of Philip's illness, and a most devoted friend both in practical terms and through constant, sometimes genuinely sacrificial, prayer.

Despair flooded through Philip as he faced the reality of what had happened in the church just now. The demon on his back was not dead or gone – just sleeping. Six years he'd been free from this particular nightmare; six years of slowly increasing confidence that – for whatever reason – he was well again. But he wasn't . . . And why, when he really thought about it, was it so terribly – so crucially – important that other people should not know what the damned illness was? Why on *earth* shouldn't he be open about it? He knew the answer, though: he was afraid. He was still afraid of losing something of himself; afraid of being vulnerable; afraid of failing to meet some absurd standard of 'alrightness' set long ago by his mother; afraid, perhaps above all, to acknowledge and expose this graffiti on the pure white sheet of his priesthood.

Being a priest, an agent of God, had become a solution to problems about inadequacy, about identity, about the hurting past. It went far beyond the vestments and other outward signs of his calling. For Philip, being a priest was like wearing a uniform inside. The very existence of epilepsy was a threat to the hard-won security supplied by that inward identity, and nobody, including God, would be allowed to risk its loss . . .

The doctor injected some kind of sedative into Philip's

arm, and almost immediately he felt himself drifting into the unconsciousness of sleep. Several hours later he felt completely well again.

But Mel and Paul were to see the vestment-shrouded figure of their father carried from church to vicarage on more than one occasion after that. Sometimes the attacks would happen elsewhere, but usually it was during a church service, when elation or stress could equally cause great tension in Philip; and it did seem to be tension that triggered his collapses. They began to happen frequently, and they were getting worse. Everyone knew that Father Ilott was a sick man. Everywhere he went people asked him about his health. His appearance changed. His face was white and drawn, his body thin and weak. Throughout Ventnor and beyond it was common gossip that the priest of St Alban's was 'always being ill'.

When Philip's mother died, the attacks became even more severe. Margaret worried and prayed, but Philip was even less able to allow the epilepsy to exist.

One day, not long before Passiontide, there was a phone call to the vicarage. A monk was visiting the island for a short retreat, said the caller. Would Philip like a guest preacher for Passion Sunday? He accepted the offer with a genuine enthusiasm. Quite apart from the relief of not having to prepare a sermon for once, it would be a real pleasure to entertain someone who had followed the path to monastic life that he, Philip, had abandoned all those years ago in London. He suggested that the monk should stay at the vicarage on Saturday and Sunday nights, and leave on the Monday morning. It was agreed and arranged. By the time Philip arrived home on the Saturday evening in question, the visitor had arrived.

Father Humphrey Whistler, a Mirfield Father from Yorkshire, was an Anglican monk, a member of the Community of the Resurrection. He was a tall, slim man with thinning grey hair, a ruddy complexion, and deep-blue penetrating eyes. He gave the immediate and attractive impression of boyishness and maturity being present together in his personality. He was the sort of person whom Philip had always classified as 'grown-up'. He wore a long black cloak and cassock, topped with a grey scapular – an impressive man.

Philip took to Father Humphrey immediately. There was a sense of well-being and security imparted to the atmosphere of the house just by the monk's presence. It was a very enjoyable first evening. The next day Philip took a childlike pleasure in introducing his guest to the members of the congregation, then he settled back to listen to the sermon.

Father Humphrey spoke without notes, straight from the heart. He was good. St Alban's was fortunate indeed to have such a man preaching on Passion Sunday. Philip breathed a sigh of relief as he listened to the well-spoken, even tones floating from the pulpit. Two days ago, on Friday, he had suffered another very prolonged epileptic collapse. He still felt extremely shaky. The thought of preaching today was too awful to contemplate. How wonderful to be able to relax and let someone else – someone so capable – do it instead. If only he didn't feel quite so unwell; it was hard to concentrate on the content of the sermon when your body was aching and your head was spinning.

The usual coffee-and-biscuits session after the service was a bright, noisy occasion, as people took turns to shake hands with the visitor and enjoy the warmth and enthusiasm with which he greeted each one of them.

As Philip climbed the steps to the vicarage with his guest a little later, the prospect of a civilised Sunday lunch was a warm, mellowing one. Reaching the house, he sat Father Humphrey down in the sitting-room while he fetched the sherry bottle and some glasses. Upstairs the children were playing more or less quietly, while Margaret made final preparations for lunch in the kitchen.

It was when Philip was seated opposite the monk, and about to raise his glass to his lips, that the peace was blown to fragments by a few words. Humphrey Whistler, holding his host's eyes effortlessly with his own warmly challenging gaze, spoke with a confidence that was positively unnerving.

'You are not a well man, Father, are you?'

Philip automatically translated the intention behind the words into an accusation.

'Well,' he replied defensively, 'I don't keep very good health, no, but I don't think . . .'

'I must tell you,' continued the monk with unrelenting calm, 'that I don't think I'm here just to preach a sermon and give you a day off; I think I'm here for something else.'

Very, very carefully, Philip raised his glass to his lips and took a tiny sip. Outwardly he managed to retain control, but inside he was panicking wildly. What did this man know, and where had he got it from? Who had he been speaking to, and what had his informant said? Was *the* secret blown somehow? Worst of all, was the secret part of himself about to be invaded and interfered with by this priest-monk with penetrating eyes?

'What do you think that something else could be?' pursued Father Humphrey.

Philip was using every ounce of energy to control the way he looked. There was none left for speech.

'I think I'm here to offer you healing,' the monk said quietly.

For an instant there was a rigid stillness in the room. Then, filled with the violent rage that only profound fear can produce, Philip swallowed the rest of his sherry down in a single gulp, slammed the glass down on a small occasional table by his chair, shot to his feet and disappeared from the room, his mind continuing to scream questions. What did Humphrey Whistler think he was going to do? How could Philip get rid of him without breaking the rules of etiquette he'd always lived

by? How could the whole dreadful situation be made to
go away? In the kitchen Margaret was standing at the
stove, stirring something.

'Margaret!' hissed Philip, speaking in tones intended
to convey righteous anger rather than abject fear. 'That
man – that Father Humphrey – has just said that I need
healing! And *he's* going to offer it to me, he says! Don't
you think it's just about the limit, Margaret? I mean –
what a cheek! For two pins I'd tell him to leave, I would
really! Don't you agree?'

Philip had no doubts about what his wife's response
would be. Hadn't she supported him on that occasion
when he had announced his impending departure to
Peter Smith in Leavesden? She had agreed with him
then. She would do the same now. He waited for her to
echo the anger and indignation in his own voice.

But Margaret loved Philip more than that, and she
had suffered a great deal herself lately from the private
cost of Philip's public excellence.

'Well, if he's come to help, he's come to help, hasn't
he? You'd better listen to what he says, darling.'

She hadn't even turned round to speak – just continued doing what she'd been doing, as calmly as if it
had all been a very minor matter indeed! Philip couldn't
have been more furious. Fancy not agreeing with him!
Dreading the thought of facing the monk again, but
unable to think of anything else to do, he walked stiffly
and fearfully back into the living-room. Humphrey
Whistler was still sitting in his chair, apparently quite
unperturbed by Philip's abrupt departure and subsequent return. He went on speaking as though nothing
had happened at all.

'I repeat what I said, Philip – I'm not here just to give
you a rest from preaching. I believe I'm here to bring
you God's healing. You are a sick man. Would you be
prepared to receive the laying on of hands?'

The stricken silence that followed was broken when
Margaret rang the little bell in the hall to announce

that dinner was ready. The meal was not a comfortable occasion. Philip was only too happy to escape for his customary lie-down in the afternoon. Perhaps if he didn't say anything else about the healing business, Humphrey Whistler would just assume he wasn't interested and go away on Monday morning without bringing the subject up again. It was a slim hope, and it proved to be ill-founded. That evening, when both Margaret and Philip were present, the monk calmly reiterated his intentions.

'I honestly do feel,' he said with kindly authority, 'very strongly indeed, that this is the Lord's opportunity for Philip to receive the laying on of hands and anointing with oil. You really have no reason to be afraid, Philip, and you do want to be healed, don't you?'

Just at that moment, Philip was far from sure that he did, but the combination of Margaret's quiet acquiescence in the idea and the monk's impressive assurance was very hard to resist.

'Well,' he capitulated gracelessly, 'all right then, if that's what you want. It can't do any harm I suppose.'

'Good!' Father Humphrey leaned back in his chair and smiled at Margaret. 'Now, my dear, perhaps you could just telephone around to all those church folk who you think would be specially interested in coming to a service of anointing . . .'

Philip's jaw dropped. What was he suggesting?

'I shall say the Eucharist tomorrow morning in the church,' the monk went on, 'so we shall need these good people to come along and pray for Philip as I anoint him, shan't we?'

'NO WE SHAN'T!' cried Philip inwardly. That wasn't what he'd envisaged at all. He'd pictured Humphrey Whistler doing this anointing business in private – perhaps with just Margaret present, but certainly no one else. Here in the house would do, wouldn't it? Or in the church, with the door locked so that no outsiders could get in. Why did God seem to be insisting on him accepting ministry in public? What kind of priest was it who needed his deficiencies remedied in front of the very people who were supposed to respect him as their spiritual leader? This thing was *private*, for goodness sake! Surely Margaret would see . . .

'Right, I'll get on with that.'

Margaret stood up and moved to the phone. She began to ring people and ask them to come along to pray for Father Ilott at the early Eucharist tomorrow. Among those she called were Richard and Val Dawes. Philip groaned in his spirit. The whole affair was slipping out of his control. Between them, Humphrey Whistler and Margaret were driving him towards the worst imaginable sort of humiliation, the open display of a gash in the fabric of his priestly invulnerability. With Richard Dawes watching! It sounded like some kind of death.

'Your ministry is being destroyed by your constant collapses,' said the monk, breaking into these dark thoughts with his unhurried voice. 'Your ministry is a special one and can only continue if you are healed. Let me tell you exactly what we shall do tomorrow . . .'

Philip listened dismally as the man opposite him explained the practical details of the healing Eucharist. In the background, Margaret's voice went on softly repeating the same words again and again to different people as she spoke on the telephone.

'. . . thought you might be able to . . . Thank you very much . . . See you tomorrow then . . .'

It was going to happen, and there was no way of escape. Before retiring that night, Humphrey Whistler and Philip prayed together. The monk's prayers were strong and expectant; Philip's were hesitant and shot through with fear. Then the night came.

He hardly slept at all. From late on Passion Sunday until dawn came, Philip prayed fitfully that tomorrow's wretchedly unwelcome cup would pass from him. But it was a woefully incomplete Gethsemane. He just couldn't bring himself to say 'nevertheless, not my will, but thine be done'.

By eight o'clock next morning the church was quite crowded. Most of the people contacted by Margaret had responded positively, including the Dawes. The general atmosphere was a mixture of puzzlement and willingness. No one quite understood what was going on, but if being there would help the vicar in some way, then that was fine.

What about Richard Dawes, though?, thought Philip, as Father Humphrey proceeded with the Eucharist. What was he thinking as he sat next to his wife in a pew near the front of the church? More to the point – what would he think when the priest he disapproved of so strongly knelt to receive ministry at the front of his own church? What would he think when –

'Would you come forward please, Father Philip?'

Father Humphrey had finished reading the gospel. It was time.

Rising heavily to his feet, Philip moved forward and knelt before the monk, his back rigid with nervousness and fear. He noted with some surprise that the hands laid gently upon his head were trembling or vibrating, as though full of some restrained power. Then the prayer began. But why, wondered Philip, was Humphrey Whistler praying in some foreign language? What exactly was the strange tongue that positively bubbled out of the monk's mouth? Latin perhaps? No, not Latin. He knew a little Latin. Could it be Greek or Aramaic? No, it was neither of them. Was it possible that . . . ?

Somewhere in the back of Philip's mind was a vague memory of hearing about people in today's church rediscovering the gifts that God had given the early church – the church in the time of Acts. The gifts were things like prophesy, discernment – and speaking in tongues. Most of what he had heard was negative, though, priests who spoke in tongues being regarded as mad. That sort of thing. But Humphrey Whistler wasn't mad. He was about as far from being mad as anyone Philip had ever met. He was almost threateningly sane and insightful. What was more, the combination of the firm, quivering pressure on his head and something indescribably pure in the strange language that filled his ears was producing a sensation quite new to Philip. It was as though he was being held, so that he could behold – what?

Father Humphrey began to pray in English. Anointing Philip's head with oil, he asked very deliberately that the spirit of illness would depart, and that Father Philip would be released from the bondage of sickness and evil. This prayer was such an uncannily accurate echo of Philip's secret feeling about his epilepsy being an evilly unclean phenomenon that a new fear took over. Suppose this thing inside him – this evil thing – were to be set free here in the church, how would he cope with it? How would everyone else cope with it? As the monk brought his prayer to a conclusion, Philip clenched his teeth and willed the service to end before some dreadful emotional or spiritual explosion could take place. More than four years ago, when he first offered the body of Christ to the people of Leavesden, it had seemed as though he had gained a control over his ministry and himself that could never be removed. Now he felt like a naked child, anxious only to find a hiding place.

At last the service was over. No explosions. No drama. Just, as far as Philip was concerned, a numbness and a relief. The question of whether he was healed or not seemed irrelevant. He formally thanked the congregation for coming, then accompanied Father Humphrey back to the vicarage. All he wanted now was to get rid of his visitor and be left in peace. But even after the monk had hugged Margaret and Philip, bade them keep in touch, and left in a friend's car, there was no peace to be had.

Philip felt exposed, embarrassed and vulnerable, sure that nothing could ever be quite the same again. He was no longer (in his own eyes, leave aside anyone else's) the priest, the one who offered ministry to those who needed it. Givers shouldn't need to receive. Soon it would be all over the parish that Father Ilott had received this public ministry in church. He felt raw, as if he had been found out in some crime or vice. Far from being a healing experience, that early morning service had left him feeling broken and wounded. For some reason the memory of his crucifixion dream came to mind. Was it connected with these events? If so, he hoped there was to be a corresponding experience of resurrection.

It was not easy to climb up into the pulpit on the following Sunday. Nobody had mentioned the Monday-morning Eucharist, but there was an air of wondering watchfulness among those who had witnessed the prayer for Philip's healing. They wanted to know if anything had resulted from it. On one level Philip knew that something *had* happened. In some mysterious way the excruciating shame of being forced to receive had allowed him, during this run-up to Easter, to identify with Christ's suffering in a completely new way. But that wasn't what they wanted to know. They wanted to know if his illness had been healed.

It hadn't. It was worse.

As Philip made his way painfully through the hard work of Good Friday and Easter, he felt like crying out to God that he was abandoned and humiliated. Bad enough to have to undergo the agony of revealing that the robe of his dignity was not seamless. But then, after all that, not to be healed! What was God thinking of? Over and over again, as the attacks increased in frequency and intensity, he said to himself, 'So much for being humbled! So much for letting everyone see me at my lowest! So much for Humphrey Whistler and his strange unknown language. I've never felt so ill in my life. It just hasn't worked.'

One weekend, about two months later, the children came home to find their father lying unconscious in the hall. Very worried, but showing great presence of mind, they pushed a cushion under Philip's head, then ran to fetch Margaret from where she was playing netball with some of the church wives. She hurried back and called the local doctor, who came immediately to administer an injection. This time the blackout lasted for more than nine hours.

When Philip came to and learned how long he had been unconscious, he was full of deep resentment. He resented the fact that the Lord's sacrament hadn't worked in his case. What was so wrong with Philip Ilott that he couldn't be made better when the right words were said by the right person in the right place? He resented even more bitterly than before Humphrey Whistler's interference in his life. He resented the way in which his own image of himself as a suave, well-dressed and smoothly competent priest had been shattered by the monk's ill-judged insistence on doing this healing 'thing'.

But worse was to come.

The doctor arranged for Philip to see a consultant at the hospital in Newport for further advice.

Two weeks later the day of the appointment arrived. A friend drove Philip and Margaret the ten miles or so from Ventnor to Newport, then waited outside while they went in. The consultant was leafing through Philip's records when the nervous couple entered his office. The gravity of his manner as he discussed the deterioration in Philip's condition was not reassuring.

Finally, he delivered his verdict.

'Your epileptic condition is worsening,' he said, 'and there is little doubt that the stresses and strains of the work you do are major contributory factors to the illness. This recent collapse is a very severe warning. Nine hours is a very long time. It is absolutely essential that all pressure is removed from your day-to-day life. Do you understand what I'm saying to you?'

Philip hoped he didn't.

'You mean . . . ?'

'I mean', continued the consultant in very definite tones, 'that, for you, because of the sort of ministry you have and the kind of man you are, the work involved in being a parish priest is not just unsuitable, it is extremely harmful, perhaps even dangerous. You will have to find something different to do. Cutting back on your workload will not make any significant difference. Your entire lifestyle *must* change radically. That can only be guaranteed by resignation from your parish work. That is not a suggestion, Father Ilott, it is an extremely serious medical prognosis.'

If Philip had felt broken before, he was in pieces now. Not only was he to lose his dignity, but also his parish – in essence, his priesthood. It would, he thought, be like having his soul taken away – that internal tangibility of Godlikeness, his identity, his own self. What would happen to the faith of those who had witnessed the laying on of hands and anointing for healing? What would they make of this abysmal failure? And what must I have done, asked Philip silently, as he and Margaret endured the silent return car trip from Newport to Ventnor, to deserve this happening to me? Being in that consultant's room just now had been like going into some divine office – or shed – to be sacked by God.

Back home, in the privacy of their own sitting-room, Philip and Margaret wept brokenly together as they often did when bad things happened. Usually, though, there was some tiny glimmer of hope at the dark centre of what seemed like hopelessness, even if it was just the knowledge that time would soften even very hard facts. This was different and they knew it. They had each other and the children, but the context of their lives was about to be wrenched away, and there was nothing they could do about it.

For several days after the hospital visit Philip struggled on with his work, unable quite yet to bring himself to contact his bishop or the patron of the parish to explain that he would be leaving St Alban's for medical reasons. He felt ill and lost.

Those months following Humphrey Whistler's visit were dreadful beyond words. Philip, frightened by his attacks and shattered by the doctor's pronouncement, seemed to be living out all his childhood traumas through his relationships with those closest to him. Margaret suffered most, of course, but so did others.

A clergyman friend from the mainland, Roger Pike, visited Ventnor on many occasions during this period to lay hands on Philip and anoint him with oil. So volatile was Philip at this stage that he would sometimes run like a child when he knew Roger was due to come, unable to face yet more ministry that threatened to open him up. Margaret alternated between hope and despair, patience and anger. On one occasion she told Roger to 'Go away!' because the visits and the prayer seemed so unavailing.

Further complications ensued when Brenda Wright and Roger Pike, thrown together by mutual concern for Philip, fell in love and decided to marry. Philip, emotionally stunted by pain and worry and confusion, suffered agonies of possessiveness over what he saw as the loss of a friend, and behaved quite irrationally at times. Unless something very dramatic happened soon it seemed that some awful disaster was inevitable.

Margaret went on praying. So did others. Brenda spent an entire night alone in the church, holding Philip up before God in her mind and asking that he should be healed.

Exactly three months after the day on which Humphrey Whistler had prayed for Philip's healing there came a ring on the vicarage door-bell. Philip, who was the only one in at the time, opened the door to find Dennis Allison standing on the step. Dennis was a Church Army captain who ran a holiday home at Ryde, on the north coast of the island. He had become quite friendly with the Ilotts since they came to Ventnor. This was just a social call, but there was clearly something else on the young man's mind. Over coffee he unburdened himself.

Had Philip heard, Dennis wanted to know, about the exciting things that were starting to happen in some Isle of Wight parishes in connection with renewal? Something called the charismatic movement was beginning to affect people's lives and the way they prayed and worshipped.

'Do you know anything about it, Philip?' asked Dennis.

'No, I don't,' replied Philip, placing his coffee cup down with unnecessary force, 'and I don't really *want* to know anything about it, to be honest, Dennis.'

'But people are apparently speaking in tongues and everything!' exclaimed Dennis, ploughing on enthusiastically. 'It's quite exciting!'

'What do you mean by "speaking in tongues"?' asked Philip warily. The expression was still an alien one to him.

'Well, "praying in the Spirit" it's sometimes called. Paul talks about it in the first letter to the Corinthians. Let's read it, eh?'

Together, sitting at the kitchen table, the two men, one brimming over with interest and involvement, the other wary but prepared to look, read through what Saint Paul had to say about God's gift of the Holy Spirit to people who believed in him.

'And tongues is just part of the gift,' said Dennis, 'a special language for us to talk to God in when we don't know what to say. Paul got angry with the Corinthians for using it too much in church and making outsiders think they were all mad. He says it's mostly for private use and that love is much more important. Then, when we look at Acts, you can see . . .'

There was no stopping the Church Army captain. He certainly knew his stuff. Philip began to wonder how, in the course of his own ministry, he'd managed to avoid or ignore all these biblical references to the power of the Holy Spirit, and the supernatural gifts that seemed to have been almost commonplace in the New Testament church.

Dennis invited Philip to a meeting in Ryde in a few days' time. For want of anything better to do, he accepted. Finally, the two men prayed about renewal in their own lives, and Dennis, who was in a hurry to be somewhere else, disappeared with a cheery wave and a smile.

Rather sadly, Philip carried the coffee cups over to the sink to do the washing-up. He'd got quite excited for a moment there, talking about gifts and renewal and the Holy Spirit. It wasn't for him though; he knew that. He was a sick man, about to leave the calling that had once seemed a lifetime's vocation. As for gifts, and speaking in tongues in particular, well, his only experience of that was the strange language Humphrey Whistler had used in church that morning, and a lot of good *that* had done.

Standing at the kitchen sink with an unwashed coffee cup dangling from one finger, he gazed out of the window at the magnificent sea view that had so excited them all when they first arrived at Ventnor. What a view! What a shame they had to leave it. What a pathetic whimpering end to a place and a life and a ministry that had seemed to promise so much.

A great sadness settled over him as he thought back to that day, so long ago now, when he knelt by his bed in his pyjamas and asked Jesus to be real to him. Such joy had filled him that night. His prayer had certainly been answered. And now, even if he lost his priesthood, he would still have Jesus. Like a little boy lost in the dark, he would have to put out his hand and trust that Jesus would take it. Such warmth he had experienced that night; such loving warmth. He could do with a bit of warmth nowadays – warmth in his body. Since the epilepsy had worsened he seemed to be cold all the time, chilled to the marrow.

Noticing the unwashed coffee cup still awaiting attention, Philip sighed and moved his hand forward to place it in the sink.

Then the Spirit came.

At first he felt a tingling sensation in the soles of his feet. It became a gentle, glowing heat that moved like a tide, up through his ankles, his knees, his thighs, his hips, his stomach, his chest, his arms, his neck, his face – right up to the very top of his head, until his whole body was held in the warm grasp of a power so benevolently overwhelming that he gasped with the shock of encountering it.

Releasing the cup from his fingers, Philip stood stock-still, his body and mind bathed in a wash of love, well-being and wholeness that was like and yet unlike the first meeting with the reality of Jesus; different because he knew, with a knowledge that came not from his mind but from his spirit, that this glowing baptism had healed him. There was no epilepsy any more. There never would be any epilepsy again. He was well.

'I've been healed!' whispered Philip to himself. 'I've been healed! I *am* healed! I'm well again! I'm . . .'

Filled suddenly with an overflowing gratitude towards God, he began to pray aloud, seeking words to express the passionate excitement that churned around inside him. Quite involuntarily he began to use words belonging to a language that was completely unknown to him. Like a baby babbling happily to his daddy, he let the sounds pour out of him. Somewhere in the back of his mind he listened, aghast, to the sound of his own voice. This was just how Humphrey Whistler had sounded when he prayed over Philip at that early morning Eucharist. What he was doing now must be what they called 'speaking in tongues'. Not that he cared in the least what it was called. It was exciting! It was different! It was – natural. Nor did he care what that tide of warmth and living energy was really called. It had happened. It had healed him. He could stay in Ventnor. He could go on being a priest with a parish. Thank God!

Turning away from the sink, with tears of joy in his eyes, Philip dithered for a moment, uncertain what to do next. There was no Anglo-Catholic procedure laid down for profound spiritual happenings at the kitchen sink. He smiled wryly. How ironic that, with all his love of ceremonial and well-ordered churchmanship, God should have chosen the kitchen sink, symbol of all that is most ordinary, as the scene of his encounter with Philip. It looked as if he really hadn't even begun to understand the nature of this God of his.

About to dash upstairs and destroy all his tablets, Philip paused, remembering that Margaret would be back from her shopping trip quite soon. What would he say to her? How could he convey with mere words the significance and excitement of what had happened? Would she believe that he really was healed after all these years?

He concentrated hard for a few moments, trying to plan coherent sentences to use when she came through the door in a minute. First, he thought, I'll kiss her as I always do, then I'll lead up to it gently, tell her about Dennis Allison's visit and what he said, then go on from there.

Circling the kitchen in pent up excitement as he planned, Philip actually had his back to the door when Margaret came in laden with shopping and exhausted after her long climb up the steps from Ventnor. Controlling his face as best he could, Philip turned round and moved forward to kiss her.

'What on earth has happened to you?' asked Margaret. 'Something's happened, hasn't it?'

Looking back, Philip was never quite sure why Margaret's acceptance of his experience seemed as great a miracle as anything else. She always did pray with faith. He had always thought of himself as God's agent, some-one who used hard slog in planning, preparing and working; the one who stood between God and the congregation, interpreting, mediating, representing and ministering – a sort of divine sub-contractor. That sudden awareness that Margaret's heart had been directly primed, as it were, in readiness for his healing, was the beginning of a new and rather startling realisation that God could and would pass and bypass any worldly or ecclesiastical structures at will. How, Philip wondered, should a 'kitchen-sink priest' conduct himself?

Philip sat Margaret down at the kitchen table, made her a cup of tea, and told her the whole story.

'And I'm healed,' he said finally. 'I'm well! I'm different!'

Margaret certainly believed in Philip's healing, but her first reaction was not a joyful one. After the number of hours that she and Roger and Brenda had spent in prayer, it seemed painfully ironic that a chance visit by Dennis Allison should have resulted in this metamorphosis. For a little while she felt quite resentful, but there was no question that God had done something quite startling.

'You look different, darling,' she said. 'You sound different. You even *feel* different. I believe you.'

With hands linked across the table, the couple prayed together for a minute or two until Philip could restrain himself no longer. Crying and laughing by turns, he leapt to his feet and jumped up and down on the kitchen floor out of sheer exuberance.

'You know what, Margaret?' he said, when he came back down to earth a little later, 'I feel as if I've been born again – again!'

That Sunday Philip preached with an enthusiasm and an assurance that quite surprised the congregation. By the following weekend a number of people had commented to Margaret on how much better Father Philip looked.

'Is he on different medication?' they asked.

'You're going to have to tell them, you know, Philip,'

said Margaret later. 'You owe it to them, especially the ones who came to the service when Father Humphrey prayed for you.'

On Sunday, in the middle of the notices, Philip invited as many of the congregation as were interested to come back to the church that evening for a special meeting. There was something he wanted to tell them about his health. The response was very warming. Quite a large crowd came to hear what he had to say. Philip spoke simply and without notes. He explained that three months after Humphrey Whistler's Eucharist he had, much to his own surprise, experienced healing and found himself speaking in tongues.

'And if this can happen to me,' he went on, 'there is absolutely no reason why it shouldn't happen to any of you. From now on,' he continued, rather surprised by his own words, 'these things will be part and parcel of the ministry of St Alban's.'

There was no doubt about the reaction of those present. They were very taken aback. Tongues? Healing? Holy Spirit ministry? Father Philip well again after all this time? Was it true, and would it last? After all, it had been his experience, not theirs.

Philip understood these problems, but he also knew that the Holy Spirit had come in a new way to St Alban's, Ventnor. The knowledge was a thrilling awareness inside him. Now he needed to pray carefully about the way forward.

* * *

One of Philip's first tasks was, somehow, to resolve the conflict between himself and Richard Dawes. The treasurer was still capable of making him feel like a little boy with no real responsibility. Sometimes it was fear he felt; sometimes it was very near to being hatred. He dreaded the conflicts, the times when he would have to summon up all his courage to say, 'I'm sorry, Richard, but that's the way I'm going to do it. I really feel I have a mission to fulfil here, and I'm going to see it through.'

Once when he had stood up to Richard like that, Val Dawes had been there. 'Well,' she said, 'we shall just see how long you stay the course, shan't we . . . ?'

It was not that Philip wished the treasurer ill. Winning him as a friend would have been the ideal solution to the problem. Margaret had carried a burden of compassion for Richard ever since they first got to know him. She felt that beneath his brashness there was an unhappy little boy who longed to be loved – a victim of rejection. Philip understood this particular problem more than most, of course, and Richard and Val Dawes might have been amazed had they known how much prayer went up from the vicar on their behalf.

In fact, if it is true, as scripture says, that 'the earnest prayer of a good man availeth much', then the congregation of St Alban's must have benefited a great deal from Philip's presence in the parish. Apart from his daily offices and prayer times with Margaret, there were two other rather unusual ways in which he made intercession for his parishioners.

The first of these happened in the church, when nobody else was present. Whenever somebody in the congregation needed extra prayer, extra understanding, or something beyond what Philip felt able to give, he would sit in the seat where that person usually sat on a Sunday, and claim the kingdom of Christ for them. There was something very relieving about handing people over to Jesus, especially when their problems were particularly horrendous. Occasionally he would sit in the places reserved for the young servers who assisted with the mass, and ask God to protect them, their families and their future lives. During the period of constant conflict with Richard Dawes he spent a good many hours occupying the treasurer's seat in the organ loft, praying for wisdom and courage in his dealings with the man, asking forgiveness for his own hard thoughts, and, most

importantly, asking that their relationship should be
healed, or at least stabilised.

'We realise you're having trouble with Richard,'
people would say, 'but, let's face it, he's jolly good value
as far as practical things and youth work are concerned. Does it really matter if you disagree over some
things?'

Philip had no doubt at all that it really mattered, not
just from the point of view of difficulties over finance
or innovation, but because his development as a man
and as a priest in this particular parish would be
seriously obstructed so long as he was unable to feel
truly in control of his legitimate areas of responsibility.

Philip's other, much more unusual, way of praying
for his ever-lengthening list of folk with special needs
was suggested by the long flight of granite steps leading
from the road above the church to the village of Ventnor
far below. Each Sunday a large proportion of the congregation made a tiring mini-pilgrimage up St Alban's steps
to their place of worship. It really was quite a climb.
Funeral services were particularly difficult. Conveying a
coffin up or down to the church could be a very perilous
business. Sometimes people tripped and fell as they
negotiated the unlit steps. One of Philip's sacristans was
confined to bed for several weeks after falling headlong
and almost fracturing both knee joints. It seemed to
Philip that the idea of sanctifying the steps through
prayer offered a satisfyingly tangible exercise.

At first he tried to do it during the day. Using the
scores of granite steps as a sort of giant rosary, he prayed
for a different person on each step as he ascended. This
worked reasonably well until, as frequently happened,
he met someone coming down the path on their way to
the sea. After the inevitable conversation that followed
such a meeting, he would usually forget who he had
been praying for and get into a complete muddle, especially when there were a number of encounters in the

course of one climb. It was when he found himself going back down to the bottom to start again that he realised how absurd the whole thing was getting. To end up muttering irritably about being interrupted by the very people he was trying to pray for didn't make any sense at all.

He decided to do it by night. Remembering that there are certain parts of the world where pilgrims are in the habit of ascending flights of steps on their knees, Philip determined that he would do the same. He told no one of his intention, not even Margaret, partly because of a slight feeling of embarrassment, and partly because it seemed more appropriate that it should be a private matter between himself and God. In any case, Margaret wouldn't worry about where he was – he was always out somewhere.

It was a very strange experience. On dark nights there was no illumination at all on the stone stairway. For that reason, presumably, Philip never met another living soul as he made his way laboriously on his knees from the lower road to the church. Now and then, though, the moon would be full and bright, and the steps would be softly lit as he went. On those occasions he would sometimes stop and look out towards the sea, gleaming like a silver salver in the distance. Whatever the degree of darkness, Philip actively enjoyed these private times of prayer, believing that God was warmly and willingly present to receive his prayers and intercessions.

Each upward journey ended in the vestry of St Alban's, where he used a clothes brush to remove dust or dirt from the knees of his trousers in case Margaret should become curious. (In the winter, or during bad weather, it was back to the pews for prayer.)

The last few steps before reaching the church were for Margaret, Paul, Mel and other members of his immediate family. The first and lowest ones were used to pray for and about the people who were the most problematic to him. For a long time he prayed the same prayers on those first three steps.

'Father, bless Richard and Val,' on the first step.

'Lord Jesus, bless Richard and Val,' as he knelt on the second step.

'Holy Spirit, bless Richard and Val,' on the third.

By the time Philip received his 'kitchen-sink' healing, a tremendous amount of prayer had been sent up on behalf of this man who had been such a blight on his peace since coming to the island.

The final solution to the problem came about, in fact, because of the brand new personal confidence which seemed to be a by-product of Philip's fresh experience of the Holy Spirit. It happened at a committee meeting of the Parochial Church Council, where, once again, the subject of church decoration had been raised by Philip, and once again the church treasurer had objected strongly to precious finance being wasted on 'tarting up the building'.

'But, Richard,' Philip argued, 'you decorate your own house and make sure it looks nice, don't you? Shouldn't we do the same with the church building?'

'I'm afraid I don't see the connection,' was the cool retort.

'But surely . . .'

The argument continued with rapidly escalating tension and ill-feeling, until Richard Dawes, realising that Philip was not going to retreat from his position, played what he obviously believed to be his trump card.

'Well,' said the treasurer dismissively, 'if you still insist on spending money in this way, I shall feel unable to retain my position on the PCC. I resign.'

Philip knew perfectly well what the next bit of the script was supposed to be, as did the other council members around the table. Father Philip would now say something conciliatory, such as 'No, no, that would be unthinkable, Richard,' and back down; or, at the very least, he would compromise. And of course it *was* unthinkable. Philip knew that. How could one deprive the people of St Alban's of the services of a man so central to the life and activity of the parish? How, in any case, would he ever find the courage to pursue the conflict to such a dramatic conclusion? He had never been able to do so before. But something new was living in and fuelling his own spirit. It was with considerable surprise that he heard the next words that came out of his mouth.

'Very well, Richard, I accept your resignation as from now.'

No one in the suddenly hushed hall was more aghast than Philip. What on earth had he done? He would have eaten his words if it had been possible. Could the church really manage without Richard Dawes' involvement? Would these other people support him or not? At the moment they just looked shocked and rather frightened. The treasurer (or ex-treasurer) rose slowly to his feet and walked out without another word, leaving Val, his wife, uncomfortably stranded in the midst of the embarrassed silence that followed.

The estrangement lasted for two or three months. Eventually, there was a reconciliation after Richard came to see Philip to apologise for the way he had spoken and to admit that some new lessons had been learned. Thereafter the relationship improved, and in time the two men became friends and developed a mutual respect that would have seemed impossible in those early days.

For Philip it was a very important victory to win, partly because it could only be good for the church community that someone had at last stood up to such a dominant character, but, much more crucially, because he, Philip Ilott, had for once neither run away nor compromised. It seemed to indicate the possibility of a new inner steadiness, a freedom to be more adult in problematic situations and relationships, and he associated that freedom with his recent experience in the vicarage kitchen, when the Spirit had done something different in or to his heart, and his illness had been healed.

Now he was fascinated and excited by the prospect of finding out how to make that healing available to others.

10

Isle of Wight – Miracles

'. . . thou hast set my feet in a large room.'

Philip spoke the words quietly to himself as he entered the upstairs meeting-place at the Church Army holiday house in Ryde. It was a month since his healing, and now, at Dennis Allison's invitation, he was attending one of the new revival meetings to talk about what had happened to him.

The previous evening, in his regular Bible-reading time, Philip had come across Psalm 31. Some lines caught his eye in a particular way: '. . . thou hast considered my trouble; thou hast known my soul in adversities; and hast not shut me up into the hand of the enemy: thou hast set my feet in a large room.' For some reason those words had seemed to leap off the page at him. Now, as he surveyed this huge room where the meeting was about to take place, he wondered if something important was going to happen. It was not the kind of connection he would have made before, but a new sense of the immediacy and close involvement of God in everyday affairs was beginning to give him a quite different view of the world. Here he was, about to take his place on one of the chairs ranged around the edge of this enormous upper chamber, perfectly happy to accept that the Holy Spirit had, through that Bible reading, prepared him for whatever was about to occur.

Seventy or eighty people listened in an enthralled silence as Philip described his recent experiences. His audience came from a wide variety of denominational backgrounds, and they were all quite fascinated by what they heard. As he finished, a profound hush fell on the room. Something stirred in Philip, an inward urging that he had never known before. Slowly it resolved itself into a conscious awareness that he was to speak in tongues in front of all these people. Hesitantly at first, then with increasing confidence, he allowed the words of his new language to bubble up from the well inside him that never seemed to dry up. As the words slowed and came to a halt, there was a short pause, then another voice began to speak from the other side of the room. It was a young man who was completely unknown to Philip, an islander who (Philip learned later) knew nothing about the parish of St Alban's, or the position of the house and the church on the hill that dropped so sharply down to Ventnor village. The words he spoke seemed to be a combination of an interpretation of Philip's tongue (another gift he had only recently learned about) and a prophecy, literally speaking out the words of God. The very air in that room seemed to be charged with the presence of the Holy Spirit as Philip absorbed the personal relevance of what was being said.

'I am going to bring new life. There will be a new springtime throughout this island, and my presence will be experienced in all its power. It will come like a bud on a tree, to be followed first by the blossom, and then by the fruit. It will take time. You must be patient. There will be times of trial and suffering, but understand that you must stay firm. And the house on the hill is the place of healing . . .'

Philip felt the hairs on the back of his neck rise as these words sank in.

'The house on the hill is the place where all will be made well. The house on the hill is the place to which all will be drawn.'

Philip knew that the young man was talking about St Alban's. He hadn't yet begun any kind of healing ministry at the church, but this seemed to be a clear indication that something new and exciting was about to happen. He could hardly contain the thrill of expectancy that followed those inspiring words. To see people actually made better through the power of God, to witness the close loving reality of God's touch on hurting people, here on the Isle of Wight, and in his own church – what could be more fulfilling?

The meeting ended with an informal communion service, led, at Dennis Allison's request, by Philip. Philip had been a little uneasy about this beforehand. It was in the days before the Anglican communion was made available to all those in good standing with their own church, and the thought of breaking bread with Roman Catholics, Methodists, Pentecostals and members of the United Reformed Church was more than a little disquieting. In the atmosphere of the meeting itself, however, his reservations and unease simply disappeared. The people in this room were not members of separate churches – not today. Today they were all members of the one true church, the church of Jesus Christ, and Jesus himself was here in their midst, just as he had promised he would always be when two or three gathered together in his name. Quietly, in a mood of contained ecstasy, the bread was passed from person to person, followed by the wine. Each person used the name of his or her neighbour in offering the sacrament: 'John, the body of Christ . . . Mary, the blood of Christ . . .'

It was a new and invigorating experience for Philip, made even richer by the promise contained in the prophecy given earlier, that healing was coming to St Alban's. That night, at home, he described the whole meeting in minute detail to Margaret, who had stayed at home to look after the children. They both determined to hunt out reading material about the new revival movement in an effort to understand the current in which they now seemed to be flowing. Not that Philip felt any desire or obligation to abandon or dilute the catholic side of his churchmanship. Rather, he experienced an enrichment of his sacramental life that ran parallel with a greatly increased sense of expectancy in prayer, Bible study and the new house groups that were growing directly out of his fresh understanding. In his personal prayer, Philip found himself praying less for gifts like prophecy and tongues than for an overall gift of love that would enable him to serve his parishioners in the best possible way. Contained within that love, he was sure, would be all the specific gifts that might be needed.

In response to the Spirit's leading at the meeting in Ryde, Philip decided to initiate a service of healing to be held once every month in the context of Benediction, a service which might be described as God's postscript to the day. In a sacramental act somewhat similar to Holy Communion, the priest holds up a large round wafer and makes the sign of the cross over his congregation, almost as if they are being blessed by the setting sun as the day draws to a close. Philip felt that healing should occur within the framework of a sacramental act rather than being an isolated process, and the Anglicanism of the service seemed appropriate because, at that stage, he had no reason to expect that anyone other than members of his own congregation would be likely to present themselves for healing on the fourth Sunday of every month. The PCC was not consulted. Philip simply announced at a morning service one Sunday that the first opportunity for laying on of hands would take place in two weeks' time, and that all were welcome to seek healing for themselves, or by proxy for someone else.

The church was packed for that first service. It was as though the St Alban's congregation knew that something out of this world had happened to their priest and they wanted to share in the miracle. After a hymn and a scripture reading, Philip spoke briefly about some of the miracles of Jesus and explained what was about to happen, then he invited those who wished for prayer to come forward to the front of the church and await the laying on of hands.

Almost the entire congregation responded to his invitation, each person hungry for help in some area of his or her life. It was a tremendous encouragement for Philip to see so many people doing something completely new to them because they had 'caught' his faith in God's caring presence. One by one he listened to their whispered problems. Arthritis, back pain, migraine, tummy troubles, family conflicts, marriage breakdowns – there were as many problems as there were people. In each case Philip, still very much in unknown territory, laid his hands on the person's head and prayed a prayer of healing.

'In the name of God most high, and through his infinite love and power, may release be given to you. In the name of Jesus Christ, Prince of Life, may his eternal life flow through you. In the name of the Holy Spirit, may you be kept entire to the glory of God and the praise of his holy name.'

Then came a prayer for the particular need.

'May Our Lord enter into your arthritis and begin to heal it, and remove it according to his will.'

To Philip's knowledge, nobody received specific physical healing on that first occasion. He was undismayed. The question of what people would think if 'nothing happened' never really occurred to him. Not many months earlier that would have been his major concern. Now, on the other hand, he experienced a new freedom in being obedient and leaving the outcome of his prayers in the hands of God. At the same time he was full of expectancy and an immovable certainty that all would be well. He was slightly disturbed by the strength of this certainty. He'd known nothing like it since his ordination. It seemed to have been implanted into the foundations of his spiritual attitude – perhaps, he reflected, in the space where his stubborn self-reliance had been.

Ironically, but predictably perhaps in Philip's case, the first person to be healed of a specific physical illness was not a member of Philip's own church. Down on the extreme edge of the parish of St Alban's was a school for 'delicate children' run by nuns from the convent of the Society of St Margaret. Almost a hundred boys and girls suffering from asthma, cystic fibrosis and a variety of other ailments were lovingly cared for by the staff of St Catherine's School. Not all the staff members were nuns. One lady was a member of the St Alban's congregation, a regular attender whose husband played the organ for evening services. Aware of Philip's own healing, and excited and warmed by the new monthly healing service, she made a special request one day for Philip to come to St Catherine's, or perhaps for some of the sick children to come up to the church. Nothing loath, he contacted the school chaplain and the sister-in-charge. With their permission and co-operation, a day was arranged for Philip to minister to some of the children in the school chapel.

It was desperately moving to see the children lined up in front of him as he spoke. Although they ranged in age from nine to the early teens, most of them, because of the wasting effects of long-term illness, were small for their age and very slightly built. After addressing his young but attentive congregation, Philip invited any who would like to be specially prayed for to come and kneel at the communion rail so that he could lay his hands on their heads.

'If you like,' he said, 'you can just ask Jesus to come and live in your hearts, and I'll pray with you about that.'

Quite a lot of children came up and knelt rather uncertainly at the wooden rail. Philip moved from one to another, taking infinite pains over every whispered communication, praying quietly with each small supplicant in turn until he came to the end of the row. The others had returned to their seats and there was just one girl left. She was a plain little creature, very pale, very thin, very small. Her hair was dark and straight, and her brown eyes were magnified hugely behind cheap National Health Service spectacles. She was probably nine or ten years old, a skinny little scrap of anxious humanity peering up nervously as Philip stood before her. Sensing her apprehension, he spoke very quietly.

'What's your name, sweetheart?'

Her answering whisper was so subdued that it was impossible to understand what she had said. Kneeling down and placing his ear next to her mouth, Philip repeated the question.

'My name's Naomi,' breathed the little girl. 'I'm ten.'

'And what would you like Jesus to do for you, Naomi?'

Naomi hung her head. The worry lines on her forehead deepened, but she said nothing. Philip waited, drawing back a little.

'It doesn't matter what the problem is, Naomi,' he said, 'if you've got Jesus living in your heart. Can you tell me what's bothering you?'

Naomi's face lifted again. As she looked into Philip's eyes, the thick-lensed glasses were slightly misted.

'That's it,' she whispered, 'he can't.'

'Who can't do what, darling?' He was willing her to put her big problem into words. Clearly something was very wrong.

'Jesus.'

'Yes?'

'He can't come and live in my heart.'

Philip thought for a moment. He was bewildered, but determined to help. He spoke gently and with as much assurance as he could muster.

'Naomi, Jesus can come and live in anyone's heart. You only have to ask him. Nothing makes him happier than to make friends with little girls like you. I promise you that's true, it really, honestly is.'

Naomi was obviously not convinced. She shook her head slowly and earnestly from side to side.

'Jesus can't come and live in my heart,' she repeated. 'He can't.'

What on earth could it be? What could a little thing like this think she'd done that was so awesomely bad as to prevent her from asking Jesus to be her friend? Philip spoke even more quietly.

'Why not, Naomi? Tell me why Jesus can't live in your heart.'

'Because,' said the very small voice, 'I've got a hole in my heart.'

Philip swallowed hard and looked down for a moment. By the time he looked up and spoke he was able to control his voice properly.

'Naomi,' he said, 'Jesus knows all about that hole in your heart, and he can heal it. He wants to make you better. Let's pray together and tell him that's what we want him to do.'

Even as Philip began to pray over the small figure, he wondered at his own confidence in more or less promising a sick child that she would be healed through his prayer. The sense of responsibility was alarming, to say the least. But something told him that in this particular case it was the right thing to do. It was his first experience of specific guidance in matters of healing, but of course the accuracy of that guidance could be confirmed in only one way. It was therefore with a profound sense of joy and relief that Philip heard a few weeks later how, after a routine set of tests, her doctors were unable to find a trace of Naomi's hole in the heart.

Later, on a different occasion, another little girl was healed of cystic fibrosis, a tragically life-shortening condition. Why these particular children should have been selected for healing when so many other cases of suffering remained untouched was beyond Philip's comprehension. All he knew was that when certain people came forward for prayer a special kind of knowledge entered his awareness, providing, at times, a quite alarmingly specific insight into the reasons for their infirmity. As he learned to trust this silent voice, so it accompanied his ministrations more and more, until it became a constant and welcome part of the monthly healing meeting at St Alban's.

One lady had been enduring appalling spinal pain for a long time. Almost completely encased in a surgical corset, she dragged herself laboriously to the altar rail one evening, and, kneeling in exhaustion, waited for Philip to make his way along the row to her. She was a complete newcomer to the church. Philip knew nothing about her, not even her name, but as he leaned forward to ask what she wanted prayer for, certain specific Christian names entered his mind with the sparkling clarity that seemed to characterise the Holy Spirit's communications. Philip, informed solely by this inner voice, told the pain-filled supplicant that her back problems were caused entirely by problems in her family relationships, particularly with her husband and one of her children. Her amazement on learning that Philip knew not only the difficulties she was experiencing but also the names of the two people concerned was matched only by Philip's own astonishment that God was so graphically, so intimately, involved in the everyday affairs of ordinary men and women, and that he, Philip Ilott, could be used as a channel of that involvement. It seemed that there were endless depths to the business of understanding that there really is a God who really does things. For the first time Philip knew a little of what had been happening when Father Cross turned away to pray for guidance on the day before that train journey from Chester to London all those years ago.

A few days later the lady with back problems returned. She no longer wore a surgical corset and she was no longer in pain. Her eyes alight with happiness, she described how she had taken the corset off as soon as she arrived home after the service. The pain had disappeared immediately, and showed no sign of returning. Her real problem had been the emotional burden she was carrying. That realisation, and the resolution of the family conflicts, brought an end to her physical suffering and a new, dynamic spiritual awareness.

As more and more people experienced healing through Philip's ministry, it became clear that very few consistent rules applied to what was happening. The physical act of laying hands on people and the actual prayer for healing remained more or less unchanged, but there was no doubt that God healed those he chose in whatever way seemed best to him. The fact that a person was healed of arthritis on one day was by no means a guarantee that someone with a similar ailment would be healed on the next, or in the same way. This tended to make life exciting for Philip, if a little unpredictable. Once a man or woman had received the laying on of hands and left the altar rail, there was no way of knowing how God would deal with them.

For example, a woman who had endured a stomach ulcer for some time came back to see Philip a few days after coming up for prayer. Her expression was an odd combination of satisfaction and puzzlement.

'The thing is, Father,' she said, 'that something funny has happened. I didn't ask for it, and I'm not sure I particularly want it, but I've got it, and it seems to do the trick.'

Patiently, Philip enquired what 'it' might be.

'You know – a language. "Speaking in tongues" you call it, don't you?'

'Ah!' exclaimed Philip, 'I see – and you say that's helping?'

'Well,' she explained, 'I was going round the house as usual, doing my work, when it just started. And it keeps coming back. I mean, I can stop it if I want, but I don't really want to, because I feel so much better afterwards, you see.'

Once more the Holy Spirit silently instructed Philip in what to say.

'What's happening,' he said, 'is that God is using

tongues to stir up the emotional life within you in order
to heal the ulcer. Speaking out in that new language is
releasing the acidity that has been making you ill.'

Whatever Philip or the lady concerned may have
thought of this novel analysis of the situation is not
strictly relevant, because as the tongues continued the
ulcer diminished, until it disappeared altogether, and
the lady was free to continue to exercise her gift, or not,
as she pleased.

It was wonderful to see God making people better.
But, for Philip, it was no less wonderful and warming
to see how the quality of relationships within the church
was changing as well. People were more loving with
each other, much more open about themselves, and far
more prepared to discuss the deeper things of life than
they had been previously. Gradually church was becoming something that you did, rather than a place you
visited once a week. It was the answer to the prayer that
continued to express Philip's most fervent wish: 'Please
give me – give all of us – the gift of love.'

Love continued to grow, especially in Philip's relationship with the Dawes. Val became very ill and received
the laying on of hands on a number of occasions, and
later (a moment that brought a long-delayed tear of joy
to Philip's eye) Richard Dawes himself knelt at the altar
rail to ask for prayer.

Life attracts life. Perhaps unsurprisingly it was not
very long before the monthly service began to attract
people from a wide variety of other denominations. So
great was the demand on occasions that Philip had to
enlist the aid of a Methodist minister and a nun from
the convent to assist him at the times of prayer for
healing. Baptists, Methodists, Pentecostals, Anglicans of
various shades – they all sought out the house on the
hill, looking for life and healing.

A lifelong Methodist told Philip how a group from
their church had been steadfastly praying for revival
on the Isle of Wight for years. Never in their wildest

imaginings had they envisaged an Anglo-Catholic church being at the centre of such a revival. The Pentecostals were even more bewildered. Most of the Benediction service was a complete mystery to them, as were Philip's robes and the general ethos of the church building. In the centre of all this strangeness, though, they sensed, and in many cases knew for themselves, the love and healing presence of Jesus which seemed to sanctify everything else that happened.

Within months it had become impossible for Philip to contain his healing work within a single monthly service. Not only were there many calls on his time from outside organisations and churches, but an increasing number of needy individuals were beating a path to the vicarage door, each one desperately hoping for private help with his or her particular problem. Philip worked harder and harder, doing his best to accommodate every request for counselling or prayer. His new insight, that the real counsellor, healer and helper was always the Holy Spirit, was opening up unlimited vistas of effective pastoral work. As long as he, Philip Ilott, maintained himself as a clean and uncluttered pathway for the Spirit to walk into people's lives, then just about anything was possible.

So frequently did Philip's work extend beyond the parish boundaries now, that some members of St Alban's began to feel and express a little resentment about having to share their priest with so many other people. Philip was aware of this element of ill-feeling, and managed to meet it with the right combination of firmness and diplomacy.

He was, however, much less aware of the negative effect of his new work on his own family. From the children's point of view, things should have been much better. Daddy wasn't ill any more, so he should have had more time to play with them. In fact, his healing marked the beginning of a period so dominated by the needs of people outside the family that it was only during holidays away from home that they saw much of him.

Philip had always worked hard. But now he was as married to his work as he was to his wife, and possibly more of a father to his congregation than he was to his children. Like so many genuine, devoted Christian workers before and since, Philip loved his wife and children, but was blinkered to their immediate and essential need for more of his input into their lives.

How easy it was, though, for that to happen, when hour by hour and day by day such tragically urgent cases arrived to eclipse the more routine requirements of family life. There was, for instance, the case of baby Harry.

One day Philip was working in his den underneath the house when there was a knock on the door. It was Margaret.

'Darling,' she said in hushed tones, 'there's a family here with a baby. They're asking if it would be possible for you to pray for him. He's very sick.'

'Of course,' replied Philip, laying down his pen and rising to his feet. 'Tell them to –'

'Darling, I must just explain to you,' interrupted Margaret, her eyes full of concern, 'he really is very sick. He's got encephalitis and water on the brain. There's no cure for that. All they can do is drain off the fluid and put a tube into his head. It's such a serious condition. If you build their hopes up and then . . .'

Margaret's voice faltered and stopped, but Philip knew what she was saying. If he agreed to pray for the child and the child died anyway, it might be worse than if he hadn't given the family any grounds for hope at all. All he could do was go forward carefully and trust that he would be clearly shown what to do. He nodded slowly.

'You'd better ask them to come down here, Margaret,' he said quietly, 'then we can decide what to do.'

A few moments later Margaret ushered two ladies through the door. The one holding baby Harry was his mother; the other was his grandmother. They were both strained with pent-up worry and grief. Carefully, Harry's mother parted the shawl wrapped around her baby to reveal the grotesquely swollen head so typical of his particular condition. Between them, the two women explained how, after Harry was born and his illness diagnosed, they had heard that people were being healed at the church on the hill in Ventnor. Did Philip think that anything could be done for Harry?

It was a difficult moment. Philip looked intently into the sleeping baby's face for a minute or two, trying to concentrate on what he knew for sure. God loved Harry. He knew that for sure. God didn't want people to suffer, not from grief or pain. That was something else he was quite sure about. On the other hand, he also knew from experience that not everybody who asked for prayer was healed. He was no nearer knowing the reason for that than he had been when that first Benediction service was held, but it was a fact. As he prayed silently for guidance and courage, an idea formed in his mind, a way to approach this particular situation. He just hoped that it really was an inspiration from the Holy Spirit.

'I'll pray for Harry,' he told the two anxiously waiting women, 'but we'll all lay hands on him while I do. Let's pray for him now, while he sleeps.'

Harry's mother and grandmother were more than willing to do anything that might help. Together the three adults placed their hands very gently on the tiny body while Philip prayed for the still slumbering child.

'In the name of God most high, and through his infinite love and power, may release be given to you, Harry. In the name of Jesus Christ, Prince of Life, may his eternal life flow through you. In the name of the Holy Spirit, may you be kept entire to the glory of God and the praise of his holy name. Dear Father, come into little Harry's sickness and begin to heal and remove it according to your will. Knowing that you love him, we ask this in Jesus' name. Amen.'

It was the first of many such sessions, and each one

followed almost exactly the same pattern. Mother and grandmother would arrive with Harry at the door of the den. All three would then lay hands on the baby while Philip prayed. Harry's father, a self-styled agnostic, chose not to involve himself in what initially must have seemed a pointless activity.

Curiously, Harry was fast asleep on every single occasion that Philip saw him during this period. His mental picture of the little boy was of a baby with closed eyes. Yet, perhaps because of the intensity of his desire that Harry should be well, Philip developed a great fondness for the defenceless little soul who lay so quietly in his mother's arms. In between visits, Harry's mother kept in touch with Philip, reporting on the results of regular tests carried out at the hospital in Southampton. It was inexpressibly thrilling to hear that a gradual but definite improvement in the child's condition was running parallel with the visits for prayer. Eventually, in a memorable letter, Harry's mother reported that the encephalitis was completely cured. The doctors could find no sign of it.

Nearly two years had passed, and in all that time Philip had never seen Harry awake, never heard him make a sound, and never encountered him other than in his mother's or his grandmother's arms. Then, unexpectedly, the priest-in-charge of the parish where Harry's family lived contacted Philip to suggest a visit to Harry's home to see the little boy in action, now that he was well. Also, he added, Harry's mother and grandmother were longing to meet Philip again, as was the boy's father, whose agnosticism had become a pale shadow of its former self.

Excited and a little nervous, Philip and Margaret set off on the appointed day to have tea and help celebrate Harry's second birthday. The house was charming, an old brick farm-cottage with chocolate-box roses growing round the weatherbeaten front door. There was no one in sight as they knocked, but the door was opened almost immediately by Harry's mother, who beamed a welcome and ushered them in to meet her husband and reacquaint themselves with the little boy's grandmother, who was busily preparing the table for tea. It was lovely to come into such a warm and appreciative atmosphere, but so far there was no sign of the birthday boy.

'He's playing in the back garden,' explained Harry's father. 'I'll call him in.'

A few seconds later Harry was in the room, flushed with running and bright-eyed with health. He stopped as soon as he came through the door and stood motionless for a moment, staring at the two visitors by the door.

What happened next was one of the strangest and certainly one of the most moving things that Philip had ever experienced. Two year old children are a friendly but cautious race. They take their time when it comes to strangers, circling around warily, as it were, before making any real advances. This was not the case with Harry. There was only one way to describe the expression on the little boy's face as his eyes met Philip's for the first time. It was a look of recognition and joy. He ran straight across the room with a little cry, and threw his arms out to be picked up by Philip. Sitting down on a nearby chair, adult and child cuddled each other like old friends, while the rest of the family looked on in amazement.

There was no doubt about it, somehow Harry knew that something had happened between himself and this man who had come to his birthday tea. They already had a relationship that had developed through a species of communication that was nothing to do with basic human senses. Harry seemed to accept it quite naturally. Here he was, sitting on the knee of an old and familiar friend. Why should anything else matter? For Philip though it was yet another mystery to ponder. *How* had Harry recognised him? He had no idea. It was God doing things again, that was all he knew. You just had to accept it.

His whole experience of the healing ministry was like

that, in fact. It was no use posing as a deep and spiritually insightful human being (however tempting that might be just occasionally), because it was God who did the healing, God who provided the specialised information, and God who laid down the means and process by which each individual received the help that they needed. Philip had become neither perfect nor powerful since his healing, just more available, and perhaps more constructively childlike in his capacity to feel awed and humbled by the Holy Spirit's dramatic use of such a flawed agent.

Certainly it would have been impossible for Philip to believe that he had achieved anything approaching perfection. Quite apart from the imbalance between work and family, there were still many things in his life that troubled him, especially since his father had joined the household.

Healed physically, and filled with the Spirit in a new way, he was still a slave to the phantoms and monsters of his early years, and they could have a crippling effect on family life. There was, for instance, his strange inability to unwrap presents. It upset and infuriated the children. At Christmas, or on his birthday, they would very carefully choose presents for daddy, wrap them up in suitable paper, then offer them excitedly when the right time came. But he wouldn't open them! Sometimes it was two days before Philip could bring himself actually to investigate the contents of those lovingly prepared packages. It wasn't fair – he knew that, but he didn't know the reason for it and he didn't know how to change.

This and other problems in his life were somehow connected with the past, that at least he was sure of. It was frustrating. So many wounds from his early life had been healed, and he had really hoped that this new phase in his spiritual experience might mean that only the present and the future need concern him now. On the other hand, he now knew with more certainty than ever before that God could change things. Not without a flutter of fear, Philip decided to set about excavating the memories that for years his conscious mind had been too nervous to acknowledge. Then, when those dark and secret hurts were out in the open, God would heal them – wouldn't he?

But what sort of memories would they be?

11

Isle of Wight – Memories

'You bloody bitch! You've always got your own selfish way, haven't you?'

'Don't be a damned fool! What about that child you gave me that I never wanted?'

Philip was five again, and a terrible argument was going on, even worse than usual.

Daddy had come home on holiday from the war that morning, and there had been rows from the moment he walked through the door.

All through lunchtime and during the afternoon a storm had been growing in the Ilotts' house. Now it was bursting out in a thunder of loud shouting voices, stamping feet and crashing doors.

Usually, daddy didn't get very angry. Mammy was too strong for him. He was more likely to go quiet, or cry. Sometimes, though, mammy would say something so harmful and nasty that daddy went absolutely mad, so angry that he didn't seem to care what he said or did. This was one of those times.

It had started with mammy telling daddy that he might as well have stayed at the war for all the use he was to her. Daddy said it was the other way round. Mammy didn't love him any more; there was no love left in their house at all, and he wished he could go away for ever and never come back again.

They fought each other with words all day, and by the time it got to four o'clock the air was so full of jagged, dangerous feelings that Philip was sure they would start fighting each other with fists and nails and teeth before very long.

He paced worriedly to and fro in the hall, listening to the awful noises coming from the living-room. Suddenly the sounds of slaps and punches were added to the spitting voices.

'You bloody useless fool . . . !'

'You stupid bloody bitch . . . !'

Philip burst through the door, unable to stand it any more. He must stop them before they really hurt each other. After all, it was mainly his fault, wasn't it? Mammy kept on saying that, right in the middle of the worst bits of the argument.

'. . . that child I never wanted . . . If it wasn't for that child you made me have . . .'

There in the living-room, etched against the brown curtains with the brass rings on top, like people in a scene from an old film, his parents were battling as if they wanted to kill each other – and if it weren't for him being born everything would have been alright.

It was up to him to do something to stop them fighting. Full of an unspeakable anguish, he threw himself down by daddy's feet, pressing his face against the rough khaki of the army uniform and trying to wrap his arms around his father's legs. All he wanted – all he had ever wanted – was love, and here were the two most important people in his life hating each other, and hating him, when they should be warm and loving and like a family ought to be. If only he could do something to stop this horrible fight. He raised his voice, trying to make them hear him.

'Stop! Mammy – daddy, please stop! Please . . .'

With a single infuriated kick of one leg, daddy sent him spinning away across the floor, so hard that his head nearly banged into the fireplace surround. Dizzy but determined, he picked himself up and, running back across the room, tried to force his body between mammy and daddy again. He couldn't stop the tears now. They seemed to be flooding out without stopping. He couldn't really see properly, he could only shout and hope they'd listen.

'Mammy, please don't fight any more! Daddy, please can't you . . .'

Momentarily united by fury at his interference in their conflict, the adults seized him roughly and threw him with breathtaking force against the wall beside them. He was conscious of his head thudding against something hard, then everything went black for a while. When he came to, mammy was kneeling beside him, her eyes ablaze with annoyance and scepticism.

'You bloody boy,' she hissed, 'you did this on purpose to frighten us.'

'Mammy, I didn't! I was . . .'

'You put it on, you little rat . . .'

'Philip, darling, are you alright? You've been miles away.'

Amazingly, Margaret's voice was breaking right into the middle of that terrible scene at the Ilotts' house in Newcastle. Quite bewildered, Philip blinked and looked around him. He wasn't in Newcastle at all. He was sitting in a steak-bar on the Isle of Wight. He wasn't five years old either. He was grown-up, married, the priest-in-charge of St Alban's. His wife was sitting next to him, looking concerned. She was touching his hand, waiting for an answer.

'I – I think I'm alright, Margaret. It was another of those memories. A nasty one – really nasty. It was way back when I was little and . . .'

Philip stopped abruptly as he realised with a little shock that the mild-mannered elderly man contentedly chewing on his steak at the other side of the table was the same man who had thrown him across the room in the incident that had returned to his memory in the last few seconds.

It was happening a lot now, ever since he had started this 'healing of memories' business. And you never

knew where or when it was going to happen. It could
be anywhere and any time. He would suddenly find
himself reliving an event from the past, an event that
had not entered his conscious mind since the day it
occurred. Most of these memories were very painful
ones, hidden for years because they were too hard to
face. It was a strange, disturbing experience, but it was
definitely from God, and it was beginning to have a
cleansing effect on the murkier parts of his personality.

At first Philip had been unsure how to go about the
task of getting in touch with such inaccessible parts of
himself. Perhaps he knew the answer all along, really.
It was Roger Pike he needed. He wrote a letter requesting
his fellow priest to visit, explaining his present needs
and suggesting a date. He was glad when he had taken
that first step.

It was so hard to offer healing to others when he felt
so flawed himself, but as the date of Roger's visit drew
near, Philip began to lose his nerve. Did he really want
to gouge out yet more unsightly bits and pieces from
wherever they were hidden? Hadn't he been healed of
epilepsy and touched by God in all sorts of ways? Surely
that was enough, wasn't it?

By the time the day of the visit arrived, Philip was just
plain frightened. He didn't want to be vulnerable again.
He didn't want to share things and talk about things and
perhaps crumble to pieces when he really opened up
about his childhood. Better to clench the memories in
the back of his brain – never let them go.

Margaret knew Philip was going to run when Roger
came, just as he had run before his healing. And she
was right – he did run. He ran out of the house and
down the steps, not stopping until he found a place to
hide at the bottom, in a tree-shaded corner, with his
heart banging away like a hammer in his chest. There
the great healer crouched, praying that his visitor would
give up waiting for him and go back home.

Margaret sent Roger out to search for Philip, guessing

that he had probably headed for lower ground. The priest went all the way down to the bottom of the steps, actually passing the man he was looking for at one point, then all the way back up again to tell Margaret his quest had been unsuccessful. Philip hung about near his hiding place for a long time, pretending he was either on his way up or on his way down whenever he encountered someone on the steps. It was a miserable hour and a half, and it seemed to go on for ever. At last, with slow, reluctant steps he made the long climb back to the house.

Roger had gone, but Margaret was very angry. What on earth was the point, she stormed, in asking a man to lunch because you need his help, dragging him all the way from the mainland, then running away like a frightened rabbit as soon as he appeared? Not to mention the fact, she added, mentioning it very pointedly, that she, Margaret, had been left to do the entertaining and provide the feeble explanations for her husband's eccentric behaviour. Did he want help or didn't he? And if he did, what was he going to do about it?

Margaret didn't often get as angry as this, but when she did, she was almost invariably right. Philip felt very ashamed and very unhappy. Once again, after feeling that things had really changed for the better, he was faced with a weakness in himself that seemed quite at variance with the work he was doing.

'I'm really sorry, darling,' he said rather tearfully. 'I just couldn't face finding out the truth about myself. I really don't know what it might turn out to be.'

A day or two later Roger, totally forgiving and understanding, made contact with Philip to assure him that he would be willing to risk the trip to Ventnor once more if he was wanted. Philip knew that nothing would be resolved until he did see Roger; his own spiritual instincts and Margaret's promptings assured him of that. He screwed up his courage and invited Roger back. This time he managed to avoid running away. The three of

them, Roger, Philip and Margaret, sat in the vicarage
sitting-room on the appointed day, a little nervous, but
quite resolved to see it through, whatever 'it' might be.

Roger anointed Philip with oil, praying as he did so
that his fellow priest would be given peace to accept
whatever the Holy Spirit showed him.

'Philip,' he said quietly, 'we've got to ask Jesus to
enter into the past – your past. We believe that what the
Bible says about him being the same yesterday, today
and for ever is true in every way. I can assure you that
he can be that through every period and incident in your
past life, healing and helping with the things that are
still causing you problems now. What we've got to
do, very simply, is to start talking a little about your
childhood and the things you remember that could have
hurt you. Then the Lord will bring to mind the things
you *don't* remember, and enter into those as well.'

Philip wanted to co-operate, but he just couldn't. It
was as though the worst of his memories were somehow
built into one of the supporting walls of his stability. If
he allowed them to be removed – knocked out – wasn't
it possible that the entire edifice of his identity could
come crashing down? He wasn't able to mention a single
thing to Roger. At the same time he felt so annoyed with
himself. He seemed to have been playing out this kind
of scene over and over again ever since his conversion.
Two steps forward and three steps back. Apparent liber-
ation followed by inevitable reminders that, while God
might do wonderful things through him, he, as a man,
had a very long way to go.

Roger wasn't troubled by this temporary inability to
relinquish old memories. Laying his hands on Philip's
head, he prayed that his friend would relax in the Spirit
over a period of time and be able to let go of the past.
Philip trusted that this prayer would be answered, despite his dumbness in Roger's presence, and he waited
with some trepidation to see what was going to happen.

He didn't have to wait very long. Within a few weeks

of Roger Pike's visit, extraordinary things began to happen to him in picture form. Vividly, like images on a television screen, whole sections of hitherto unremembered experiences would flash before his eyes. Even more dramatically, as with the living-room fight memory, he sometimes seemed to be back inside the child that he once was, reliving the event as though it was happening now. It might occur during a meal, or while he was with the family, or in the church, and simply take him over for a matter of minutes. Fortunately, Margaret understood what was happening when Philip's attention seemed to be so heavily distracted. She would quietly squeeze his hand while the experience lasted, and gently remind him that he was with people who loved him as he returned to the real world.

He discovered why opening presents was such a problem for him. It was something else that happened when he was a boy.

It was his birthday, and he was very excited. Mammy had told him there was going to be a special treat on the morning of his birthday. Treats were rare in Philip's house; he could hardly contain himself when he awoke. What was the treat going to be? Downstairs, he ate his breakfast with undue haste, then waited, all a-quiver, to hear what was going to happen. Mammy and daddy were both there. His birthday present, wrapped in brightly coloured paper, lay on the table awaiting his attention a little later. Mammy leaned back and lit a cigarette in her long black holder. She drew smoke into her mouth, then blew it in a long thin stream in the direction of the ceiling. Then she spoke.

'Daddy's going to take you swimming, Philip. That's your birthday treat.'

Philip felt the blood draining from his face. Disappointment and fear chased each other in giddy circles around his mind. Swimming? He hated swimming! Surely mammy knew how frightened he was of water? A little while ago he'd banged his head badly when someone towed him through the water on the end of a rope at the swimming pool. Going to the baths wouldn't be a treat. It would be more like a punishment. Why had she chosen swimming? Why? His lips moved soundlessly as he tried to think of something to say. He didn't want to go to the swimming pool, but if he told mammy that, she would be furious with him. She would –

'Well? What do you say? Aren't you pleased?'

'I – I don't really like swimming, mammy. Do I have to go swimming?' His voice was hardly more than a whisper.

The explosion that followed was worse than anything he might have expected. Mammy shouted and screamed about his ingratitude and selfishness, and lots of other bad things. Daddy stayed quiet, trying to say things now and then, but not managing it. Philip just waited dumbly for it all to finish. Mammy got angrier and angrier, until, at the moment when she seemed to have run out of hurtful things to say, she picked up his birthday present from the kitchen table and held it towards him. Not sure what to do, he half rose from his seat and twitched his hand nervously an inch or two in her direction.

'You'd better have your bloody present, you ungrateful little wretch!'

Drawing her arm back, she threw the package as hard as she could in Philip's direction. Missing him, it smacked into the wall behind his head and fell to the floor.

'Well, open it then!' shouted mammy. 'Or do you not want that either? I don't know why we bother to do anything for you!'

Philip did want his present. He wanted it very much. He knew what it was going to be, and he'd been even more excited about his present than about his 'treat'. It was going to be a wristwatch, the first one he'd ever had. He had imagined himself wearing it, flicking a casual glance at his wrist every so often, just to check on how the time was going. He wanted that watch so much that it ached. Mumbling something, he stood up, turned round, and bent down to pick up the package from the floor. Sitting back at the table, he fumbled with knots and paper until the watch lay revealed before him. It was smashed to pieces.

'That's your own stupid fault!' said mammy, as she drew on her cigarette once more.

Philip cried for the rest of the day, and although the actual incident of the watch disappeared from the front part of his mind, he feared and distrusted gaily wrapped presents from that day onwards.

Some memories were tiny, fleeting glimpses of the past, like still photographs. He would see himself being shut in a dark cupboard as a punishment; looking through the bars of his cot when he was *very* little, longing for mammy to stop being annoyed and take him out for a cuddle; being in bed with her when daddy was away at the war, longing for her love but terrified by what seemed to be her expression of it; and there were mental snapshots of himself as a baby, dressed in his all-in-one, blue, hand-knitted suit with white buttons down the front.

It was an extraordinary visual album of his early life, organised and selected by the Holy Spirit, and inhabited by Jesus in a way that brought great hope to Philip. He never sought out memories, never 'picked the scabs' off old ones, never tried to analyse new revelations or pin down their significance, and never tried to hold on to the tail-end of his new experiences. He let them go, and as each one appeared and disappeared, peace remained and a little area of healing was accomplished. Inevitably, this tutoring and healing process fed into Philip's ministry to others, increasing and deepening his understanding of their needs, and raising his expectations that God would help them.

Without doubt the most important outcome of Roger Pike's prayer for Philip was an occasion on the Ventnor Downs, when Philip felt that he encountered and forgave his mother. That moment when they wept together just before she died had meant a great deal, but the *words* had not been said. With her death the opportunity seemed to have gone.

One day, several months after his mother's death, Philip was up on the Downs, walking the family dog, a poodle called Nicky. Nicky was a sweet-natured creature who had been introduced to the Ilott children after midnight mass on Christmas Eve. His name, reasonably enough, was short for 'Saint Nicholas'. Mel and Paul fell in love with the little bundle of white fluff immediately, and he became a great favourite with everybody. Philip particularly enjoyed having a good excuse to walk regularly across the gently undulating Downs, often praying aloud to God in a very personal way as Nicky sniffed and scampered around looking for rabbits. There was something about the peace, and the breadth of sky and sea above and below, that was able to draw things from the innermost part of him. On this occasion, a sunny morning in late spring, Philip had turned for home, when he found himself speaking aloud to his mother. A sensation of terrible sadness filled him as he reflected, yet again, on the incompleteness of their relationship. The words tumbled out of him.

'Oh, mother, if only we'd had time to make things right – to get it right . . . you know how much I wanted it to be sorted out. If only I could tell you that now – if only I could!'

'But I know that – I know that's how you feel . . .'

The voice that replied to Philip was not exactly audible, but it punched its way into his mind with such strength and clarity that he stopped dead on the cliff path, stunned into immobility as he realised that his mother was replying to him.

Human beings are funny creatures. At that precise second Philip noticed that Nicky had decided this would be the perfect spot for a canine lavatory. Surely this was profaning a sacred moment? He moved towards the

innocently squatting animal, stopping abruptly as he
realised the absurdity of his response. He turned out
towards the sea, conscious that tears were starting to
blur the white and blue wash before him.

'You can hear me, then . . . ?'

The silence was warm and receptive. He went on
speaking.

'You can hear me talking to you, and saying how sorry
I am for the way things were – the things you did. I want
you to know that I understand you couldn't help being
you, and I forgive you – I really do.'

'I know that you understand that now,' said the voice,
'and so do I at last. I love you, Philip.'

'I love you, mammy! I love you!'

Philip stumbled home with Nicky, crying with the joy
of such an unexpected reconciliation. Over breakfast he
explained to Margaret what had happened, and they
both wept with happiness, all over the marmalade. It
seemed that Edith Ilott, through death, had died to
herself so that Philip could live with her in a new experience of the mother and son relationship. He found
himself greatly looking forward to meeting her again one
day.

Sadly, he was unable to experience a similar kind
of reconciliation with his other, living parent. Philip's
resentment went very deep. He found it impossible to
forgive his father. On the contrary, he maintained a
distance between the two of them that was never really
bridged. His bitterness about his father's weakness in
earlier years was one area that was certainly not healed
during this period, not least because communication
between the two men was almost non-existent, other
than on a fairly shallow basis.

Philip never spoke to his father about the healing of
memories, despite a nagging awareness that this very
private, lonely man, who was so generous to the family
and loving towards his two grandchildren, might have
been helped enormously by the news that the past was

not unredeemable. On the other hand, Philip's father never mentioned his wife, nor did he respond to any comments or questions relating to her, for his was a very complex grief. Occasionally Philip would say of a picture or a piece of music, 'Don't you think Mum would have liked this?', but there was never a trace of reaction. There were no photographs of Edith Ilott in the room that her husband occupied; no mementoes, no keepsakes, no evidence that she had been such a large part of his life. What he thought about his wife in retrospect was something that nobody knew for sure.

* * *

By the time Philip reached his seventh year on the Isle of Wight he still had some sharp thorns in his flesh, but it had been a very rewarding time, especially in terms of his spiritual development. People were being healed, God was working, there were endless calls on his time. It was invigorating, thrilling stuff – seven fat years, and there seemed no reason to believe that the next seven wouldn't be just as good, or even better.

12

The 'Filymead Experience' (1978–1981)

'I'll tell you what, Father, when you go it'll be like taking the presence of God off the streets.'

It was the village postmaster speaking, and Philip was amazed – amazed and deeply moved. The man who had just sold him five second-class stamps was not a churchgoer, and this was the first conversation they had ever enjoyed that even remotely touched on religion.

'It's very nice of you to say that,' he responded, his voice catching a little. 'I certainly have no wish to go. On the contrary, I think I'd be happy to stay on the island for ever – I really would . . .'

It was the truth. He had never wanted to leave St Alban's, but now the choice had been taken away from him. Towards the end of his seventh year on the Isle of Wight, Philip paid a visit to the mainland to lay a proposal before the Bishop of Portsmouth. For some time now he had felt the need to establish a rest-house for clergy somewhere in the St Alban's parish. Many clergymen experienced stress at some point in their careers, and very often the last place they wanted to take their problems was to an officially appointed person or institution. Philip was all too familiar with the feeling of wanting to run away, and hoped to provide a non-judgemental, relaxed environment, where his brother priests could take refuge and find professional help if they wanted it. He would be the chaplain. It was an exciting idea.

Sitting in the bishop's Portsmouth house, with his notes balanced on his knee, Philip explained the project with his usual enthusiasm and thoroughness. When he had finished there was a short silence.

'To be honest, Philip,' said the bishop, 'I thought you'd come to see me about something else.'

'What?' asked Philip, completely taken aback.

'You have been at St Alban's for nearly seven years now. That is longer than any other priest in the last thirty years. I thought you might have wanted to see me to ask for a move.'

'No,' replied Philip, 'I came to see you about this clergy-house idea. I really don't want to move. I'm very happy where I am.'

'Nevertheless,' pursued the bishop, 'I believe you should be considering a change now. In fact, if you hadn't contacted me, I was about to suggest we meet to discuss this very matter.'

From that moment, it seemed to Philip, the die was cast. There were further discussions between the arch-deacon of the island and Philip's PCC about the need for a clergy-house, and the unlikelihood of such a vision materialising if Philip was not there to pursue it, but the pressure to move became overwhelming.

The church authorities, influenced perhaps by the fact that some Isle of Wight clergy were distinctly uneasy about the revivalist aspects of Philip's ministry (the monthly meeting, for instance, where the congregation sang in tongues), were adamant that the time had come for Philip to seek a parish of his own. In vain, Philip made enquiries about vacant parishes in the same diocese, but it appeared that there were no Anglo-Catholic churches seeking an incumbent, much less one who brought the charismatic 'package' with him.

Philip felt angry about the clergy-house project, which would almost certainly never happen if he left St Alban's, and terribly sad about leaving the parish and the island. There was no point, though, in dragging his feet. For the sake of the parish and his own family, he would have to look for another position in a different part of the country. He and Margaret prayed for guidance, of course, as they always did, but it was difficult for them both, much later, to understand why God allowed the three dark years that were to follow. After that period was over, they developed a name for it. They called it the 'Filymead Experience'.

Filymead was a small country town, or large village, of some four and a half thousand souls, many of whom were extremely wealthy. Set in the midst of beautiful Sussex countryside, it consisted of a few rather stylish shops, three or four timbered public houses, some beautifully preserved buildings of the mellow red-brick type, and a selection of rather superior council houses around the edges of the village. The parish church was an impressive building, well-maintained and beautifully situated just above the High Street, almost opposite the vicarage across the road, which was made up of two charming timbered cottages knocked into one.

Philip, who had already endured one rigorous interview in Oxford before being offered a second interview in Filymead itself, was impressed by his first sight of the village. He thought it was beautiful. As his day in the parish wore on, however, he began to feel rather worried. Attractive as the environment was, there was little doubt that St Brandon's was a very *social* church, a place where large music festivals were held and community activities were more frequent and more significant than spiritual ones. The only people he was introduced to were very well-to-do and upper middle class. Philip was quite stunned by the size and quality of the two churchwardens' houses. Their monied, elegant lifestyle was outside his own experience, and might be more than a little threatening if he was expected to emulate his predecessor.

The last incumbent had been ideally suited, it seemed; a man who was able to initiate and host dinner and cocktail parties with cool and civilised efficiency. A brilliant administrator, he had forged strong links with other churches in the village and succeeded in breaking down barriers between 'high' and 'low' elements in his own congregation. A single man, he had provided precisely the kind of social competence that the wardens were hoping to find in the person they appointed in his place. It was worth considering, one of the churchwardens pointed out to Philip, that the next rector of Filymead was very likely to be appointed a rural dean in the not too distant future.

Philip knew nothing about cocktail parties, had no gift for administration, and didn't want to be a rural dean; he also had severe doubts about his ability to play out this figurehead role, and even greater doubts about whether he would want to even if he could. Then there was the transport problem. This parish had an area of seventeen square miles, and he still hadn't learned to drive.

'You do drive, don't you?' they'd asked earlier.

'I haven't got a car myself,' Philip had replied, evading the question rather, 'but my father can drive me anywhere I need to go.'

Back at home that evening, Philip described his day in detail to Margaret. As he had expected, she was not at all impressed by the figurehead business, but then he might not be offered the job in any case. A few days later the bishop contacted Philip to say that the Filymead churchwardens were a little concerned by some of his comments about 'healing ministry', and 'services of praise', as well as one or two other odd things. Could Philip offer assurances, the bishop wanted to know, that he would go sensitively into the parish if he was offered the living?

'Of course,' replied Philip. 'Of course I would be sensitive.'

Within a week he was formally requested to become the next vicar of St Brandon's, Filymead, as soon as he was able to take up the post. He accepted.

Why did he decide to go to Filymead? That was a question that Philip asked himself many times during the years that followed. Was part of it that he was flattered? Yes, probably. He was the fourth applicant for the job, and the others had all been turned down. Those rich, sophisticated people had decided that he, Philip Ilott, had what it would take to keep the social wheels turning in that very classy parish. Then there was the possibility of becoming a rural dean. It was true that Philip didn't actually want promotion as such, not since he'd really seen God working, but there was enough of the old status-loving perfectionist remaining in him to give the idea a little glow, especially when the acceptance of his application made it a real possibility.

So flattery did play a part. But there were other reasons as well. At that time the local suffragan bishop used the parish church in Filymead as his episcopal centre, regularly conducting services of ordination at St Brandon's. Philip felt that his particular brand of ministry could be very useful to young people preparing for a lifetime of work in the church. He was also very attracted by the strong musical tradition that existed in Filymead, conscious though he was that its roots and expression were secular rather than spiritual. But it was not possible either then or subsequently to separate out the real determining factors in his decision. Being wanted is, of course, in itself a lively incentive, and not necessarily an inappropriate one. He was particularly cheered by the bishop's private comment on the phone that he was fed up with the St Brandon's churchwardens turning applicants down all the time, and that he was therefore jolly glad that Philip had got the job.

It was autumn, and Philip decided to leave Ventnor in time to be involved with the celebration and excitement of Christmas in his new parish. That would also avoid the much greater sadness of leaving old friends at such an emotional time of the year. But first they had to be told he was going.

On the evening before the Sunday on which he intended to announce his plans, Philip wrote an identical letter to every member of the Parochial Church Council, setting out his intentions, together with details of the church to which he was moving, and the date (13 December 1978) when he was to be instituted at Filymead. Later that night, when it was dark, he asked his father to drive him round the parish so that the letters could be delivered. At each PCC member's house, Philip, in an agony of tension, crept up to the front door as quietly and as quickly as he could, popped the envelope through the letter-box, and ran in tip-toed panic back to the car before anyone could open the door and find him there.

During the following morning's service he publicly announced his plans to a shocked congregation. The general reaction was one of deep dismay, and as the news spread it became clear that the man in the local post office was by no means the only non-churchgoer who would miss the priest-in-charge of St Alban's. Philip's characteristic energy and hard work had brought him into contact with people all over the island, and his bright enthusiasm had made its mark on each one.

The next few weeks were very hard for the Ilott family. Warmed by the love and sadness expressed in the response to news of their departure, Philip and Margaret dreaded the prospect of leaving the island and starting all over again somewhere else. Mel and Paul, settled at school and as attached to their home area as most growing children are, were simply devastated by the idea of going to this horrible Filymead place, leaving behind all that was familiar and comfortable. Philip's father had done his best to be positive, generously offering to pay for the new vicarage to be completely recarpeted, but he too had found a kind of peace in Ventnor, and was as apprehensive about moving as all the others.

It was a horrible time. Philip's last service, a mid-week Eucharist, was the most difficult of all. He entered the church from the sacristy on the north side, together with servers and acolytes bearing incense and candles. The number of people in the church took his breath away. Every seat was filled, every aisle was jammed with standing people, all determined to carry the departing priest through his final service on the tide of their good will and prayers. With some difficulty, Philip processed through the church, eventually arriving back at the front to sing the first hymn, 'Forward! be our watchword . . .'

The sermon. He talked about Mary, the mother of Jesus, and how she had discovered the real nature of her vocation at the cross. He too was receiving his new vocation at the cross; he didn't want to go, but the cup had not been taken from him. In a low voice he added the recently received and very unwelcome news that St Alban's would no longer have a priest-in-charge of its own. The patron of Godshill would look after both churches. It was part of an economy drive. It would save a salary . . .

The peace. Most difficult of all. It was so difficult to look out at that sea of faces, each one the small map of a relationship, and say for the last time, 'Let us offer one another a sign of peace.' Steeling himself against the pain of saying farewell, he descended into the body of the church to shake hands with, kiss, and hug people who would soon be part of his past. Everywhere he went there were tear-stained faces, watery smiles, loving arms. Richard Dawes was one of the people he hugged. Exchanging the peace went on for a very long time. Somehow he got back to the altar without bursting into tears, but only just.

The whole Ilott family stood by the church door at the end of the service, shaking hands with members of the congregation as they left. Then it was over to the church hall on the other side of the steps for a farewell 'do' that was just as crowded as the service had been. As well as the folk of St Alban's, there were people from a wide variety of other denominations. Pentecostals, Roman Catholics, Methodists, Baptists, all linked by the common bond that they had been touched by the Holy Spirit through Philip's ministry. There were gifts and speeches. Philip was too emotional to say much, but he had to say something to all these people who had come to say goodbye.

'From the bottom of our hearts, we thank you for your love, and commend you to the love of God, because we don't know what your future will be . . .'

The next morning, the morning on which the Ilotts were travelling to Filymead, Philip awoke to find that God was baptising the Isle of Wight with a cloudburst rivalling the one that had raged outside his train on the journey from Chester to London. There was no sense of delicious anticipation this time though, just cold dread. As they were about to leave the vicarage for the last time, an unexpected visitor arrived. Edwin Curtis, a tall, white-haired man in his early seventies, with twinkling blue eyes and bushy eyebrows, was a retired bishop, a very wise and kindly man. Arriving on the vicarage doorstep with his wife that morning, both dripping wet from the rain, he announced that he had come to offer the Ilotts a final prayer before they left. Kneeling on the floor of the desolate, denuded hall, each member of the family received a blessing from Edwin, who finished by saying a prayer for the parish on their behalf.

Away they went in Philip's father's car, five people, a dog and some gerbils, heading for the ferry. The crossing to the mainland was very rough, for the storm continued unabated. Rain obscured everything in the outside world, including the dark mass of the Isle of Wight itself, as the ferry drew away and moved in the direction of Portsmouth. It made no difference to Philip. Seven years of his life lay behind him. If he had looked back he would have wept.

That first night in Filymead was not quite as bad as

Philip had feared. The heating had been turned on in advance, so the house was nice and warm. The new carpets had been laid and looked beautiful. Someone had left a white cyclamen, a box of chocolates and a bottle of wine in the vicarage as welcoming presents. They had to sleep on the floor as their beds had not yet arrived, but they preferred that to splitting up and accepting the temporary local hospitality that had been offered.

From the following morning onwards, and for the next three years, Philip was almost perpetually absorbed in and distracted by the task of finding a compromise between what he felt he should be doing, and what the dominant, socially oriented section of St Brandon's expected him to be.

It began very early on, with the PCC, which seemed to consist of retired or active professional people such as a bank manager, a lawyer, a retired headmaster, a school inspector, all of whom were very well-dressed, very businesslike and very assured. Philip did not, in any objective sense, believe himself to be markedly inferior to any of these people, but it was a totally new situation for him, and he had to fight a constant, wearying, internal battle to avoid feeling overwhelmed and insignificant.

In the first few days the tension of endless introductions, and an almost neurotic concentration on being 'proper', caused a physical exhaustion that flattened Philip. People had certainly been welcoming and responsive, but adjusting to a world where sherry or cocktail parties replaced 'a chat over a cuppa' was more tiring than climbing St Alban's steps. One afternoon, within a week of arriving, Philip felt that if he didn't sleep he would die.

'I'm going to bed for a while, darling,' he yawned in Margaret's direction. 'I'm afraid I just haven't got any energy left.'

'You do that,' said his wife encouragingly. 'No one's likely to come.'

Upstairs, he undressed quickly, and dropped his tired body into the double bed that now graced the master bedroom. Delicious, enveloping, warmly embracing sleep came almost instantly. Never mind the parish, never mind the PCC, never mind anything except going to . . . He was gone.

'Darling, the bishop's here! Get up quickly – you must come down and see him!'

Dragged from unconsciousness by the jagged hooks of guilt and duty, Philip sat bolt upright in bed. His brain seemed to be spinning like a gyroscope inside his skull. He looked at his watch.

'Five minutes!' he moaned despairingly to himself. 'I've only been asleep for five minutes!'

'Darling – the bishop!' repeated Margaret from the door as she disappeared downstairs again.

'Oh my God!' muttered Philip irreverently to himself as he clambered out of bed and stumbled around drunkenly, looking for something to wear. 'Our first meeting, and he finds me in bed! He'll think – my goodness, he'll probably think I've been in bed since last night.'

As he hunted frantically for the shirt he had removed a few minutes ago, he imagined how the bishop was picturing this new addition to his clergy team. Fat and bloated, probably; bleary-eyed with sleep and drink; an unshaven, indolent disgrace to the priesthood. So anxious was Philip to dispel this inaccurate impression, that he tripped as he was attempting to haul his trousers on, and hit the floor with a mighty crash that must have echoed through the entire house.

'What on earth will he have made of that?' whimpered Philip as he completed his dressing at last and stumbled down the stairs.

He needn't have worried.

Peter Ball, the Bishop of Lewes, was very understanding. Middle aged, healthy looking but tired, dressed in a full-length dark-grey habit, he had a charming, boyish smile, with perhaps a hint of toughness in the eyes.

'Please don't apologise, Philip,' he said gently, 'I quite understand. I just wanted to put a face to a name and welcome you to this parish. I really do hope that you will all be very happy here.'

He took his hand from inside his cloak and presented Margaret with a box of *All Gold* chocolates.

'I do pray,' he said simply, 'that you will find gold at the bottom of your garden.'

Philip and Margaret loved Peter from the beginning. He seemed so warm and humble and fatherly. Those first impressions were not mistaken. Peter later proved to be a real support, and a dependable father in God.

The day of Philip's official institution into the parish arrived. The service was a sung Eucharist, and the church was packed. As well as Philip's new parishioners, there were a number of folk from St Alban's present, keen to support their ex-priest on such an important day. They were staying with various members of St Brandon's, and were plainly staggered by the affluent lifestyles of their hosts. Philip felt quite embarrassed for one or two of his old flock who were finding it particularly difficult to fit in with their surroundings.

Peter Ball's sermon (typically, as Philip was to discover) arrowed unerringly into the centre of the vital issues. The priest was a violin, Peter said, that must be played by the master, because only the master's tune would resonate properly with everyone and everything else. Each string of the violin, he went on, must contain precisely the right tension. And the tension existed and was set up by the difference between what the people wanted from their priest, and what God wanted from him. Jesus was the one with the bow. He must be the one who made the music, because he played so delicately and would not break the strings. The priest is a fragile instrument, he concluded.

'Yes,' said Philip very quietly to himself as he listened, 'that's what I feel like – that's exactly what I feel like, a very fragile instrument. I just hope I don't end up breaking . . .'

'Receive the cure that is yours and mine,' said Bishop Peter a few minutes later as he handed Philip a seal that symbolised the parish being placed into his hands.

As he took the seal, a shiver of fear passed through Philip, and he knew suddenly, with chill certainty, that he was in the wrong place at the wrong time. He wouldn't be there long. He was on his way through. The sermon had touched him on a very profound level, making him very aware of just how vulnerable he was. All the healing and the special knowledge, the miraculous happenings and the spiritual fireworks of the past seven years; that had been God working through Philip Ilott, not Philip Ilott himself. He was fragile, and he might break. Like John the Baptist in prison, he doubted the message that his own mouth and hands had been powerless to withhold such a very short time ago.

The moment passed and the service finished. Now he was the vicar of Filymead. There was no going back, only standing still or moving forward. Later that same day, he snatched an opportunity to ask Bishop Peter a question.

'Father,' he asked, 'what would you say is my first job here?'

'Get them in the mud, Philip,' was the bishop's reply. 'Get them in the mud as soon as you can.'

It was an enigmatic response, and at the time Philip was far from sure what Peter was really saying. The only image that his words conjured up was one of pigs wallowing and rolling around in the muck.

As he came to know the parish better, he realised that the bishop's words conveyed a real understanding of the best and worst of Sussex church life, exemplifying as it did the Church of England's general tendency to remain success-orientated, and to extend a slightly patronising benevolence towards the poor.

On the positive side, St Brandon's was perfectly organised, well attended, and genuinely integrated with one large section of the local community. The potential was great, but the task was enormous. It is easier, Philip reflected, to bring true spirituality to a man who is lost in the darkest of sins and completely unchurched, than to reach someone who is comfortably and worthily established in his local church, but unaware of his need to find Jesus.

The 'Filymead experience' came very close to destroying the Ilotts. Because of its position in the very centre of a quite small community, the vicarage and the lives of those who lived in it were terribly exposed. Like some ecclesiastical goldfish, Philip was constantly on view to the public eye. Sometimes the sense of being trapped was unbearable. There was nowhere to walk to in Filymead, and the vicarage was as vulnerable to visitors as vicarages always are.

If he had felt approved of, it wouldn't have been so bad, but he didn't. As the first year wore on, he felt increasingly deskilled and incompetent as criticisms were levelled at almost every aspect of his ministry and his personal lifestyle.

Sermons were a prime target, especially the ones that tried to speak to people on a personal level. One Sunday Philip spoke on the subject of 'acceptance'. He pointed to the east window of St Brandon's, and asked his congregation to take note of the Victorian designer's composition.

'What we see,' he said, 'is that Jesus, our risen Lord, is at the centre of the picture, and all around him, sharing in his victory, are all kinds of ordinary people: peasants, shepherds, soldiers, all the people who make up the real body of the church.'

He went on to talk about Filymead, and the need for spiritual unity to override considerations of class or income. He mentioned the council estate, and asked why it was so poorly represented in the church. What, he asked, should we all be doing about it?

To his amazement, Philip received a number of critical letters over the next day or two, suggesting that his choice of sermon content left a lot to be desired. Sitting at his desk in the vicarage, he angrily tore the letters to shreds and flung them into the waste-paper basket, muttering through his teeth as he did so about 'bloody people who want academic, high-falutin irrelevancies every Sunday!'

Nor was it only the subject-matter that came under fire. Split infinitives, misplaced prepositions and other grammatical errors, as well as grotesque misuses of the comma in Philip's parish letter in the church magazine, were mentioned in frequent communications, usually from the churchwardens. Preaching and writing had always been areas of strength and achievement in his previous work. Here, in Filymead, he began to experience something close to terror each time he attempted to prepare a sermon or write the monthly letter. Programmed to thrive on encouragement, like most human beings, Philip now found himself stumbling in his spoken delivery from time to time, and composing prose that, all too often, could only be recommended for its grammatical exactitude. Sermons became something of a weekly nightmare – done with by the end of Sunday, but triggering worry again by Tuesday or Wednesday with gut-gnawing regularity.

Philip's attempt to introduce the ministry of healing to Filymead made quite an encouraging start. One of his very early visitors at the vicarage was the Roman Catholic priest, Eric Flood, a charming man who smilingly told Philip how much he envied his married status, especially after meeting Margaret. The two men had much in common, including a desire to see the healing ministry find its proper place in the church. Philip's self-appointed mentors were quite happy to hear about the plans the two men had for a regular joint healing-service. This, after all, was the kind of social glueing exercise that their vicar was there for. The healing aspect, their reaction seemed to suggest, was just a convenient hook to hang such an experience on.

The healing-services did get under way, but did not survive for very long. First, Eric Flood left Filymead to become priest of another church. His successor took little interest in healing. Then, Philip invited a well-known evangelist with a real gift of healing to address one of the meetings. This man, full of enthusiasm and faith, but lacking perhaps in sensitivity and common sense, spoke at exhausting length. The things he said were all very sound, and were in line with Philip's point of view, but the sheer length of his talk and the exclusive nature of his particular religious language only succeeded in alienating the people who were there, to the extent that most of them vowed never to come again. Numbers and interest dwindled from that point onwards, and eventually the meetings died a very quiet death. As far as Philip knew, not a single person was healed.

Even the new vicar's choice of personal transport was a matter for heated controversy. For some time Philip relied on his father's help, but after passing his driving test he was told that some people in the parish wanted to buy a new car and make it available for his use. All Philip had to do was choose a vehicle. Grateful for such practical assistance, Philip decided that a Renault Four would be quite sufficient for his needs. Leading PCC members were horrified. A Renault Four? A little two-door car? A *foreign* car? It was unthinkable! What he should be looking for was an English car with four doors, something respectable and substantial. How could you pick the bishop up from the railway station and bring him back to Filymead in a Renault Four?

There were some things that Philip would not back down from, and this was one of them.

'If Jesus could ride on a donkey,' he told them firmly, 'then the bishop can ride in a Renault Four.'

He won that one.

But he lost a lot more than he won.

There was, for instance, his attempt to establish a 'watch and pray' presence in the church on Maundy Thursday. Philip posted up a list of times for people to enter their names by. The idea was that someone would be praying at any given time up to midnight. The response was poor. One gentleman, noting the rather naked list, spoke to Philip as though he was trying to put together a chair-arranging rota.

'I see there aren't many names down on your list, Father,' he whispered confidentially at the church door. 'I won't put myself down now, but if you really get stuck – give me a ring. Okay?' When the day arrived, Philip and Margaret found themselves on their own after the first two hours.

Attempts to institute a Holy Hour service were not much more successful in terms of attendance. The Holy Hour was a time when the eucharistic bread was exposed on the altar while people worshipped and adored Jesus. Philip's part in it was to say a few simple prayers. One day, when Holy Hour happened to coincide with general election day, he was astonished to see three solid 'eleven o'clockers', a man and two ladies, enter the church and kneel in prayer before the altar. As the hour came to an end, he walked to the door and greeted his unexpected visitors, not one of whom, he was quite sure, had the slightest understanding of what 'worshipping and adoring Jesus' might mean. Still, it was good that they'd come.

'Evening, vicar,' said the man, in gruff county tones. 'We're off to vote now.'

'Oh,' replied Philip. 'Well, I was absolutely delighted to see you at the Holy Hour this evening.'

''Fraid we had no idea what the service was all about,' boomed the man, 'but we noticed there was something going on in the church, so we thought – well, we've got to get these socialist buggers out somehow, so we came in to pray . . .'

The tension between the worldly and the spiritual was everywhere. Philip frequently took communion to housebound or bed-ridden folk. When one of the church-wardens visited one afternoon, he was out doing just that. The man shook his head doubtfully at Margaret.

'I don't know,' he said darkly, 'I think it might be a lot more useful if he were to do something like shopping for these people, something practical.'

Margaret was never less than lively in her defence of Philip, especially when he was in the right.

'I don't agree at all,' she said spiritedly. 'There are no end of laypeople in the church who can do all the shopping that's needed. Only Philip can take communion to these folk, and if that's not important then I really can't think what is!'

Philip continued to take the precious bread and wine to anyone who wanted to remember Jesus in that way but who was prevented by age or illness. There was a great deal of opposition to this throughout his stay in the parish, but those who received his visits loved him for it.

There was general agreement also, even from his severest critics, that Philip had a very special gift for bringing comfort and constructive help to bereaved folk. His ability to enter into the centre of their suffering in a straightforward non-fussy way was quite exceptional. Years later he was to hear that many people still remembered how Father Philip had brought the love of God to them when they were at their most desolate. They, at least, seemed to think it almost as useful as having their shopping done.

Philip did his best to follow Peter Ball's advice and get the people in his parish 'in the mud'. But it was a fearsome task: these people his mother would have been so impressed by – especially the PCC members – didn't like the mud. They didn't want to get in it. They particularly didn't want to be led into it by their new vicar, whose primary function, as defined by one leading light, was to be *seen* at coffee-mornings, bazaars and flower shows.

The nearest Philip came to fulfilling his bishop's injunction was during the period when restoration work was being carried out on the church building. The mess and muddle was dreadful, and the work was scheduled to take a number of weeks. One of the churchwardens surveyed the chaos left by the builders after their first week of work, and shook his head in what was fast becoming a depressingly familiar way.

'Well, there's no question of worshipping here tomorrow,' he said. 'We'd better use the school chapel up the road.'

'No, we don't need to,' replied Philip. 'This is our church, and this is where we'll worship.'

'But the mess . . .'

'We'll clean it up,' said Philip brightly. 'We'll come in every Saturday and clean it ready for Sunday services. That's what we'll do.'

It was probably the best thing that happened during his time at St Brandon's. At first the response was about as good as it had been for Maundy Thursday prayer, but gradually the numbers increased, until, towards the end of the restoration period, there were about twenty people turning up each Saturday to assist each other in the task of making their church usable on the following day.

The sight of Philip and Margaret, dressed in jeans and carrying a selection of cleaning equipment across the High Street from the vicarage to the church, became a regular feature of weekends in Filymead. More than once a passer-by crossed the road to avoid being seen in conversation with such inappropriately garbed persons, but, on the whole, the church cleaning was a success. Hard work, side by side, in uncomfortable conditions, was as good as a sermon on love.

The strain of coping did not ease. It got worse. It was as well for Philip that there were a few people in Filymead he did relate to warmly and easily. Ironically perhaps, the two people who impressed him most with their friendliness and humility came from completely opposite ends of the social scale.

Mr Clout was the local man who looked after the vicarage garden. Employed by the church and inherited by the Ilotts when they came to Filymead, Jim Clout tended the lawns once a week and generally looked after the old brick-walled garden that stretched out behind the house.

It transpired that Jim had never actually entered the vicarage, and he had to be coaxed in gently by Margaret to have his morning coffee. He soon relaxed, however, especially as his vicarage morning fell on the same day that Margaret did her washing. Sitting amid the confusion, he would sip his coffee and chat happily about his work and his family. Often he brought a present of plants or flowers from his own garden and presented them to Philip and Margaret with a sort of nervous pleasure.

His wife was a Sunday school teacher, but Jim himself was not a churchgoer. It seemed from the way he spoke about such things that he did not consider himself sufficiently 'upper-crust' to belong in that world. He was very much in awe of 'important' people.

Jim Clout would have been astonished to learn how important he was to the new vicar and his wife. Philip and Margaret loved his kindness, his simplicity and his humility, and they treasured their friendship with him as a warm ember in a very cold grate. Philip often thought about how much God must love his unchurched gardener.

Then there was Sir John Glubb, a very distinguished ex-military man, famous for his colourful exploits as a leader of Arab forces in the Far East. Now retired, the great man had settled with his wife, Rosemary, in a large house on the outskirts of Filymead. The Glubbs attended matins, one of the morning services at St Brandon's.

One day Sir John phoned Philip and asked him to visit his house as there was something he wished to discuss. Philip's heart sank as he replaced the receiver on its hook. What now? He had hardly exchanged more than a couple of words with this VIP whose presence was such a feather in Filymead's social cap. Some complaint presumably – another highly civilised attack on his speech or his grammar or his clothes or his theology or the way he combed his hair. It could be anything!

Sir John Glubb's house turned out to be very dark. As Philip entered by the side door a mynah bird squawked 'Hello!' from his cage in the porch. Inside, the walls were hung with pictures and photographs of Sir John dressed in Arab costume, while objects not in day-to-day use were draped in a curious fashion.

Sir John, surrounded by cats, greeted Philip. He was a small man, no more than five foot six in height, who almost always wore a raincoat with the hem falling down, and brilliantly shined black shoes.

Settled with a drink in the dark sitting-room, the two men exchanged minor pleasantries before Philip's host came to the point.

'Father Philip, I have a problem.'

Philip braced himself. Here we go, he thought.

'As you know, I am a matins man. Always have been actually.'

'Yes, Sir John,' said Philip, wondering what was coming.

'Well, the fact is – numbers have been dropping off, dwindling as it were, and I wondered . . .'

'But the numbers for the Eucharist have been going up,' interrupted Philip, rather defensively.

'Well, quite,' agreed Sir John. 'Precisely right. Look, let me put it to you like this, Father. As I said, I've always been a matins man, but really, you know, I need to be

where the people are, where I can be most use. If I'm
any use,' he added somewhat worriedly.

'I don't quite –'

'So what I need from you, Father, is a spot of advice.
What do you think I should do? Should I stick with
matins and support the minority, or should I shift over
to where the majority are and show that – well, show
that I'm part of the way things are going, as it were?
You're the expert, Father, what do I do?'

For a moment Philip was too taken aback to speak.
Amid all the disapproval and conflict that he was already
experiencing, it hardly seemed possible that, of all
people, this man was asking for his advice.

After a lengthy discussion Sir John decided that the
sung Eucharist was the service for him, and he and
Philip parted on very warm terms. From that day Sir
John Glubb provided Philip with one of his few areas of
encouragement in the church. A truly humble man, with
a real concern for the community, he frequently and
generously expressed appreciation for Philip's sermons,
and generally offered acceptance to the new vicar. At
church services he had a habit of sitting at the end of a
pew, with one leg extended slightly into the central aisle.
Philip, entering from the vestry at the back of the church,
always liked to see that limb, with the highly polished
shoe attached, sticking out reassuringly in front of him.
He reflected whimsically now and then on the fact that
he must be the only person in the world who drew
comfort from Sir John Glubb's leg.

If Philip had been the only member of his family to be
negatively affected by the problems he encountered at
St Brandon's, the 'Filymead experience' might not have
been so disastrous. But they all suffered, each in his or
her own way.

Philip's father felt unwanted and uncomfortable from
the start. Each Sunday he would walk across for the
eight o'clock communion service, and return each time
without a word being said to him by his fellow communi-

cants. He was not very good at making friends, in any case, and as the months passed he became terribly lonely, clinging to Philip and the family with a desperation that could be highly claustrophobic. Every week, on the morning of Philip's day off, he would appear in the kitchen and ask the question that (in Margaret's words) gave Philip 'the screaming habdabs': 'Where are *we* going today . . . ?'

The children hated Filymead. They hated it because it wasn't Ventnor, and they hated it for being what it was.

Because he attended a state school, Paul made few friends among the sons of other church folk, most of whom were educated in private schools. And although at school Paul was doing extremely well academically, what Philip's critics wanted to know was 'Is it the right kind of school?' and 'Doesn't he want the name of a good school behind him?'

Even Paul's clothes were wrong. Money was too short to allow Margaret to buy him a suit to wear to church, and his casual dress was noted and commented upon, as indeed was Margaret's own.

It was Paul who created the name of 'Rev' for Philip. Philip felt uncomfortable with the informality of 'Dad', and Paul and Mel were adamant that they would never choose to identify with the majority of Philip's parishioners by addressing him as 'Father'. So at Paul's instigation they started to call him 'Rev', and the name stuck.

Between Philip and Mel there existed what can only be described as open warfare. Mel was just coming into her teenage years as the family moved to Filymead, and already some tensions had arisen between herself and her father.

Mel sensed that her development along tomboyish, non-academic lines was far removed from Philip's expectation that the little girl he loved so much would fit into a traditional feminine mould as she grew older. Paul seemed to be successful in every way that her father judged to be important, while the things that she did and said frequently provoked him to annoyance or quite intense anger. She was a very dominant young female, quite unaware, of course, that her father had spent most of his life attempting to escape the mental and emotional clutches of the even more dominant female who had given him birth.

Already, during the Ventnor period, there had been some harsh and hurtful exchanges between the two of them, as for instance (before Philip learned about the watch-throwing episode) the occasion when Mel plagued her father incessantly about the fact that he had still not opened a Christmas present, until, goaded beyond restraint, he lost control and allowed the child in him to shout that he hated her. He didn't hate Mel. He loved her. The trouble was that she uncovered parts of him that were still raw and unmatured. She reacted to his flawed humanity, not his priesthood.

Filymead brought all these tensions to a head.

Mel loathed Filymead from the bottom of her boots to the top of her head. She loathed what she saw as the hypocrites who dressed up in furs to go to church on Sunday, but wouldn't notice her mother in the High Street on a weekday. She hated the fact that there was always somebody in the vicarage to do the typing, or hold a meeting, or discuss something with the vicar, or stand around at a wine and cheese party – always someone to be polite to, always someone who had a greater claim on her father's time than she had. She hated the fact that they didn't like his sermons, and that they weren't interested in him doing youth work. She hated all the posh ones for being posh and not like the nice ordinary people at St Alban's. She sensed the disapproval directed towards her family coming in waves from the 'toffee-nosed' ones, and fancied that they looked down on her particularly. She hated feeling stupid at school and having no friends because, as in Paul's case, they lived too far away.

And what was it all for? Why did her father spend so much energy and time trying to get on with and fit in with these ghastly people who only cared about their beautiful houses and their stupid cocktail parties, and their posh children at posh schools, and their boring expensive cars? They didn't really want to hear what he had to say, and they looked down their noses at his wife and his father and his son and his daughter. *Why* should they get all the time and the smiles and the work and the attention? Why should they?

Like many a vicar's daughter before and since, Mel reacted strongly to the situation she found herself in. Of course, the exact nature of these reactions varies according to temperament. Some girls withdraw and become very quiet, others openly rebel and kick over the traces. Mel did the latter, but on an epic scale.

'Right!' she said to herself. 'If that's the way it's going to be, I'll really give them something to disapprove of!'

She did. She made friends with all the local punks, and brought them back to congregate in full view outside the vicarage. She started to smoke. She dyed her hair pink and green and any other colour that took her fancy. She wore the shortest mini-skirt ever seen in Filymead, and the tightest tops she could squeeze herself into. Her make-up ranged from the exotic to the bizarre, her socks were psychedelic and multicoloured. Often she would stay out until the early hours of the morning, occasionally not returning until the following day. By her own, later admission, she set out to upset everybody as much as she possibly could, and there is little doubt that she succeeded.

Philip could not handle it at all. The constant, intense effort required just to survive as the vicar of this horrendous parish left little space for anyone or anything else. All his time and energy was given to talking and joking and explaining and compromising and being tactful with people who didn't understand him at all. When he succeeded he liked the success too much; it was his mother's kind of success. When he failed he was desolate.

Why was Mel making things so difficult? His own early teenage years had been rather strange, but, from what he'd gathered, at Mel's age you would normally be working hard at school, coming home and helping around the house, then reading or playing happily until bedtime came. Why was she setting out to embarrass him and make life difficult for him at a time when he most needed support from his family?

Why did she bring those people home with her? Why? He'd seen them coming the first time as he stood looking out of the dining-room window. He'd nearly gone spare! What would his parishioners say when they saw the vicar's daughter bringing the local layabouts home to tea? In a youth club, yes – there he would have *welcomed* them – but not here, not with his daughter!

Margaret persuaded him they should all come in and sit in the kitchen. These were Mel's only friends, and we must welcome them, she had said. He'd agreed, but that didn't mean he accepted it. He boiled and raged with anger about it. She brought them to church as well. He should have been glad, but he couldn't be. It just made him angry and worried. Sometimes he thought he would burst.

Sometimes he did burst.

Terrible arguments with Mel. Terribly vicious tennis matches of hurt and counter-hurt.

'You're not my real dad anyway!'

'If you were really my daughter you'd never behave as you do!'

'You never talk to me – you just preach! Why don't you go and preach at your hypocrites?'

'At least they don't set out to embarrass me like you do. I'm ashamed of you and everything you do!'

These explosions of verbal and sometimes physical conflict were certainly hard for Mel, but they nearly destroyed Philip. Mel's rebellion had the effect of un-

leashing dangerously negative forces in him. Coping
with the demands and expectations of the parish while
such teeth-grinding fury and frustration swirled around
in him was so difficult that on occasions he could hardly
breathe for the sobbing tension in his breast. How could
he condemn anyone else for being hypocritical when his
weekly sermons on love and acceptance were written
against the background of an almost complete breakdown in his relationship with his own daughter?

Sometimes, when the stabbing anguish in his heart
became like a physical pain, he longed to find a hiding
place, somewhere where he could simply *be*, without
the imminent prospect of excessive demands or disapproval or conflict. The inside of the church, with all
the doors firmly locked, was the only place where he
could truly be alone. Once inside, he would lie on the
floor of the Lady Chapel with his arms extended, like a
human cross, and cry his eyes out for Mel and the rest
of the family, for the parish and for himself. It wasn't
prayer – or perhaps it was the purest kind of prayer: an
abandoned release of his innermost feelings. The healing
ministry, the healing of memories, all the God-guided
events of his seven fat Isle of Wight years seemed to
Philip to be temporarily dissolved in the copious tears
that he shed during those solitary hours in St Brandon's.

One Sunday, when Philip was conducting the sung
Eucharist in church, quite distracted because Mel was
going through an even more difficult time than usual,
he seemed to see something, apparently floating in mid-
air, at the back of the church. The object (not a Bible this
time) began to move towards the altar, until it was close
enough for him to identify it as a baby wrapped in a
shawl. Right over the bread and wine it floated until it
lay directly before him so that he could see its face. It
was baby Mel. Right in the centre of his work and his
priesthood, there on the altar itself, with the body and
blood of Jesus, was baby Mel, needing to be loved like
an infant now that she was an angry, confused teenager,

just as she had needed love when she first came home
to Philip and Margaret all those years ago. When Philip
got home he told Margaret what he had seen in church
that morning. His father, who was listening, began to
weep. He too was upset about Mel. During the Ventnor
years Mel had become very close to her grandfather.
Now the relationship had reached a very low point. It
was one of the few times that the two men knew a
genuine closeness.

Philip understood the baby vision. He knew that he
should look beneath the raucous symptoms of Mel's
rebellion, and continue to love and care for the vulnerable child in her that was as much a part of him as Paul
and Margaret were. He knew he should do that, but he
couldn't – not yet – and she certainly didn't make it any
easier. Later, under very different circumstances, he was
able to do it, but for reasons that were as dramatic as
they were unforeseen.

The final and perhaps the most patient sufferer of all in
the 'Filymead experience' was Margaret, who frequently
had to act as referee and peacemaker in conflicts between
Mel and Philip. Her clothes, her children's clothes, her
husband's skills and ministry, Paul's school, and just
about everything about Mel, had been criticised and
commented on continually since their arrival. More em-
bittering still was the way that, in her view, the St
Brandon's style of Christianity had turned her children
away from the church. But Margaret took her divine
commission very seriously indeed, and she loved each
member of her family devotedly and without bias. As
Mel was to express it later, 'Mum was always *there*. We
never had to fit in with her life – she fitted her life round
us.'

Why was Filymead so unhappy for Philip and the rest
of the family? Why did God let them go there? Was it a
mistake? If it was, whose mistake was it? What was the
point of all the Isle of Wight happenings if everything
was to fall to pieces on the other side of the Solent? Was

Philip really in the wrong place at the wrong time?

Those were the questions Philip asked himself again and again as time went by and things got worse. There were no easy answers. The clash between Mel and himself would have happened to some degree wherever the family had gone, but this particular place had made it worse, there was no doubt about that. Maybe, he thought, I should have gone for a different parish. There'd been a church up in Birmingham, for instance, that he'd seriously considered. It was nothing like St Brandon's. As far as he could gather, it was a sort of tin tabernacle set in the middle of some desert of an industrial area. Perhaps he should have pursued that one. On the other hand, you could say that all these negative experiences were just part of the learning process, something you had to work through and benefit from in ways that wouldn't be clear until much later. It was pointless to speculate really. It was so easy to say 'if' and 'perhaps'. He would probably never know what had made Filymead go so wrong.

There was one thing, though, one factor that was quite different from all the others – something rather sinister.

Philip had heard about black magic, and he was aware that covens were said to be particularly active in the south-east of England, but he had never personally encountered the movement or its effect on others, as far as he knew. It was after he had been driving the Renault Four for a short time that his suspicions were aroused. He had been somewhat accident-prone since first arriving in Filymead, tripping and falling in a way that was not at all typical. The resultant injuries were slight but irksome. Philip attributed this unprecedented physical clumsiness to his own growing feelings of inadequacy and awkwardness about the role demanded of him by the PCC members. He may well have been right. What happened with the car, though, was much more than that.

It began one morning as he drove back into Filymead

after visiting an elderly couple who lived on the edge of the parish. In doing so he was obliged to pass a house where one of his sternest antagonists lived. This person particularly objected to Philip's 'preoccupation' with the person of Jesus, and the whole spiritual thrust of his message.

A few days previously, Margaret had been walking Nicky the dog past this same house, when she felt herself being pulled, as if by an invisible force, into the path of an on-coming lorry. Desperately frightened by the nightmare-like immobility of her limbs, Margaret struggled against the strange pressure, managing to regain the pavement just in time. Knowing as well as he did that two of his wife's major characteristics were complete truthfulness and an ability to remain level-headed in all situations, Philip had taken this unusual event very seriously, but beyond registering where it had occurred, he made no significant connection between the near-accident and the person who lived in the house overlooking the scene.

Now, as he approached that same spot in the car, he was thinking about something completely different. Without warning, as though two hands had reached over his shoulders, the steering wheel seemed to be wrenched from his grasp and swung wildly to the left, pulling the vehicle on to two wheels. Philip struggled to right the car, but whatever was gripping the wheel had a strength beyond anything he was able to combat. Bracing himself for the inevitable crash as he reached the place where the road curved round into the village, he felt the steering wheel suddenly relax in his frantically clenched hands, and just managed to negotiate the corner without hitting anything.

Pulling into the garage at the end of the High Street, he stopped and sat quite motionless for a moment or two, staring ahead through the windscreen, still clutching the wheel so tightly that his knuckles were white. Certain that a mechanical defect was responsible for what had happened, he left the Renault with a mechanic and walked home, pale and trembling, to tell Margaret what had happened. It was only when the garage mechanic reported on the following day a total absence of any mechanical basis for such a steering failure that they made a first tentative connection between Margaret's experience and this new one of Philip's, only to dismiss it as purely fanciful.

When the same thing happened, not just once more, but on a number of occasions, including a time when Margaret was in the car with Philip, the connection did not seem fanciful at all. After each incident Philip, anxious to avoid reacting hysterically, took his car to be inspected by an increasingly sceptical garage mechanic, who never did find anything wrong.

Eventually, putting together their own experiences and information gathered from other sources, Philip and Margaret became convinced that some form of ill-wishing had been directed towards them by one person in particular, and that she was not alone in her attempt to harness dark forces and repel the light in that part of the country.

In the end Philip did have a serious crash. It was in a different part of the village, and it was caused by another driver swerving into the Renault, but Philip, who was unconscious for a time after his car mounted a bank and rolled over, was sure that, for someone, this was a victory to be celebrated.

Eighteen months after the service of institution, Bishop Peter visited the vicarage once more. He wasn't expected, but this time Philip was up and Margaret was out shopping.

'How are things going?' enquired Peter without any preamble.

'Do you really want to know, Father?' asked Philip sadly.

'I think I do know,' said the bishop gently. 'You're going through a depression, aren't you?'

'Yes, in a way I am,' admitted Philip, vastly under-stating the case.

'I knew at your institution,' continued Peter, 'that you felt you had come to the wrong place at the wrong time. With God's grace anything is possible, but you may have been right.'

The seeds of Philip's decision to make an early move from Filymead were sown during that conversation. In the following year a parish became vacant in a seaside town near Hastings, about thirty miles away to the south-east. Philip's application was very favourably received. When the invitation came to take up the post of vicar of St Barnabas' Church, Bexhill-on-Sea, he accepted immediately.

In September 1981 the Ilott family said their goodbyes, packed their bags, and headed south, licking the wounds of the last three years as they went. Many problems were still unresolved, but on the day of their departure they had one overwhelming thing in common. They were all passionately glad that the 'Filymead experience' was over.

13

Bexhill – Through the Door of Suffering (1981–1989)

He was dreaming again.

Before him, set in a brick wall, was a small wooden door. It was a beautiful door, a little like the one in Holman Hunt's *Light of the World*, but half the size and with no thorns or briars surrounding it.

As Philip studied the sight before him, he realised two things. First, the door was just the right height and width to admit him in his wheelchair. Secondly, there was no handle or latch fastened to the dark, knotted wood. There was a large keyhole of gleaming brass, but no sign of a key. He felt very drawn to the door, intensely curious about what might lie on the other side, but as he wheeled his chair a little closer he happened to glance up. Written across the brickwork above the door in large capital letters was a single word: BEWARE.

'Beware of what?' Philip asked himself. 'I can't go through in any case. I haven't got a key.'

Suddenly aware that some tall structure was overshadowing him, he turned his head to discover that the place where his wheelchair stood was at the foot of the cross of Jesus, and there, lying on the ground beneath it, was a large key. He knew it was the key to the door, and he knew that he was being offered the freedom to pick it up and use it, or leave it at the foot of the cross, just as he pleased. He hesitated for a moment, glancing

round once more at that word of warning etched starkly
into the wall. Meeting whatever lay on the other side of
that door was going to need all his courage.

Turning back, he reached down over the side of his
chair to pick up the key. Although small, it turned out
to be terribly heavy, so heavy that he had to swing his
chair right round and use both hands to lift it from the
ground. At last, after great effort, he managed to insert
the key in the lock; it turned with surprising ease, and
as the door swung slowly open, he wheeled himself
through to the other side. There, he stopped abruptly,
transfixed by the sight that met his eyes. It was a garden
full of people, and they were all suffering. Maimed or
disabled by sorrow and need, they turned pleading eyes
in Philip's direction as he appeared; some held out their
hands in dumb supplication, the tears coursing down
their faces as they begged for healing. He moved towards
them . . .

Philip's institution as vicar of St Barnabas', Bexhill-on-
Sea, was conducted at a Eucharist, presided over by
Bishop Peter on St Michael and All Angels' Day. This
Eucharist of the Angels, in which Gabriel, Michael and
Raphael are remembered, was an exciting event for
Philip. So far, what he had seen of his new parish
suggested that he would soon be able to settle back
into his old hyperactive pattern of ministry, putting all
thought of Filymead out of his head, and picking up the
much more positive threads of his Ventnor experiences.
This service was to mark the commencement of better
times.

During the following month, Philip's father died after
an illness that began before the family left Filymead. He
remained a lonely man to the end, but as with his
mother, Philip was able to bring the sacrament to his
father at that time with an intimacy and emotional closeness that exceeded anything they had known previously.
The gap between them was not completely bridged,
though. Philip had always judged his own feelings about

his father to be illogical and unfair, but those feelings went very deep, and God could not yet reach them.

Philip's relationship with Mel was still very strained, but his first year at St Barnabas' was as professionally satisfying as he had hoped it would be. The Christmas services went well, and the exacting programme of Holy Week was as exhausting but as thrillingly dramatic as ever, Philip's favourite service of all, perhaps, being the one entitled the Veneration of the Cross. This began with the cross being carried into the church, the figure of Christ lifted high above the congregation as they sang the same words three times:

> Behold the cross; behold the wood of the cross,
> On which hangs the crucified Lord.
> Come let us worship . . .

After processing three times, the cross was brought to the front of the church and, as psalms and hymns were sung, the congregation came forward one by one to kneel and to worship Jesus, who had died for them. Philip was in his element, drained physically by the interviews, confessions and service preparation that always made Easter a busy time, but glad to be appreciated once more in a church whose tradition so closely matched his own.

By the time May came there were enough confirmation candidates taking instruction for a special service to be held for that purpose in the following September. It would be the first time for twenty-seven years that St Barnabas' had justified a visit by the bishop for its own confirmation service, and Philip was justly proud. It was to be a great occasion.

But something else happened in May as well.

Philip woke one morning to find that he was unable to move his head. It felt as if it was clamped in one position. In addition, he felt very, very sick. The local doctor was puzzled and called in a specialist. The specialist visited Philip at home and diagnosed an ear infection.

The steroids he prescribed were helpful, but Philip was still left with a raging headache, as though something was causing intense pressure within his skull. Then the hearing in his left ear went completely, and he returned to the specialist. There was talk of a hearing aid, much discussion about possible prognoses, and in the end, another fortnight on steroids, which again brought some relief. By the time the Ilotts set off for their annual holiday in August, the doctors had decided that Philip was suffering from a viral infection that had caused some inflammation to the base of his brain.

The journey to Torquay was hot and uncomfortable. After driving all day, the thing Philip wanted most of all was a shower. It left his body tingling with warmth, as showers generally do, but on this occasion the tingling didn't go away. It lasted throughout the holiday, his left leg being particularly uncomfortable.

By the time they returned to Bexhill at the end of a not very refreshing break, Philip was in extreme discomfort, still suffering blinding headaches, and now more or less dragging his affected leg behind him when he walked. The specialist was no wiser than before. Was the leg problem a touch of sciatica? He wasn't sure. He prescribed more steroids.

By the time of the September confirmation service, Philip was looking very ill. The steroid treatment had resulted in a big weight increase, and he now found himself perspiring heavily and unable to stand still in one position for more than a few seconds because of the irritation in his legs.

As the autumn wore on, he suggested to his doctor that instead of waiting for the National Health Service to admit him for tests, he should go to St Luke's Hospital for the Clergy, in Fitzroy Square, the same place where he had visited Father John Crisp on the occasion of his first confession. The doctor agreed, and he went.

At St Luke's he was given a private room, very good meals, and his own television to watch, all under the eagle eye of a very dominant matron who initiated their acquaintance by saying very firmly, 'Now, Reverend, if you have pain, I want to know – we don't encourage martyrs around here!'

It wasn't until the end of Philip's ten days at St Luke's that he was seen by a neurologist. He was made to walk up and down the hospital corridor, then examined thoroughly.

'Right,' said the neurologist, as he concluded his examination, 'I want to see you in my hospital soon for tests.'

'But what's wrong with me?' asked Philip.

'I don't know for sure,' replied the neurologist.

Philip went into hospital five times in the following year, each visit involving weeks of lengthy and sometimes humiliating tests. One involved lying facedownwards on a trolley for half an hour, with the whole of his naked body exposed to other patients (all waiting for the same test) every time someone went in or out of the door. Some, like the injections into his spine, were just excruciatingly painful.

The neurological ward was a very depressing place. The patients included a number of young men suffering from afflictions such as Parkinson's disease or tumours on the brain or spine. It was not uncommon for patients to receive letters from wives or girlfriends who felt unable to accept the pressure and complication that those illnesses were likely to produce, and the resultant unhappiness was very distressing.

Many of Philip's fellow patients, discovering that he was a priest, opened their hearts to him, not realising in their own misery, just how worried he was about himself.

The tests went on: blood tests, eye tests, body scans, two lumbar punctures – everything that could be investigated was covered.

In between hospital visits, Philip continued to work in the parish, but the acute pain he was now enduring made it impossible to be fully active. Secretly, he was convinced that he had a tumour on his spine.

As the relentless battery of tests came to an end at last, all that Philip desired was to know for sure what was wrong – *whatever* it was. After the second bout of testing he had been told that it was probably a viral encephalitis, something that would right itself if he rested sufficiently. In vain, he now awaited a definite diagnosis. He would have to wait, they said, and see if it settled down.

Life became intolerable for Philip and those closest to him. He lost his balance and fell on steps and stairs. He lost sensation in his fingertips and dropped things. He was constantly worried and deeply depressed. He lost his temper with the family, and particularly with Mel, their relationship having reached a very low ebb indeed. Later he began to realise how much Mel had been a scapegoat for his anger towards himself and his illness, although her response was never exactly placatory, to say the least.

The conduct of church services became increasingly difficult. He would leave home feeling ill, and arrive at the church feeling worse. For Philip, who had always taken such a pride in his public ministry, it was like being crucified every Sunday. He would lose his place in the service, recite prayers twice, and handle objects with a clumsiness he had not displayed since the worst of the Filymead days. It reached its climax at mass one Sunday morning.

As Philip reached forward to pick up the cup containing the consecrated wine, he lost his footing a little and jerked forward, hitting the chalice with his half-opened hand and knocking it on to its side so that the wine flowed in a purple tide over the white altar cloth.

Philip stood and stared in a horrified trance as the blood of Christ spread across the altar in a slowly widening stain, and dripped on to the floor beneath. It was him there as well, him and his life being poured away –

wasted by an illness they couldn't even name. There seemed to him to be a significance, an exposure, a stigma in that simple accident. He could no longer control or accept the cup that had been offered to him.

The parish, the family, everything that had ever meant anything to him was slipping away from his numb grasp. He was seeing all that he had loved and cared for through a mist of pain and despair and sheer weariness. Nothing was quite real any more – everything he did seemed to require such an enormous effort. He became silent and depressed at home, a brooding presence preoccupied with what he saw as his complete failure in every area of life.

Fearing that an emotional breakdown was following close on the heels of his physical deterioration, Philip went back to his doctor and simply asked to be returned to hospital until a definite diagnosis had been reached. Inwardly he knew that this final result, when it came, was going to be devastating.

He resolved to use the weeks that remained before the date of his readmission to hospital in some kind of constructive preparation. Roger Pike came to mind. Roger now had a parish at Cowes, on the Isle of Wight, and when contacted was very willing for his old friend to come and stay for as long as he wished.

Philip was not at all sure what to expect from this visit. In his confused and negative state of mind he was not able to feel very optimistic. But it was Roger's prayer that had hastened the healing of his epilepsy, and triggered all those long-lost memories, so anything could happen. He travelled down to the Isle of Wight in a rather blank frame of mind, and with no inkling of just how important those few weeks were to be.

Philip kept his own written account of the visit, a daily record of truths revealed by the Holy Spirit in the course of Roger's ministry to him.

. . . Roger presided over the Eucharist this night, after

first blessing me with holy water. The collect seemed to speak to me vividly.

'Leaving his father and all that he had without delay, he was obedient to the calling of Jesus Christ.'

A collect choosing the theme of letting go. It was a Eucharist resurrection for my mother and my father, my grandparents and my forebears, seeking to loose me from the bondage that I had felt in my attachments to them, the obsessive thought patterns, fears and prohibitions inherited from contact with my loved ones. Roger ministered to me the ministry of deliverance. I had forgiven my mother but I had never consciously done so at the Eucharist. I was asked to let my mother go, and not to see Margaret as a mother figure in my life. I asked Jesus to tell my mother again that I was sorry – that I forgave her, that I would let her go in Jesus. I let myself go from her in Jesus. I let my father go. I asked Jesus to tell him I was sorry, and that I forgave him for not standing up to my mother, for not being the father I had wanted. I let him go in Jesus. I let myself go from him in Jesus. Likewise with my grandparents, especially my maternal grandmother and grandfather, also my French greatgrandfather. As I did so, as Jesus set us free from each other, I saw that at times we had all ignored one another out of fear of each other – silences that were hurtful. I saw how this had been carried on in my own life – in my own relationships with my own family at the times when I shut myself off. The sins of the fathers visiting to the third and fourth generations. Roger directed me to let go of St Alban's. My first Eucharist had been on July 25th, the same day as this Eucharist – an anniversary day. Then Filymead, the blame and the hurt. I had to let go of them. Then Melanie and my worries over her. Then Margaret as a figure that I'd looked up to in the wrong way. The obsessive patterns lived out in my relationships, inherited from the attitudes of my parents to me and mine to my mother, enslaving me now. That I might love Margaret properly as my wife, and be free of wanting to re-live my mother's obsession and possession of me in Margaret. Latterly I had thought of myself as becoming my father. I hadn't thought about this before. It shocked me. I was actually being like my father towards Margaret. The experience of Jesus bringing reconciliation to my departed loved ones and to me with them was deeply moving. I began to cry as the ribbons that attached us were let go. With my mother – the umbilical cord being broken at last. The parable of the seed. The grain of wheat dying in the ground. The soil was Christ. Roger spoke to me of being born again literally into Christ's line, breaking with the past – the old family line and the bondage.

The blood. Emotions in the blood. The feeding on the placenta, on the emotions of my mother, long before the nervous system had developed. And there was the blood of Christ, his atonement – in the Eucharist – the feeding on Christ.

I had called to mind with Roger my sense of claustrophobia and agoraphobia. He explained they were birth experiences, pressure in the birth canal itself, the fears of my mother because she didn't want me, the pain of my mother transferred to me growing up. Can't face it – feeling trapped – can't find a way out. Safe inside and yet trapped inside.

Later on in the same week Roger called me into his study and talked about the healing of my memories.

In the womb of my mother I had felt afraid – alone in the dark. I could picture it all – noise and conflict. I could feel myself holding my head with my ears covered to shut out the noise – noises in my head – what were they? – Brenda, Roger's wife, said that at five weeks the head was taking shape. It would have been the moment, the time when my mother knew she was pregnant. There would be strife and distaste, arguments and conflict – yes, I felt all that. I could hear dad saying he was proud. My mother didn't feel pride at all.

This was the place of healing for me, at the Eucharist. I had to surrender the pain and panic of my mother with me in the womb, me not wanting to come out and my mother not wanting me to come out. The surrender of my birth – the giving of me to Jesus who was saying, 'I was *there* at your birth. I knew you before you were born. I was *there* in the womb.'

Dad did everything for me for the first months of my life. The first touches of love were from my father, a male contact. God in my father. Longing to relate to my father. Longing for my father and his love – but dad was taken away by the war, so I was left with my mother, who in my father's absence took me to her bed. She could cope with a little boy's love.

I know she molested me. I remember it quite clearly. I think I know how she felt, but I hated it. I had to let go of it. It sickened me. I disliked even the smell of a woman.

I can remember so clearly hating my mother for what she wanted from me, but didn't want from my father. My father I had to forgive because he didn't love my mother in the way she needed.

Lord Jesus, please tell my mother that I'm sorry she was so afraid, that she didn't want me, couldn't accept me – had a rough time with my birth. Please tell her I forgive her, I loose her and I loose myself from her. I love her and I understand.

I love my father and I understand. Please, Jesus, help me not to fall again into the patterns videotaped on my young mind of being trapped and belonging nowhere – of panic when meeting others, and the places and journeys which meant more pain – all symptoms of my birth experience. Help me to know that Jesus was there. Thank you for the train journey – the picture of the crucifixion in my dream long ago and for my conversion – for trying to show me Jesus' sacrifice was giving me the love that I always needed but didn't understand.

The Eucharist, the highlight of my priesthood, was the one event I knew where I belonged. He was showing me he was at my birth – when I wanted love, yet I wanted to die. Jesus was showing me a way out – a way of being born again. Jesus was healing me at the mass – my body and his body being consecrated at the mass – held together. My childhood being lifted up just as the bread is lifted up. My blood, his blood – my life with my family at last being broken and being brought into line with Jesus. Thanks be to God! Thanks be to God!

John Fourteen: Many mansions. I go to prepare a place for you. In my Father's house are many resting places. And stopping places – wayside caravans, shelters along the road where travellers may rest from their journey. The custom in the East is for travellers to send someone forward to prepare resting places along the road so that they might find comfort and shelter. Our Lord was the one who was going before me. He treads the way of faith before us and makes ready to welcome us. We have a long journey of many days before our pilgrimage is finished, but there are, by God's mercy, many stopping places – otherwise of what avail would be the promise of our Lord to pledge a place for us? The Lord calls and points us, here and now, to what is for each one the next stage – the next stopping place on the way to perfection. As we follow we find him there, welcoming us and leading us to himself. If I go to prepare a place for you I will come again and receive you to myself until the last stage is reached. Press on, says St Paul.

I am with Roger in the study again. I am a baby in the pram. My father is caring for me. My mother I can't find anywhere. My father seems to love me but he's afraid to commit himself completely to me. My mother wants all of his attention. My grandparents arrive and my mother rushes upstairs. My grandfather picks me up from the pram then decides they should leave and I'm given to my father. I am afraid, divided. Who loves me? Is love always given with pain? I am in the pram again and a hand rocks my pram. Our Lord is there. I cannot see his face, but now I am in his arms every time that I am alone. I see a beautiful garden banked with flowers. It travels into the distance and I hear a voice saying, 'I made all of this out of love. It is mine. It is all yours.'

I know where he is and this is where I belong. He is my true home. He shows me the beauty superimposed on the material. This is true reality, the only reality that matters.

My father loves me. To my mother I am an intrusion into the world of order and stifling precision – I am a baby bringing mess and chaos. I demand attention and my mother cannot cope with that. My father leaves in 1940. I'm nearly four years old. Mother's attention for the next six and a half years is all on me. Her fondling and obsession, her fear and need. I feel and I am afraid. It repels me, and yet, like a moth to a flame, I cannot resist. It's all that I know. It's the only love that I know. The mother image I want to be freed from gives no privacy and it stunts my sexual growth into manhood. I long for my father to come home, for his touch and his gentleness which makes no demands. Jesus is in his gentleness.

My father is away and I'm tied to my mother's strings. I feel panic and suffocation, and when father returns from the war he takes *my* place. I resent being in the background again even though I wanted to be free from my mother's sexual advances. I miss those touches which at their giving made me feel unclean. Strange, but that is how I felt. I sought my father. I needed his love desperately. No privacy. Deep frustration – anger and resentment is all there again. Panic in the dark where mother puts me. The same fear I had in the womb is in the cupboard where she puts me under the stairs. Nowhere did I belong. No real bedroom – no place to play. Just a shed in the garden. Sometimes I was locked in there, not allowed to come out and yet strangely there was peace.

Even now in a locked room where no one can penetrate I find a passing peace.

Then comes the most wonderful sense of pale blue light – a warm glow. It fills my eyes and it fills the room. Roger is with me and he feels it too. We speak of it together – it is the blueness of the light of Our Lady herself – the same beauty as I once saw and knew when I was ill.

. . . Margaret's letter arrives relating her vision at Walsingham. She woke and felt an overwhelming sense of inner suffering – terrible and indescribable to her. Is someone ill? It became more and more intense. She found herself weeping but didn't know why. She opened her eyes and the light outside her bedroom was shining in front of her, making a large cross out of the old beams holding up the ceiling. She cried out: 'Oh no, Lord! Not Philip! Please not Philip!' Then a voice: 'Out of his suffering will come victory.' Margaret asked Mary to be a mother to me, the mother I'd not experienced. She had often asked this of Our Lady for Melanie. Margaret left with a sense of peace, the pain gone completely. It was a wonderful confirmation of Our Lord's will and the pattern of ministry received. In my pilgrimages to Walsingham I'd sensed the presence of Mary so clearly.

A member of Roger's congregation, Joyce Patterson, a lovely free and open lady, approached me after mass with a prophecy she'd had laid on her heart for nearly two weeks. It took courage for her to tell me.

'Philip, you are to experience suffering – the Lord is saying, "I have given you so much. I have loved you, but there is more to come – more suffering. That suffering will be your salvation. You are to return to your wife and love her as your wife. No longer is she to be your mother." '

How could she have known this? She didn't know me and Roger had said nothing.

'You are definitely to be healed of your inner turmoil. How much God loves you, and loves you to love others! You have so much to give others. That will come through your suffering. I feel your suffering is going to restrict you in some way and yet that very restriction is going to be your freedom. I don't think you will return again to be a parish priest. There is a house somewhere in this. A house where spiritual needs are going to be met. This needs much discernment on your part and you must be true to it.'

I am detached from the bloodline of my mother into the bloodline of Jesus, receiving salvation as I receive the blood of Christ in the Eucharist. I am now in the bloodline of Jesus. I can be cleansed . . .

Philip returned home to Bexhill, his physical condition as bad or worse than it had been before. The truths he had learned and lived through on the island were now inside him, real experiences that he hoped and prayed would strengthen him for what was to come.

In a way, going back into hospital was easier than enduring the failure-ridden ethos of home and work, but there were all those tests to go through again. Proceeding on the tentative hypothesis that Philip was suffering from an operable tumour on the spine, the hospital investigated every aspect of his physical and neurological condition. Back in the same depressing ward where emotional trauma continually aggravated physical sickness, he did his best to encourage and be encouraged by his fellow sufferers as he awaited the final verdict.

It was autumn when he heard, the season when nature gracefully, but with pungently sweet sadness, agrees to die so that, later, the spring can come again – Philip's favourite time of the year.

The doctor told him the news in circumstances almost bizarrely similar to those in which he had learned about his epilepsy at the Charing Cross Hospital. This, too, was a teaching hospital, and most key moments were observed by a little bevy of white-coated seekers after knowledge, a very understandable and necessary thing, no doubt, but very hard for the patients sometimes. They all gathered round the specialist as he sat by Philip's bed on this particular morning, waiting and watching to see how he would react when he heard what was wrong with him.

'Reverend Ilott, we have some news for you at last,' said the doctor, leaning forward to take Philip's hand. 'I'm very sorry to have to tell you that you are suffering from disseminated sclerosis.'

There was a short silence.

'Is that the same as multiple sclerosis?' asked Philip in a small, calm voice.

'Yes it is,' replied the specialist. 'Exactly the same.'

He explained that the cause was degeneration of the myelin coating which is wrapped around nerve fibres. When the damaged patches become scarred, nerve messages can't travel properly and they get garbled or lost. Instructions sent to different parts of the body are disrupted.

Philip nodded. He'd known folk with MS, but it had always been a complaint that other people suffered from, not something you would ever experience at first hand. Now he'd got it.

'It's a most capricious disease,' continued the specialist, 'up and down, stable and unstable – there can be remissions and there can be relapses. It's very difficult to predict its effect in individual cases.'

Philip's dominant emotion as the news sank in was one of relief. At least he knew now! He knew what was wrong. *They* knew what was wrong. There would be medication – ways of coping . . .

The consultant's next words sliced through his optimism.

'The next question is: "What's going to happen to you professionally?" There's no way you can carry on with your job if you've got MS, you see, because we can never be sure which way it's going to go.'

For a moment Philip was back in Newport, facing a different consultant but listening to very similar words.

The shock of being told that his priesthood was coming to an end was no less now than it had been then. The epilepsy had been healed after that, so that he could keep his parish. Would the same thing happen now with the MS? Why had he been healed before if he was going to go through the whole thing again? What *was* God doing?

He managed to control his voice.

'What do I have to do, then, doctor?'

'Well,' came the reply, 'I'll have to write to your bishop and put him in the picture, and then decisions will have to be made about where you go from here – what sort of work will still be open to you, that sort of thing. But whatever it is, I'm afraid it can't be what you've been doing. It would be unfair of me to pretend otherwise. What securities does the church present you with in the case of illness?'

Philip shook his head slowly. He had no idea. He'd never thought about it.

'You've got decisions to make,' said the consultant. 'Not immediately, but you need to start thinking about the future.'

Later that day Margaret visited. She kissed Philip and sat down beside him.

'Any news, darling?'

'Yes,' said Philip, like a child, 'I've got multiple sclerosis. I can't be a priest any more, Margaret.'

After many tears and troubled words, Margaret returned to Bexhill bearing the doctor's letter for the bishop. That evening she informed the churchwardens of the situation and put a notice up on the church door, explaining that the vicar had been diagnosed as having multiple sclerosis, and that the future was uncertain. He would continue in his post for the time being, the notice said, and further announcements would follow as decisions were made.

Philip came out of hospital. Sticks enabled him to walk, but only with great difficulty. The journey by foot from the vicarage to the sea and back again was long and painful, and he dreaded meeting parishioners in such a vulnerable, enfeebled state. It was now late autumn, and only injections administered by the district nurse were keeping the MS under any sort of control.

Eventually, while Philip and Margaret were staying in Eastbourne, attempting to think through their plans for the future, Margaret suggested they should hire a wheelchair from the Red Cross to make it easier for Philip to move around. Philip, seeing it as a temporary measure, agreed that it would aid his 'convalescence', and almost enjoyed the release from pain and strain. It was a rather ancient, heavy type of conveyance, though, and Margaret, although happy to do the pushing, found it very hard work. Unhappily for Philip's optimistic talk about convalescence, he lost the use of his legs completely over the next week or two and was permanently confined to a wheelchair.

As the specialist had said, it was time for decisions to be made. There was absolutely no pressure from the church or the bishop. They were all consistently kind and patient, knowing what a hard and unwelcome path Philip might have to choose. Parish work was becoming almost impossible now. It involved so many different activities, some of them in places not accessible to a wheelchair. Often, because of extra pain or discomfort, he would be obliged to cancel his appearance at meetings or services at the last moment, and although people rallied round and coped in a heart-warming way, the situation was very far from satisfactory.

But how do you decide to leave behind your art, your talent, your sense of happiness, your fulfilment, your one-ness with creation, your most complete expression of who you are? Philip couldn't quite do it. Then he remembered Walsingham, the famous place of pilgrimage in Norfolk. He had made a number of trips to this unusual village over the years, and always found it a place of peace and spiritual refreshment. He would go there, he decided, and ask Mary what he should do.

Two ladies in the parish, regular pilgrims who had offered to help in any way they could after hearing about the MS, agreed to take Philip to Walsingham with them and care for all his physical needs; quite a heroic offer, because he now needed lifting in and out of cars, on and off his wheelchair, dressing and undressing, as well as all the more intimate requirements that disability produced. Margaret stayed behind in Bexhill with Mel. It was a very painful parting.

Late November in Walsingham.

Philip spent most of each day in the Shrine Church of Our Lady of Walsingham, built on a site that had been a place of healing and prayer for a thousand years.

Inside the main body of the church stood a small brick building, shaped like a house, and intended to represent the Nazareth home in which Jesus was brought up. It was known as the 'Holy House', its walls and ceiling blackened by smoke from countless candles lit by visiting pilgrims over the years. Above the altar on the east side stood a statue of Mary with the child Jesus on her knee.

In the small, dimly lit confines of this silent place, Philip sat in his wheelchair for hour after hour, letting his mind and spirit relax, in the hope that he would find comfort for his soul, and wisdom to aid his decision-making. Certainly he did very quickly feel surrounded by the love and care of God, and Mary's presence in the little house seemed more real than what is commonly called reality. It was good to rest for a short time in this other world, where the weight of his individual circumstances and personality simply dropped away, allowing him to float freely in a rhythmic swell of spiritual love that seemed to fill the physical space around him.

Then, towards the end of his stay in Walsingham, one memory began to fill his mind, returning again and again as he sat quietly in the half-light. It was not a lost memory, and it was not from his childhood. It was something that had happened in the middle of the night when he was living on the Isle of Wight, before he was healed of epilepsy. He'd just had an attack, quite a bad one, and woke to find himself in bed, with Margaret lying peacefully beside him. But there was someone else there as well, a glowing presence, instantly identifiable through the same special sense, perhaps, that little Harry was to use when he recognised Philip at his birthday party a year or two later.

She spoke to him.

'Philip, will you endure more suffering? There is one more thing that is required of you, and it will not go away.'

'I can't take it – I can't . . .' replied Philip faintly.

'For the sake of my son and the world – you can.'

Later, Philip learned that Margaret had been awake and had heard him speaking as he sat up in bed, but of his holy visitor she had seen and heard nothing.

Now, in Walsingham, that experience, or dream, or vision was speaking to him in such a way that his illness and the loss of his parish seemed to be a fulfilment of Mary's words. No sooner had this understanding found a home in his spirit than another memory claimed his attention. The dream of crucifixion that had so puzzled and troubled him after his conversion in Germany returned with every graphic detail as clear as it had been on the night he dreamed it.

It was a call to obedience and an answer to his question. As he let the two memories inhabit and inform him, Philip knew that the time for resistance had gone. He must let go of his parish and, if necessary, his priesthood – not give up, but let go. That was the thing that was now required of him, the cross that he must carry for the sake of Jesus and the world. It was far from being a dramatic realisation. On the contrary, there was a quietness and a gentle inexorability about the way in which the knowledge had settled into his heart. That night he resolved to offer his resignation as soon as he returned to Bexhill.

The following day happened to be Armistice Day. One of the ladies took Philip, in his wheelchair, for a walk around Walsingham after the morning service. Nearly everyone they met was wearing a poppy, a sign of mourning for the fallen of two world wars, men and women who had not wanted to die, but were ready to, if that was the price demanded of them. Philip felt a new closeness to them on that bright autumn morning, as the wheels of his chair ploughed through piles of dead leaves along the pavements, leaves that had fallen gently and without resistance from the branches of the half-naked trees.

Two overwhelming questions still needed to be answered as Philip announced his resignation in the Easter of 1984. Where were the Ilotts going to live, and what was Philip going to do? Church authorities, distant geographically as well as sympathetically, insisted on dealing with Philip as though he was a very old man who was about to die, suggesting for instance that a large house would not be necessary because it was 'about time the children left and found somewhere to live'. Obviously, their attitude seemed to suggest, Philip and Margaret would want to subside quietly into a retirement flat and watch television for the rest of their lives.

They reckoned without God and Margaret!

Unknown to Philip at the time, Paul wrote a letter on Margaret's behalf, to the Church Pensions Board, strongly expressing her insistence that the family would *not* separate because of Philip's illness, that Philip *did* still have something to offer in terms of ministry, and that it would be a good idea if the CPB were to acquaint themselves with the *facts* of the case instead of proceeding according to the rulebook. This letter prompted an investigative visit from a CPB representative who soon gathered that Philip was not an old fuddy-duddy who could be disposed of summarily. The Pension Board offered extra money for a more substantial house, and Philip and Margaret began searching for a place to live.

House after house came on to the market, but none of them seemed quite suitable until, in the course of one of their daily walks, the couple found themselves in a pleasant residential street called Albany Road. Philip was immediately warmed by the name. He still felt a great attraction to his old shed companion.

'Wouldn't it be marvellous,' he said, as they slowly made their way along the pavement, 'if there was a house in this road that was for sale?'

'And suitable,' added Margaret practically.

They spotted a FOR SALE sign shortly after that, and speeded up a little, curious to see what kind of property was on offer. It was a very pleasant house, from the outside at any rate, and there was something else.

'Look, darling,' said Philip. 'Look at the name. It's called Albany House. That's it!'

On the following day the Pension Board's surveyor inspected four houses, one of which was Albany House. Later, he visited the Ilotts to report his findings.

'I'm afraid, Reverend,' he said, 'that only one of them is a possibility for you, and that's the one in Albany Road . . .'

A fortnight later Philip and Margaret explored their new home thoroughly, Philip being carried up the stairs in an ambi-chair. It would need ramps, swing doors and a lift to be installed, but otherwise it was perfect. Philip's study (Margaret insisted that Philip should have a study) was to be the large front-facing room on the first floor. Here he would be able to pursue the new ministry that Margaret adamantly insisted would replace the old one.

Philip was not so sure. He had relinquished his parish because he knew it was the right thing to do, but he had no idea what would take its place – if anything. Besides, he had not yet really come to terms with his status as a wheelchair-bound MS sufferer. He had been very disappointed with the response to his illness from fellow clergy and church leaders. Many said to Margaret, 'We'd come, but what on earth do we say?', as though it was a sort of cheering-up exercise that was required. Philip wanted people to cry with him, to be in mourning with him and share his bereavement. He wanted neither sympathy nor jollying along.

Notable exceptions to the above rule were, among others, Peter Ball, who became a close friend, and a local priest named Graham Bryant, who came on a fairly regular basis to lay hands on Philip and anoint him with oil. One day Graham was so overcome by the situation that he sat down opposite his fellow priest and simply wept like a baby. Philip, who found it very difficult to cry for himself at that time, was greatly helped by this. He felt that Graham was doing some of his grieving for him, bringing something out of the centre of him that he was unable to release himself. Philip greatly valued Graham's ministry and friendship, and missed him immensely when he later moved to a parish in Cheltenham.

One of Philip's assistant priests from St Barnabas' brought the sacraments to him. He couldn't face going back into the church after his resignation, partly because of the sense of loss, but also because the helplessness of his condition, the excruciating fact of being a broken, functionless priest, was too humiliating for words. Already, he had hated reading the blaringly public headline on the front page of the local paper: 'LOCAL VICAR – TRAGEDY HITS'.

Margaret was as warmly, consistently supportive and encouraging as ever, but too often others he encountered either patronised or pitied him. Philip knew instinctively that he would only truly accept his illness and physical dependency when *he* was accepted for what he was. But what was he? What would he become?

Three things were particularly helpful in putting Philip back on his feet (in the strictly figurative sense!).

The first was his dream about the door and the crowd of needy people waiting for him on the other side. If it was from God, as he believed it was, then it seemed to indicate that there clearly *was* a new ministry awaiting him, just as Margaret had always insisted. Exactly what form it would take, or when it would begin, was unclear, but it promised a future that had shape and meaning. It gave him hope.

The second thing, which happened shortly after the dream, was a very brief encounter in a nearby shop. It was Philip's first outing into town in his wheelchair, and Margaret had left him in the local branch of W. H. Smith to buy a birthday card. He studied the rack for a few minutes, taking out something that caught his eye from time to time, but invariably replacing it because it was not quite suitable. He liked to take particular care over the selection of cards or gifts for people close to him. Then he saw it – the card he wanted, up on the topmost row of the sloping rack. That one would be ideal. Drawing his chair a little nearer, he reached his hand up as high as it would stretch, to take down his selection. He couldn't reach. His fingers just touched the card, but he was unable to take hold of it.

'Blast this chair!' he thought, stretching in vain once again, '– blast this illness – blast everything!'

Suddenly he became aware that a small boy was standing next to his chair. He turned his head, and the two studied each other's faces for a moment, then the boy smiled, reached up to take the card from the top row, and presented it to Philip without a word. There wasn't even time to say 'Thank you' as the small figure slipped round the end of the card display and disappeared. But something in that fleeting experience spoke eloquently to Philip. A wonderfully natural pleasure and enthusiasm in the little boy's willingness to help had reminded him of some words that Jesus spoke: 'Unless you become like a little child . . .'

Just now, just after their eyes had met on more or less the same level, he had accepted from a little child a service that he was not able to perform for himself. To be vulnerable, and to be like a child – was that what all those hurt people on the other side of the door needed to find in him? Could it be that someone as broken and afflicted and physically reduced as he was might offer just the kind of unthreatening help that desperate folk were looking for? Could he be that vulnerable and that generous, saying 'Yes' to what God could do with his MS? He wasn't sure, but he hoped so. It sounded like an adventure.

He often looked out for that little boy when he was in town, but he never saw him again. Sometimes he wondered if it had been an angel in W. H. Smith's that day.

The third and most important element in Philip's journey towards an acceptance of his illness was not a thing at all – it was a person, someone who had exactly the qualities he needed. It was Mel.

The move to Bexhill had brought little, if any, improvement in the relationship between Philip and Mel, and as the symptoms of the as yet undiagnosed MS began to affect Philip more and more, it reached an all-time low. So negative were her feelings that for more than six months Mel hardly saw her father; she visited him in hospital just once, and then only because her mother persuaded her to go. When the multiple sclerosis was finally diagnosed, she saw it only as one more burden for her mother, who had to cope with so much already.

Mel had observed everything. She saw how, after returning home, Philip's mobility deteriorated. First he managed with a walking frame; then, unable to use the stairs, he was forced to sleep on the ground floor; finally, his legs became useless, and confinement to a wheelchair was the inevitable result. She noticed other things as well: how difficult Philip was finding it to adjust to his new lifestyle, and how people seemed to be molly-coddling him, picking up the things that he dropped before he had a chance to try for himself. She also noticed that it was beginning to matter to her.

Mel refused to indulge him, or to treat his illness with great solemnity. She built assault courses in the garden for 'Rev' to negotiate in his wheelchair, and she took him out into the town in his chair to practise getting through shop doorways, negotiating crossings, and all the other tasks that were so daunting now that he no longer had the use of his legs.

One day, in the early stages of Philip's illness, Mel took her unemployment money out and bought him a stick with a brass handle fashioned in the shape of an eagle.

'Here you are, Rev,' she said, 'this'll help you to walk.'

Philip treasured that stick.

Ironically, it was the very qualities in Mel which had angered Philip in the past that now provided such a necessary stimulus and encouragement to him. Throughout his illness she drove him from self-pity with her jokey approach to his new problems. Jovial and carefree, she insisted on trying everything, and never giving up. To hell with the rest of the world and what it thought. She and 'Rev' were going to do it, and that was that! She was daughter, mother, and kicker-along to Philip, and no one else could have done it in quite the same way.

At the same time, Mel began to notice things about her father that seemed quite new to her. Friends noticed it too.

'I like your dad. He's a good laugh.'

From Mel's perspective, Philip had broadened out dramatically since the onset of his illness. He spoke to her now, instead of preaching. He seemed to have a new ability to accept that other people had a right to go their own way without reference to his own views. He was altogether calmer and sweeter. She put it down to the medication he was now taking, and assumed that much of the conflict at Filymead and since had its roots in the early effects of the MS, while being quite aware that her own behaviour had done nothing to help.

Whether or not she was right about the medication, it was certainly true that two major changes had occurred. First, Mel and Philip were seeing more of each other than they had done for years, meeting parts of each other that had been reserved for people outside their particular relationship in the past. They both liked quite a lot of what they found. Second, and most important, Mel had at last found a way to be significant and valuable in her father's life at a time when he needed her most. Later, Philip was to reflect that if it hadn't been for Mel's help in his first 'wheelchair year', he might never have adjusted to his new way of life. Their relationship would always be a 'lively' one, to say the least, but the bond that had been forged years earlier, when Mel was a tiny baby and Philip was all she had got, had been rediscovered and strengthened.

There was no doubt that Philip *had* changed. As time went by, a new acceptance of his own condition seemed to spread arms of love and comfort to embrace the needy folk who had begun beating a path to his door soon after the move to Albany Road. That last session of ministry from the Holy Spirit through Roger Pike seemed to be crystallising now into genuine resolutions of problems that had haunted him since childhood, freeing him into a much more vulnerable availability to the needs of others. Joyce Patterson's prophecy had been absolutely accurate. This unusual combination of physical helplessness and spiritual strength was irresistible to folk who were carrying burdens that had seemed too huge, or too shocking, or too shameful to be revealed to anyone in the past.

Many people were to break down and weep in the safe

privacy of Philip's first-floor study, as they encountered, often for the first time, the profoundly disarming compassion and warmth that God chose to express through his wheelchair-bound servant. Philip had suffered too much in his life ever to impose suffering on another. There was never any condemnation. In Philip, Jesus was entering into the private world of each one who came, not to judge but to demonstrate how much he values those who suffer, and how far he has gone, and is willing to go, to bring them peace.

Many of those whom Philip counselled needed, more than anything, to be 'hugged' by God; to be reassured that they were not isolated in the darkness of angry rejection. Problems of every description presented themselves, from physical infirmity, through every kind of emotional and sexual difficulty, to quite severe mental illness.

The gifts of the Holy Spirit, so necessary in Ventnor, but pushed into a siding over the past few years, once more began to inform and inspire his ministry, at times shocking both Philip and those he was counselling with the accuracy and appropriateness of the things they revealed or the advice they offered. Healings occurred – sometimes quite dramatically; people were comforted and led into new ways of thinking and understanding; long-buried sins were excavated and confessed; lonely suffering was eased a little; the love of God, smiling through Philip, brought new hope to many despairing hearts.

Some of the most unhappy visitors in those early days were homosexual Christians, many of them in leadership positions in the church. Quite often they would be married men, finding – again, usually for the first time – a place where the hurt and bewilderment and anguish could be poured out without fear of shallow ministry or mindless, thinly disguised judgementalism. Believing, as he did, that the church as a whole was simply refusing to face this issue, Philip was determined that, in his small corner of the kingdom at least, these people would meet the kindness of God in the midst of their trouble. As time went by this became an increasingly important area of his work, especially as there were no simple once-for-all solutions to such complex emotional puzzles.

Any fears that the MS would rob Philip of a genuine priestly function were completely unfounded. Over the next few years the calls on his time were increasing. Nor was it only in the area of personal counselling. Just as people had flocked to the 'house on the hill' in Ventnor and drawn Philip out to a wider ministry on the Isle of Wight, so now the life of the Spirit was so evident in him that the demand for his ministry involved an enormously wide variety of venues and events. These included preaching and speaking engagements in all kinds of denominational settings, the leading of retreats and conferences for lay or clergy groups, and even a regular appearance on the TVS epilogue programme, *Company*, where a few people sat in informal surroundings each night discussing topics of spiritual or topical interest. Philip was a great favourite with viewers, who were captivated by his depth and sweetness. His fellow participants were equally impressed by 'the man in the wheelchair', including a rather confused member of the team called Adrian Plass, who had just come through a very difficult time himself.

Philip talked freely on television about his illness and the ministry that had grown since he had been forced to give up his parish. The things he spoke of were inspiring and, occasionally, almost beyond belief. He described, for instance, a recent occasion on the Isle of Wight when a young American companion, named Darryl, received news that his friend Jon had been killed in an aeroplane crash somewhere in America. Jon was not a Christian. Philip, who was leading a retreat on the island at the time, suggested that the resident priest, who happened to be Roger Pike, should say a Requiem Eucharist for the dead boy. As the service proceeded – it was attended only by Philip, Roger and Darryl – both Roger and Darryl were conscious of a fourth presence beside them, but as the words 'Jesus, meet Jonathan – Jonathan, meet Jesus' were said, Philip actually saw the figure of a young man standing before him, participating in the service with great concentration. Later, when he described this unexpected visitor in detail, Darryl, considerably shaken, told Philip that the person he had described was his friend Jon.

Reactions to that story varied enormously. Some viewers felt it bordered on heresy, and was dangerous. Others were content to enjoy the mystery of an event so rare and precious. Philip's spirituality caused considerable confusion in any case, just as it had done in Ventnor. Conversion, sacramental confession, Mary, physical healing, baptism in the Spirit, speaking in tongues, healing of memories – all part of one man's Christian life and experience. Some people, mainly 'hard-liners' at both ends of the church, found it all very difficult to accept. But what no one could deny – including the lady who wrote to say that 'if he had any real trust, he'd say the prayer of faith and stand up' – was the visible, glowing quality of the life inside him.

* * *

The cost of Philip's new ministry is great; for Margaret in terms of never-ending, hard physical work and care, and for Philip in sheer physical suffering. After a week spent leading a mission or retreat, the pain resulting from fatigue will often spread agonisingly down from his head and neck into both arms and hands, and along the length of his spine until it becomes almost unbearable. Only lengthy periods of massage are able to restore feeling and movement to his hands and arms at such times. A bout of flu or any other bug has the same effect. These bodily afflictions are usually accompanied by mental disorientation and an inability to concentrate. The experience of suffering is never pleasant, but Philip has learned to meet God in a place that is closer to him than the darkness of pain.

Philip Ilott loves and enjoys his family and his friends, but there are times when he longs to die; to leave the pain behind and go home to Jesus. At such times, though, he reflects that the word BEWARE was written very large over the door in his dream, and that he was allowed to choose either to pick up the key which opened it, or to leave it where it lay on the ground. He chose to pick it up, and so the work continues.

Philip's life has been a rich mixture of calm and storm. The Holy Spirit has worked hard in him and with him. He is far from perfect now, but for many, many people who are aching in heart or mind or body, he is living, encouraging evidence that there is a smile on the face of God.

14

An Unexpected Postscript
(1989)

A very surprising phone call made this postscript necessary.

The book has been a very difficult one to finish in any case. Towards the end of 1988 Philip began to slip into a deep depression. The combination of his illness and four or five years of unceasing work for the benefit of others was largely responsible. Also, perhaps, the emotionally taxing business of reliving his entire life experience for the purpose of this biography added to the burden.

My wife, Bridget, noticed the change in him. In the course of making some TV epilogue programmes together, Philip mentioned to her how dispirited he was feeling; how, as he woke each morning, the day seemed a dark prospect, whatever it might contain. For the first time in his life he blamed God for the bleakness he was feeling, and developed a hatred of his wheelchair that was quite unprecedented. As the year changed things became worse. There was no reduction in the flow of people needing help, but Philip felt that he was now operating in his own strength, and was eventually ordered by his doctor to stop work and give himself a sabbatical year, free of responsibilities, in which to recover.

My own response to this turn of events was on two

levels. First, as Philip's friend, I was very concerned. The depth and nature of his depression was unlike anything he had experienced before, as far as I knew. Bridget and I worried incessantly about Margaret and Philip, finding it hard to believe that yet another dark time was upon them.

Second, as a writer with a deadline that had already passed, I had a different set of problems. The planned title for my book about Philip was *A Smile on the Face of God*. It had been a very apt title before, but it wasn't now. I could hardly rename it *A Rather Glum Look on the Face of God*. A second deadline passed, and I was still scratching my head over how to end the book.

In April, Philip visited Quarr Abbey on the Isle of Wight to go into retreat and face God over what was happening to him. I visited for a day on 25 April, and found him in surprisingly good spirits. The discipline of the retreat was providing a very useful structure for his thoughts and prayers, and a new optimism was just beginning to take root. At that time we agreed that the book should finish with an honest description of Philip's most recent problems. Better, we felt, to leave the account of his life open-ended and unglossed than to give the impression that all loose ends were tied up and all difficulties solved.

Philip paid a second visit to Quarr Abbey a little later in the year, and knew, for the first time, a genuine happiness in solitary communion with God. He learned much more as well, but that was his greatest discovery, that it was a safe and joyful thing to be alone with his heavenly Father. But he still wondered what was in store for him. What was God doing with his life?

I still couldn't finish the book. My patient editor agreed to extend the deadline to the end of September, and I geared myself to finish the task by then. I arranged to meet Philip for a final chat about the project on the evening of 25 September, a Monday. On the Friday evening before that, the phone rang at about eight o'clock. It was Philip. The dialogue that followed was roughly as follows:

> Philip: 'Do you want to hear some news?'
> Me: (Rather grumpily) 'Only if it's good news – I can do without bad news at the moment.'
> Philip: 'I think you might describe this as good news.'
> Me: 'Good! What is it?'
> Philip: 'I'm walking again.'
>   (Long stunned silence)
> Me: 'What did you say?'
> Philip: 'I'm walking again – I can walk!'
>   (Longer stunned silence)
> Me: 'That's – that's . . . amazing!'

Philip told me how, two days before the Cyprus holiday he had just enjoyed with Margaret, he had suddenly felt what he described as a new 'physical impetus'. To Margaret's surprise, he went out in his wheelchair and bought a pair of walking-sticks to take on holiday. On the morning of departure a letter arrived from America. It was from Philip's old friend, Darryl. In it he recounted a dream he had had the previous night in which Philip was walking normally. Darryl was sure that Philip was going to be healed.

In Cyprus Philip heaved himself up on to his two sticks and staggered around on them, gradually gaining strength and balance until, in an amazingly short time, he was walking more or less normally. The high point of the holiday for Philip was standing in the River Jordan during a trip to the mainland, actually *feeling* the fish nibble his toes.

He was once again able to open doors for Margaret to walk through – a tiny courtesy, but one denied him for years. And he defended her from giant cockroaches, the first act of gallantry he had achieved since being confined to a chair.

On returning to the house in Bexhill, he got a hammer and nailed a souvenir barometer from Cyprus to the wall. He did it standing up, and smiled as he did it.

Later that same day he picked Mel and her baby daughter up from playgroup in his customised car. Mel knew nothing as yet about her father's new mobility, and when they got back to Albany Road she went into the house to fetch his wheelchair. When she came out again she nearly fainted when she met Philip, on his feet, just outside the door. It was one of those rare occasions when Mel allowed 'Rev' to hug her.

On hearing the news, Paul dashed down from the north with his family to see for himself. When he arrived he threw his arms around his father, not just once, but again and again. There was great rejoicing.

The climax came two days later, on the Saturday when Philip was due to attend a Eucharist at St Barnabas' to celebrate the twenty-fifth anniversary of the priesting of Father Timothy Van Carrapiett, the present vicar.

When Philip rang Father Timothy on the Friday evening, to warn him that he would be *walking* into the church, the vicar was ecstatic. He asked Philip to assist him in administering the Eucharist on the following day.

It turned out to be a very moving occasion.

The church was packed with laypeople and clergy who had come to honour Father Timothy. As Philip, in his robes, processed up the length of the church, heads turned and eyes opened wide with astonishment as those present recognised the priest who should have been in a wheelchair. Two hundred people received the bread and the wine at that service, and Philip was on his feet for two hours. Two beautiful hours . . .

The doctors were puzzled. They talked of remission, but were unable to explain how such normal mobility was possible after more than five years in a wheelchair.

Philip himself just thanks God that he can walk again, and prays that it will continue. The heat of the Mediterranean countries certainly seems to help Philip's particular case, and according to a Maltese doctor specialising in MS whom Philip met recently, there is a property in certain rocks common to those areas that may be beneficial, but, in a sense, such considerations are irrelevant. Things do not tend to happen by accident in Philip's life. Whatever the direct means, God has done something, and a new chapter is beginning in the Ilott saga. It is very exciting.

On the Monday following that phone conversation, Philip walked through the front door of our house and flamboyantly shook one of his legs in the air to demonstrate just how 'alright' he was. It was the first time I had seen him out of a wheelchair. Often, as I have sat at my desk over the last year or so, sifting through the tape transcripts prepared by my wife and trying to write something approaching reasonable prose, I have addressed God irreverently in my mind.

'If you had any sense of drama,' I said, 'you'd put Philip back on his feet for chapter fourteen.'

He has done exactly that.

Seeing Philip on his feet that day was wonderful. I don't know about a smile on the face of God – it certainly put one on mine.

Hodder Christian Paperbacks: a tradition of excellence.

Great names and great books to enrich your life and meet your needs. Choose from such authors as:

Corrie ten Boom	Jackie Pullinger
Charles Colson	David Pytches
Richard Foster	Mary Pytches
Billy Graham	Jennifer Rees Larcombe
Michael Green	Cliff Richard
Michele Guinness	John Stott
Joyce Huggett	Joni Eareckson Tada
Francis MacNutt	Colin Urquhart
Catherine Marshall	David Watson
Jim Packer	David Wilkerson
Adrian Plass	John Wimber

The wide range of books on the Hodder Christian Paperback list include **biography, personal testimony, devotional books, evangelistic books, Christian teaching, fiction, drama, poetry, books that give help for times of need** – and many others.

Ask at your nearest Christian bookshop or at your church bookstall for the latest titles.

SOME BESTSELLERS IN HODDER CHRISTIAN PAPERBACKS

THE HIDING PLACE by Corrie ten Boom

The triumphant story of Corrie ten Boom, heroine of the anti-Nazi underground.

"A brave and heartening story."

Baptist Times

GOD'S SMUGGLER by Brother Andrew

An international bestseller. God's Smuggler carries contraband Bibles past armed border guards to bring the love of Christ to the people behind the Iron Curtain.

"A book you will not want to miss."

Catherine Marshall

DISCIPLESHIP by David Watson

". . . breath-taking, block-busting, Bible-based simplicity on every page."

Jim Packer

LISTENING TO GOD by Joyce Huggett

A profound spiritual testimony, and practical help for discovering a new dimension of prayer.

"This is counselling at its best."

Leadership Today

CELEBRATION OF DISCIPLINE by Richard Foster

A classic on the Spiritual Disciplines.

"For any Christian hungry for teaching, I would recommend this as being one of the most challenging books to have been published."

Delia Smith

RUN BABY RUN by Nicky Cruz with Jamie Buckingham

A tough New York gang leader discovers Christ.

"It is a thrilling story. My hope is that it shall have a wide reading."

Billy Graham

CHASING THE DRAGON by Jackie Pullinger with Andrew Quicke

Life-changing miracles in Hong Kong's Walled City.

"A book to stop you in your tracks."

Liverpool Daily Post

BORN AGAIN by Charles Colson

Disgraced by Watergate, Charles Colson finds a new life.

"An action packed story of real life drama and a revelation of modern history as well as a moving personal account."

Elim Evangel

KNOWING GOD by J I Packer

The biblical portrait that has become a classic.

"(The author) illumines every doctrine he touches and commends it with courage, logic, lucidity and warmth . . . the truth he handles fires the heart. At least it fired mine, and compelled me to turn aside to worship and pray."

John Stott

THE HAPPIEST PEOPLE ON EARTH by Demos Shakarian with John and Elizabeth Sherrill

The extraordinary beginnings of the Full Gospel Business Men's Fellowship.

BROKEN WINDOWS, BROKEN LIVES

Adrian Plass

David Harper is no Superman. An out of work actor, he applies for the position of housefather in a residential school for 'maladjusted' boys. He sees himself as the new Doctor Barnardo, surrounded by tragic but beautiful children eternally grateful to him!

The gulf between day-dream and reality is quickly bridged as David, fearful of violence and racked by self-doubt, meets his charges. How do you continue to relate to someone who has just lunged at your stomach with a knife? What would you do with someone who smashes the windows in your front room, rings the bell, tells you it was he who did the deed and then collapses crying into your arms?

This entertaining and challenging novel is a fictionalised account of Adrian Plass's own early days as a childcare worker.

"Rich in material convincingly played out with a humour which never offends . . . poignant . . . an incredibly good read."

Community Care